PATIENT
OR
PRETENDER

Inside the Strange World
of Factitious Disorders

Marc D. Feldman, M.D.
Charles V. Ford, M.D.
With Toni Reinhold

JOHN WILEY & SONS, INC.
New York · Chichester · Brisbane · Toronto · Singapore

This text is printed on acid-free paper.

Copyright © 1994 by Marc D. Feldman, M.D., and Charles V. Ford, M.D.
Published by John Wiley & Sons, Inc.

Library of Congress Cataloging-in-Publication Data:

Feldman, Marc D., 1958–
    Patient or pretender : inside the strange world of factitious disorders /
  by Marc D. Feldman and Charles V. Ford with Toni Reinhold.
      p.   cm.
    Includes index.
    ISBN 0-471-58080-5 (cloth : alk. paper)
  II. Reinhold, Toni.   III. Title.
    [DNLM: 1. Factitious Disorders. 2. Sick Role. WM 178 F312p
  1994]
  RC569.5.F27F45 1994
  616.85'8—dc20
  DNLM/DLC
  for Library of Congress   93-13547

Printed in the United States of America

10 9 8 7 6 5 4 3 2 1

To Jackie, Lee, and Sara, for boundless nurturance.
To Pam, for your support.
To Phil, for your encouragement.

]

]

PREFACE

We know how to speak many falsehoods which
resemble real things, but we know, when we
will, how to speak true things.

Hesiod (c. 700 A.C.)
The Theogony

The euphemisms for people who "play sick" to get attention (factitious patients) often reflect the feelings evoked in the authors. In
the medical literature, the terms used to refer to these individuals
and their medical deceptions sometimes display a barbed humor. They
may focus on the factitious patient's interactions with caregivers ("trick-
ing and treating") or the wandering of the subset of factitious patients
with Munchausen syndrome ("hospital hobos"). At other times, a sense
of betrayal is evident ("disease forgery," "the false patient"). Some feel
encircled by the paradoxes this behavior presents, describing individuals
"dying to be sick" or "impatient to be patients."

In preparing this book, we have experienced all of these feelings and
more, including a grudging admiration for the skill and persistence
with which they carry out their ruses. Both of us first heard about
the factitious disorders in medical school, listening with disbelief as
professors described people who seemed to delight in duping physicians.
One of us (C.V.F.) was transformed into a believer during residency
training when a young man named Billy was transferred to the inpatient
psychiatry service. Billy had so skillfully simulated the symptoms of a
brain tumor that he had been scheduled for surgery before it was discovered that no tumor really existed. He managed to keep the psychiatric

ward in turmoil for three months as he continually developed new symptoms. On one occasion during a day pass, he was returned to the hospital by the Beverly Hills Fire Department after faking a seizure on the sidewalk along Rodeo Drive. He could scarcely have chosen a more dramatic medical sign or more glamorous location in which to feign illness! The other author (M.D.F.) met his first factitious disorder patient even before completing medical school. An anxious search for the cause of this young woman's profoundly low blood count ended abruptly with her confession that, like a self-victimizing vampire, she had been bleeding herself. Like so many factitious patients, she fled before treatment could be offered.

Each of us had heard of military recruits who engaged in "malingering." It is understandable, albeit illegal, that someone not wishing to serve might manipulate his way out of military duty by pretending to be sick. However, we have been more intrigued by patients who simulated disease when the payoff for appearing sick was not nearly so obvious. Of all the patients we have seen in consultation, those patients with factitious disorders stand out most clearly in our memories. This striking quality reflects their desperate need to find the caring they often had not received elsewhere in their lives. Despite his theatrical charades, it was impossible not to have some sympathy for Billy, whose childhood background had been harsh. He, like others, had learned that whatever nurturance he could receive would have to come from doctors and nurses. We have found that we must acknowledge these patients' genuine pain and frantic attempts to alleviate it.

The universal identification of factitious disorders is that almost everyone can admit either to having played sick to get sympathy (instead of asking directly for attention, nurturing, and/or lenience) or to having fantasized about how people would react to their serious illness and possible imminent death. How many times has each of us competed for the position of "the sickest" and most in need of nurturance? It's a battle for sympathy in which the implicit message is: I want you to take care of me.

Factitious disorders are an exaggerated outgrowth of a relatively harmless, normal behavior—"playing sick." And that's what makes it at once frightening and familiar. The primary distinction, however, between most people and those with full-blown factitious disorders is that factitial patients take playing sick to *pathological extremes*, profoundly affecting their lives, as well as the lives of others who support them.

In the early 1970s, it was fairly easy to read essentially everything that had been published about patients with factitious disorders and their severe manifestation, Munchausen syndrome. Since then, there has been at least a 10-fold increase in published case reports in an amazing variety of languages, reflecting both fascination and perplexity.

The impetus for this book was our growing awareness of the powerful effects that factitious disorder patients have on the lives of others. For example, a sobering ethical and legal dilemma was presented when a medical specialist discovered that a woman was simulating severe kidney disease. Her husband's promising career was being destroyed as he concentrated on caring for his "sick" wife. However, the woman threatened to sue her physician for breach of confidentiality if he told her husband her true diagnosis. Through national publicity generated by case reports and other publications, we have received telephone calls and letters from numerous family members and associates of factitious disorder patients. Often they reek of pathos. One woman wrote that she had always tried to be a good mother but that her now-adult daughter continued to have bills for unnecessary medical treatments sent to her. She could not afford to pay them and in fact had accumulated an entire dresser drawer of unopened medical bills. At the root of so many of these calls and letters have been poignant cries of "Why, why? We tried so hard to be good parents, devoted friends. How could we have been misled in this way?"

Our experiences with patients such as Billy initially led us to suspect that these disease simulators invariably came from turbulent childhood homes. Recent research, however, suggests the possibility that a number of these patients may have underlying brain dysfunction that predisposes them to pathological lying and factitious illness behavior. Such neurologic findings may explain why some patients who carry out medical hoaxes appear to come from seemingly well-adjusted families. More sophisticated psychological exploration and neurobiological research are required to understand these individuals and to learn how to meet their needs more effectively. We hope that this book will contribute integrally to these efforts.

What is it like to live the fantasy and bask in concern and love from others, some of whom would never show such emotions toward us if we weren't "ill"? Probably not what you imagine.

MARC D. FELDMAN, M.D.
CHARLES V. FORD, M.D.

Birmingham, Alabama
September 1993

ACKNOWLEDGMENTS

There are so many people we wish to thank for their indispensable support in the preparation of this book. Among them are Malcolm Ritter of the Associated Press, Shari Roan of the *Los Angeles Times*, and numerous other journalists who have become interested in our work and have helped to educate the public about factitious disorders. We would like to thank Cheryl Wilke, Joel Feldman, and Scott Ford for sharing their legal knowledge, and Drs. Mary Sheridan and Ernest Braasch for contributing their expertise and mentoring. We also express our gratitude to Diane Raybon, who provided excellent secretarial support, and to Herb Reich of John Wiley & Sons. Our agent and friend, Susan Lipson, sustained us with her vision and enthusiasm, as did our families. We'd also like to thank Ed Castro and journalists John Latta, Rod Gibson, Barry Gross, and Sharon Kingman for the assistance they so graciously gave us when their special abilities were needed. We thank the many caring individuals throughout the country who have had the courage to tell us of their experiences with "great pretenders." Finally, we thank the professors who taught us so much, and the patients, who taught us even more.

M.D.F.
C.V.F.
T.R.

CONTENTS

CHAPTER 1

TERMINAL
BY CHOICE

Lest men suspect your tale to be untrue,
Keep probability—some say—in view . . .
Sigh then, or frown, but leave (as in despair)
Motive and end and moral in the air;
Nice contradiction between fact and fact
Will make the whole read human and exact.
　　　　　Robert Graves
　　　　　The Devil's Advice To Story-Tellers
　　　　　(1938)

Jenny, one of those "invisible" people we all know and overlook each day, was a secretary for a manufacturing firm. She had earned a reputation for being dependable and efficient even if she wasn't ambitious, and these characteristics contributed to her unassuming presence. She hadn't developed strong personal relationships at work, but 35-year-old Jenny didn't seem to miss that kind of camaraderie, looking instead to her after-five existence for comfort, companionship, and security. She lived with the man to whom she had been engaged for more than a year, had a small circle of casual friends, and periodically saw her mother, who lived in the same western city. Week in and week out, Jenny's world seemed never to change, until one day it suddenly, quietly, fell apart.

Without any warnings that had been evident to Jenny, her fiancé announced that he was breaking their engagement. She needn't grope for solutions, he told her. The relationship was over and Jenny would have to move out of his apartment.

Jenny had existed to please her man, happily performing all the tasks of a homemaker, even though it meant working for hours each evening after returning from her outside job. Fancying herself an old-fashioned girl at heart, she had filled her leisure time with activities such as baking, preparing lavish dinners, and meticulously ironing everything from sheets to shirts. She yearned to be married and even had a hope chest full of items for her wedding day, but she never pressured her fiancé to set a date. And although she was hardly a creative lover, Jenny was faithful and devoted and always put her fiancé's needs before her own.

Jenny reeled with the prospect of having to leave this man. She blamed herself for the breakup even though she didn't know what she had done to cause it. Bewildered, Jenny surrendered the relationship amidst tears and pleas for answers, but without a fight. With nowhere else to turn, she went to live with her mother, a workaholic elementary school teacher whose prescription for coping was "keep busy."

In an effort to fill the empty hours after work, the lonely, depressed Jenny began sewing for the drama club at her mother's school. The children loved her kind, mild manner, and Jenny spent many hours fitting them for costumes for the semiannual productions at the school. Sadly, this wasn't enough to meet her emotional needs or rescue her from becoming increasingly introverted at work and in her personal life. Whereas she used to feel worthy of sharing in conversations, Jenny now felt she had nothing of interest to discuss. She also felt so overwhelmed by her feelings of abandonment and betrayal that she couldn't begin to express herself to anyone, let alone resolve her troubles by herself. Silence and overwork became her coping mechanisms.

After months of functioning under intense emotional strain, Jenny went to work one day and confessed to everyone there: "I have terminal breast cancer."

Jenny became an instant "somebody," the object of sympathy and attention from people who never noticed her before. Suddenly coworkers became best friends. Everyone rallied to her support. People were willing to change their own life-styles to accommodate Jenny. They offered to include her in car pools to cut down on the amount of traveling she had to do, and to share her work load, even though that meant they might have to work overtime without compensation. But Jenny declined their offers, saying that she wanted to carry on as she had before in spite of her illness. Her coworkers were moved by her spirit.

Jenny was rewarded with the kind of nurturance and support she had been craving. She had watched a neighbor suffer from breast cancer and knew how a woman would look as the disease progressed. Gradually, Jenny, too, lost her hair. She seemed to lose any incentive to wear makeup that would help hide her haggard appearance, and her already slight figure reflected drastic weight loss.

As her hair disappeared (later to be replaced by a wig), as her weight dropped 20 pounds, making her look more gaunt and pale each day, Jenny's life was, ironically, transformed into that of someone "special." Emotionally she was finally fulfilled.

Jenny cut back her already limited social activities. At home, her mother sometimes questioned her about her appointments with doctors, but also became even busier than usual to keep her mind off her daughter. Jenny's hair could regularly be found in the bathroom sink, but her mother's concern seemed muted until Jenny became entirely bald. "Oh my God, Jenny! Your hair! It's *all* gone!" cried her mother, her face contorted with horror and tears welling into her eyes. Jenny touched her smooth scalp wistfully and replied, "It's all part of the therapy, Mother. I just have to be strong and bear it. The doctors are doing everything possible. It's going to be okay, really." Jenny's calm response alleviated her mother's worries somewhat and Jenny maintained her "brave victim" persona.

Several months after breaking the news about her illness, Jenny enrolled in a weekly hospital support group for women with breast cancer. She became a diligent member, never missing an opportunity to be with the caring group of cancer patients and the social support team from the local cancer center. Jenny mirrored the appearance and tribulations of the other women in the group.

Because Jenny had emphasized the deadly nature of her illness, coworkers naturally talked among themselves about what would happen to her as she got closer to the time when the cancer would claim her life. But when months passed and Jenny's condition didn't seem to get worse, support from coworkers leveled off and even began to wane. At that point, Jenny shared another personal tragedy—her beloved grandfather had been seriously injured in a fire. A few people rolled their eyes as if to ask, "What next?" but most of her coworkers were upset by the thought of the increased emotional burden Jenny would have to bear and they pitied her. One woman spent her lunch hour reassuring Jenny and sharing intimacies about how she had dealt with the death of her grandmother. She even offered to accompany Jenny to a death and dying counseling group which was sponsored by a local church. But Jenny boldly squared her shoulders and pronounced, "I'll be all right. I'm learning to deal with these things in my cancer group."

The student body of her mother's elementary school supported Jenny as well. The children raised money to help Jenny pay for chemotherapy treatments. Jenny didn't want to take the money, but her mother insisted, saying she shouldn't disappoint the students. Feeling guilty about accepting money from the children, Jenny squirreled it away with the intention of somehow paying them back. At school, Jenny became a role model for students and teachers alike because, despite her illness, she continued sewing costumes for the upcoming school production. Students promised to dedicate the musical to Jenny. A local newspaper wrote about her courage and strength.

Although some people wondered about Jenny's ability to report to work every day, there were surprisingly few questions from her coworkers and supervisors, despite Jenny's failure to file insurance claims. It wasn't until her support group leaders tried to gain more information about her medical status that suspicions arose. "Jenny, we haven't been able to reach one of the doctors whom you said has been treating you, and the other doctor you referred us to doesn't know you," a counselor told her one night. "Can you help us?" Jenny hesitated momentarily, then quickly explained: "One of them retired and moved to Florida, but the other is my specialist. Of course he knows me. Call him again." She gently touched the hand of the counselor and thanked her for being so concerned. Jenny continued to provide the group's leaders with the names of doctors who had treated her, but it seemed that she was sending them on one wild goose chase after another. After following Jenny's dead-end maps, the leaders became convinced that she was lying.

Dr. Feldman:

They asked me how they should approach Jenny because they believed she was pretending to be ill. I told them to avoid being harsh or judgmental but still to maintain their position, and to beware of the denials that Jenny would surely issue. I advised them to let her know that she was not somehow "in trouble" and that there was immediate help for her if she would accept it. I agreed to make myself available to treat Jenny. Jenny's initial reaction to the confrontation was the same as that of many sufferers of factitious disorders when they are discovered: she vociferously denied having feigned the cancer.

"How could you accuse me of such a thing?" Jenny cried indignantly. "I shouldn't have to go through this awful grilling after all I've been through. Do I have to die to prove how sick I am? Will you believe me *when* I die?" Jenny angrily paced back and forth, her arms folded across her chest in a gesture of defiance. "It won't do you any good to refute this, Jenny," the group's leaders calmly told her. "We know that you never had cancer, but something else really *is* troubling you and we want to help." Eventually, as Jenny began to accept that the counselors did want to help her and not exact retribution, she collapsed into a chair, admitting her ruse in a flood of emotion. "You're right," she sobbed. "I faked everything right from the beginning. I just needed someone to care about me. I'm so sorry, so very, very sorry. I beg you to forgive me. Are you going to report me to someone? How will I ever be able to face everyone?" The counselors assured her that now that the truth was known, help for her emotional problems was available, and they recommended that she accept psychiatric counseling. Before the episode was over, Jenny agreed. She also promised to tell others that she had concocted the entire story and, when she lived up to her word, she felt the repercussions of her actions. Jenny sheepishly returned to work and confided in her supervisor, a no-nonsense woman who had lightened Jenny's work load because of her "illness." The supervisor was enraged by Jenny's tearful confession. She chastised her for "all the pain and anguish" she had caused her coworkers. "You took advantage of everyone and for what! You should be ashamed of yourself," the woman shouted, and with that she fired Jenny. By then, Jenny had carried out her simulation of cancer for two years.

Losing her job had compounded Jenny's embarrassment, but her mother's reactions made her wish for death. "I can't believe that you put me through all these months of worry," her stunned mother said. "I prayed and prayed for you. How could you do this to someone who loves you and who you supposedly love? What's wrong with you?" she asked, shaking her head in disbelief. "Do you know how many times I imagined myself at your funeral? I've mourned for you over these months as if you were already gone. How could you do this to me? Say something to make me understand!" But Jenny couldn't explain; she hardly understood what was happening herself.

Dr. Feldman:

Jenny's mother was concerned about the effects that Jenny's confession might have on her own job, so she broke the news at school. "Jenny is sick," she apologetically told the principal and other teachers, "but she doesn't have cancer." She awkwardly explained that Jenny had a mental disorder that led her to fake illness and tell lies, adding guardedly that she didn't understand much about it. The staff was dumbfounded and confused. Many reacted with disgust toward Jenny's mother for not having uncovered the ruse, but she defended herself, citing examples of Jenny's illness that had seemed so concrete, such as her hair loss. With her admission that she had faked her illness, Jenny confessed to her mother that she had cut her hair and eventually shaved her head to mimic the effects of chemotherapy. Jenny had also dieted to appear emaciated. Many staff members wanted more information about Jenny, contacting me themselves; but when I refused to violate my patient's confidentiality, some took their anger out on me, demanding that Jenny be given no consideration in view of what she had done. They felt she should be punished in some way for her deeds.

I was initially surprised by the backlash. I never expected to hear from so many angry callers. But they helped me realize the scope of the effect Jenny had on others. I understood their frustration and anger and I felt empathy for them, but empathy wasn't what these people were after. They also didn't want Jenny's apologies; they wanted their pound of flesh. Anything I said about Jenny at that point might only have set her up for further ridicule and abuse. The coworkers wanted me to agree with them that Jenny was wicked and deserved to be punished. I couldn't do that. Jenny was sick and needed an ally, not another accuser. I suggested that they seek outside counseling, perhaps as a group, to help them work through their feelings but they wanted help from *me*, as if being counseled by Jenny's own psychiatrist would affirm that they had been wronged. They were extremely displeased when I referred them to another doctor.

At first I was uncertain whether Jenny's was a case of malingering or factitious disorder. Factitious disorders are the conscious feigning or production of physical and/or psychological symptoms in order to assume the "sick" or "patient" role for gains such as nurturance. In contrast, Jenny would have been guilty of malingering if she had been seeking external gains such as financial benefits. It first seemed that she must be setting up a case for disability support or looking for a way to take time off from work. But when I noted that there had been no change in her work habits and that in two years she hadn't filed a single insurance or disability claim, I probed further. Soon it became clear that Jenny found the patient role inherently gratifying.

In our first meeting, Jenny bluntly admitted to me, "I'm here because I faked having cancer."

"I know, but I'm still glad you told me. How do you think you got yourself into this mess?" I asked.

"I'm not sure," she meekly confessed. "But I'm sorry that I did it, and now I don't know what to do."

When Jenny came to see me, she was teary, sad, and remorseful. But I didn't know if her sorrow was over her having feigned the cancer or if it reflected a deep depression that had led her to behave in such a desperate way. There are certain things we look for in depression, and Jenny was exhibiting many of them: a sad mood, lack of energy, an inability to concentrate. She wasn't eating well, wasn't sleeping, and was feeling helpless.

Part of Jenny's fantasy surrounding her cancer portrayal was that her former fiancé would hear about her "illness" and rush to be with her. But he and Jenny ran in such different circles after they broke up that he never even knew she was carrying out the deception. He had chosen to make a very clean break and move on with his life, while Jenny remained devastated by the separation.

After spending time with Jenny, I knew that she had to be treated for depression. I came to realize that Jenny had feigned cancer in order to feel in control. For some patients, factitious disorders become an elaborate form of denial, a way of avoiding painful emotions by focusing their attention on their bodies. They also avoid others' sympathy for the emotional trauma because it would be too hard to accept it and still move on. I thought that with her sources of support suddenly gone, Jenny was potentially suicidal, so I suggested hospitalization and she agreed to it.

I worked from the premise that Jenny also had a personality disorder which prevented her from having adequate coping skills and a clear-cut image of who she was. The depression and personality disorder were her main problems, and the factitious disorder seemed to be a manifestation of them. Psychological testing supported my diagnoses.

Jenny responded surprisingly quickly to medication for her depression, while continuing to address the factitious disorder in therapy. But before there was any marked improvement in her condition, Jenny had to conquer a new behavior that developed while she was hospitalized. Jenny had begun mutilating herself by gouging at her hands, arms, face, and ears with her fingernails, causing welts, bleeding, scabs, and infections. More frightening than her appearance was Jenny's denial that she had done it to herself. She claimed that she had to be doing it while asleep because she had no recollection of gouging herself. I really felt concerned about Jenny. I was worried that she was creating a new factitious illness.

It soon became apparent, however, that the mutilation was a spin-off of Jenny's anxiety. Jenny had to start her life over and this was overwhelmingly anxiety-producing for her. She also didn't know how to cope very well with stress. Some people rub their hands or pick at small imperfections in their skin when they're nervous. Jenny carried this to the extreme, and it had the potential to become disfiguring. Self-mutilation is scary, regardless of the underlying problem, and it creates a sense of helplessness in the treatment team. The nursing staff spent so much time putting medication on Jenny's welts and trying to catch her when she was causing them that I was getting subtle criticism from them. The nurses resented spending so much time with Jenny, tending to a problem that she was creating.

I talked frankly with Jenny about her behavior, and she agreed to wear mittens at night. She was very willing to try this because she wanted to stop mutilating herself. I suspect that at some point before we met she had even wanted to terminate her cancer portrayal but she was so caught up in it that she didn't know how to get out of it and save face. The mittens helped minimally. I plowed ahead with her treatment, continuing antidepressant medications, and over time the mutilation stopped.

Jenny also received self-relaxation training, which I believe hastened her progress. We tried to teach her to relax without medication as part of her becoming more self-reliant. This was a skill she could utilize whenever anxiety and pressure built up, instead of resorting to drastic measures to deal with stress.

Jenny reached a major turning point in her recovery when she talked with other patients and hospital staff about her ruse and found them open-minded and accepting. As part of Jenny's treatment, I asked her to call her father, who was divorced from her mother and living in New Mexico, and tell him the truth about her illness. She thought that he was going to be hostile and punitive but instead he wanted to know how he could help her.

Jenny agreed that it was important to share her feelings with her father. He visited her in the hospital, and his presence and keen interest in her condition implied that support was going to be in place for Jenny after her hospitalization. That improved her prognosis remarkably. It was important that she not have to go it alone.

Antidepressant drugs can take as long as six weeks to make a significant difference in a patient's condition, but Jenny showed marked improvement after only three weeks. When Jenny turned the corner, she turned it at a 180-degree angle and was doing 70 in the opposite direction. I think her improvement resulted from a combination of the medication and behavior therapy, plus the non-judgmental, caring way in which she was treated by the hospital staff and by her father. I never felt as confident about a factitial patient's recovery as I did about hers.

As the time drew near for Jenny to be discharged, I couldn't help but wonder, despite her excellent progress in treatment, whether she would fake another illness, if only to be able once again to enter a supportive hospital environment. But instead of trying to prolong her hospital stay, Jenny accepted her discharge and, although somewhat apprehensive about the future, decided to move to another city so that she could start over without the stigma of her factitious performance. She and her father assured me that they would contact me if the problem ever recurred. I have not heard from them since.

Although physically well, Jenny was one of the countless people who suffer from the strange psychological illnesses called *factitious disorders*. While well known to psychiatrists and psychologists, factitious disorders are often misinterpreted by the uninformed to be merely lying; a vicious way to use others for personal gain. Factitious disorders are far more complex than that, however, and surprisingly far-reaching in their effects upon the general public and medical community.

Jenny wasn't the first patient to seek nurturance by feigning cancer (cancer pathomimicry). Cancer has been the disease of choice of a number of factitial patients, and researchers wonder whether it could become even more commonplace as the general population receives cancer patients with less fear and discrimination and more support. The heroic image that cancer survivors sometimes have is attractive to factitial patients, as is the strong emotional response a cancer diagnosis is sure to draw from loved ones and associates.

In one case, a young pre-med student used feigned cancer in place of the social skills he sorely lacked to get the attention of a popular girl at school. He told her, other students, and selected members of the faculty that he was being treated for a tumor in his chest. He even showed them an irritated area on his back which he attributed to radiation therapy but which he had actually created at the hospital where he worked with the use of a sunlamp and tape.

His regular updates on his condition and his sickly appearance (he had dieted to lose weight and appear as if he were wasting away) convinced everyone around him that he was seriously ill. He maintained a high level of interest by telling his friends that he was facing critical treatment and went so far as to record farewell messages on tapes "just in case." His hoax was shaken after only a few months when his brother visited him and was surprised to hear from other students of his sibling's illness. Teachers then checked the hospital at which the young man was supposedly being treated and found that he was not a patient there. His parents asked teachers to pretend they didn't know about his ruse until the school term was over. But before then the student ended it himself by announcing happily that the treatments had been successful and he was going to live after all.

His father confronted him during summer recess and the young man confessed his actions, explaining why he had started his hoax and how it had gotten out of hand. After only a short time the girl he had been trying to attract became uninterested; however, by then word had spread that he was ill, so he continued the ruse, as Jenny had, rather than face the embarrassment that a confession would bring. Even though there were times when he wanted to stop fooling everyone, he was grateful that his hoax brought him a tight circle of concerned friends and took pressure off him to be the ultimate achiever. "It was such a relief not to be best in everything, and have to be on top of everything," he acknowledged in therapy.

He said he was relieved by his father's awareness of his actions, admitting that keeping up his ruse had been exhausting and ultimately boring. The young man apologized to his friends and teachers and, through therapy, learned how to take some of the pressure off himself and make his goals more realistic.

Two cases, reported in 1992 by Walter F. Baile, Jr., M.D., Charles V. Kuehn, M.S.S.W., and Drew Straker, M.S.W., in the journal *Psychosomatics*, parallel Jenny's case in a number of ways. However, unlike Jenny, who had no prior history of faking illness and did so only to gain nurturance, these women exhibited characteristics of Munchausen syndrome (the most chronic and extreme version of the factitious disorders) in that their lives had centered on disease portrayals. In addition, each sought financial assistance for the maintenance of her ruses, raising questions about the possibility of malingering.

One case involved a 38-year-old woman, whom we shall call Abby, who traveled from town to town faking cancer and other equally dramatic illnesses. Although Abby's simulations became more intense as she grew older, her practice of playing sick had actually begun when she was in elementary school. The eldest of three children, this woman adored her father, a military officer, who showered affection on her younger twin brothers but totally shut her out. After being enrolled in parochial school, Abby began playing sick to stay home as a way of getting extra attention from her authoritarian mother and trying to evoke some positive emotion from her father, who remained cold and distant.

Abby's mother knew that she was faking illnesses but didn't know how to help or stop her. At one point, Abby saw a psychiatrist, but he was unable to curtail her charades, which increased after her father's death.

As she grew older, Abby created a new setting for her performances, another version of a family environment, by gravitating toward clergy-men (father figures) and religious communities (Abby's second families). She carried this so far that she actually entered a nunnery and became a novice. Though now surrounded by a nurturing, supportive "family," Abby soon resumed her sick role by feigning leukemia. She asked the other nuns to pray for her because she was fighting a terrible illness, but she never shunned her responsibilities, putting up a good front even though she felt "weak." Abby's acting was convincing enough to draw pity and concern from other nuns, and her ruse was discovered only after she told her mother superior that her cancer was in remission. When the older nun telephoned the physician whom Abby said was treating her to applaud his success, she learned that Abby didn't have cancer or any other life-threatening illness.

Abby denied that she had pretended to be sick, but she soon left the nunnery with the explanation that such a life wasn't for her after all. She moved from one Catholic parish to another under the guise of a terminally ill patient, seeking counseling and guidance from priests while putting herself at odds with them if they challenged her or with-drew their support. In one parish she claimed to be a victim of AIDS, and a priest arranged for her to receive psychological counseling to deal with her illness. Abby said she would take advantage of therapy, but she never showed up for her appointments, always making excuses about having "bad days" due to her illness.

To keep her audiences engaged, Abby told tall tales, and the longer she remained in a place, the more outlandish her lies became. When, for shock value, she claimed that she had had an affair with a priest, the kindly priest who had viewed her as an AIDS patient reconsidered her other stories and confronted her. Abby accused him of being indiffer-ent to her problems, which she insisted were real, but the priest could no longer be swayed. Like a compulsive gambler gone bankrupt, Abby moved on to new sources of wealth in other venues. In one town she claimed that she had been raped and sought counseling at a Catholic rectory.

Abby was given room and board by many parishioners who were moved by her "plight" and wanted to help her. When she sought financial assistance at a cancer center, however, Abby exposed herself to scrutiny. She told social workers there that she had been treated several years earlier for uterine cancer, which had now spread to her liver, and that she had only six months left to live. They wanted to know where she had been treated so they could request her medical records, but she was vague and said that most of her medical care had been received in public clinics. She further explained that a doctor at the cancer center was treating her free of charge and, to avoid red tape, he had not registered her as a patient. She had convoluted answers for every question.

Lies to counselors snowballed into tales of tragic loss. Abby claimed that her fiancé had been killed in Vietnam when she was 20, that a priest friend had been killed in Guatemala, and that her brother had died in an auto accident, which led to her mother's suicide. She exaggerated her education, saying that she had received bachelor's and master's degrees in nursing and had worked at several cancer centers before being called on to nurse her father after he had suffered a heart attack. In her fantasies the father who had shunted her aside needed her, but in reality Abby never nursed her father or carried out any of the heroic deeds for which she claimed credit.

Abby's portrayal of illness was so convincing that therapists were taken in by her. When they visited her for outpatient counseling, she was often bedridden and surrounded by gifts from parishioners. Abby appeared to be enduring chronic pain, yet she maintained such a positive attitude that her counselors asked if they could videotape her talking about her illness and funeral arrangements. They also invited her to speak to a graduate social work class on death and dying, and she readily agreed. The students were overwhelmed by Abby's presentation, and when she told them that one of her dying wishes was to ride in a hot-air balloon, they collected $125 so that her wish could be fulfilled. There wasn't a dry eye in the house when Abby was finished.

Abby's needs were met beyond her expectations. But as the amount of attention she was receiving escalated, her story became increasingly inconsistent. A therapist started checking the facts and learned that Abby had never seen the doctor who was supposedly treating her. When Abby was confronted, she hinted that the doctor was lying for reasons that she could not divulge. But after the confrontation with the therapist, Abby never returned to the cancer center.

Abby lived with parish friends for four months before her hoax was irrefutably uncovered and she moved on. She was described as being devious and clever. However, it was her mysterious trips out of town under the pretense of visiting other friends, whom she never satisfactorily identified, that aroused the greatest suspicion among her caregivers. Looking for answers, they hired a private investigator, who discovered her string of illness deceptions and located her mother, who was very much alive. The detective learned that Abby's employment history was a patchwork of short-term jobs, usually at doctors' offices or hospitals, which doubtless provided her with the information she needed to make her portrayals believable. After being discovered, Abby returned to live with her mother, who was not surprised to hear that her daughter was still faking illness.

In the second case reported by Baile and colleagues, a 19-year-old woman faked cancer and other illnesses for 1½ years after her lover/cousin left her and her grandmother died. She told relatives and church members that she had cancer and went so far as to photocopy and alter bills and records taken from a hospital to make them appear as if they were hers. The records included notes about ovarian and cervical cancer and contained bills totalling $3,000. To keep her ruse believable, she allowed parishioners to collect money for alleged out-of-town medical care.

This young woman went to a pediatric cancer clinic complaining about leg pain, saying that x-rays and an isotope bone scan had been performed at another hospital and that a doctor had referred her to the clinic because she might have cancer. She made a follow-up appointment and when she didn't keep it, a concerned nurse contacted the "referring" hospital. The nurse learned that the teenager had indeed been there a year earlier but that no bone scan or x-rays had been performed and that she had not been referred to the clinic.

Relatives said that this young woman believed that her parents held her responsible for their divorce, which took place when she was eight years old. After her parents separated, she lived with her grandmother, who died several years later from cancer. They speculated that she had first feigned illness to try to keep her cousin romantically involved with her. Her fear of abandonment seems to have been a great motivation for playing sick. Her feelings of guilt from age eight laid the groundwork for her own shaky, self-defeating relationships.

After being told that her illness clearly was psychological, not physical, she chose to live with her mother, a nurse, and reportedly ended her disease portrayals.

For patients with Munchausen syndrome, the need for room and board, as well as burning psychological needs, can motivate behavior. In both of the above cases, the patients realized some deliberate material gain—one in the form of room, board, and gifts; the other in contributions for medical expenses that were never incurred. (In contrast, Jenny hadn't solicited money or planned on keeping what was given to her. She also rejected other forms of concrete assistance that were offered by coworkers.) Although some material gain was involved, what sets these two cases apart from pure malingering is that the women appeared to be motivated primarily by their emotional needs: one played out her ambivalent feelings for her father through her relationships with clergymen and their parishioners, and the other had reacted to ego-bruising rejection and great personal loss. Overall, it seemed that their material gains were merely means to an end—the credible portrayal of a long illness—rather than ends in themselves.

Even though Jenny's deception lasted two years, longer than in most simple factitious disorder cases, she was not diagnosed as having Munchausen syndrome because hers was a single deception, and feigned illness was not all there was to her life; she held a job and pursued a few outside interests. Some of Jenny's actions were typical of virtually all factitial patients, but it is also true that certain aspects of her case are atypical. First, Jenny was able to carry out a deception involving a serious illness for a long time in one place; most disease portrayals last a relatively short time before the patient is discovered and takes the portrayal elsewhere, abandons it, or switches to a different illness. Second, Jenny did not flee when confronted; rather she accepted the advice to admit the deception to her coworkers and employer. And third, Jenny then accepted and profited from treatment, which is contrary to most psychiatrists' experiences with factitial patients.

The two Munchausen patients, like Jenny, suffered from additional mental disorders including borderline personality disorder, which is characterized by unstable and intense relationships, conflicts with identity, feelings of abandonment and loss, mood swings, and self-destructive and manipulative behavior. As all three of these patients were carrying out their disease portrayals, they flitted around medical professionals like moths around a flame. Jenny and Abby surrounded themselves with counselors and therapists and, in Jenny's case, authentic cancer patients, while the teenager allowed herself to be x-rayed and repeatedly examined. Even though their dramas were carefully played out, the question still remains: how were they able to fool health care professionals who are exposed to genuinely sick people all the time?

Many of them are truly convincing actors and actresses. In two of these cases, as in so many other cases of factitious disorder, the women knew people who authentically had the disease they were going to feign. They were aware of what these individuals had gone through, what they looked like as the cancer progressed, and how they reacted to treatments. Jenny was an especially good mimic.

It isn't as hard to fool doctors as one might expect. Time and time again we see in the factitious disorders literature that patients expose themselves to multiple tests, exploratory operations, and diagnostic procedures. These tests may be repeated several times, even by the same doctors, because the doctors want so much to believe their patients. They just assume they missed something the first time.

And as in any business, physicians want to satisfy their patients. If a patient says, "You're missing something; I'm still in pain," doctors make every effort to please the patient and so they perform more tests. In other situations, a doctor may say, "Everything looks normal, but since you're so sure of the ailment let's just go ahead and treat it." As a result, people end up with unnecessary medications and surgeries. Doctors often find it very difficult to believe that somebody would actually feign a serious illness or self-induce dangerous symptoms.

It's the same with counselors and other health care professionals. Their first thoughts are not about whether or not someone is faking an illness. Although Jenny never actually presented herself to physicians, she did something that may well have been more exotic—she enrolled in group therapy. Surrounded by people with breast cancer, she said that she too had breast cancer. This lie actually represented a very primitive way of reaching out for help. It was so literal that it was pathetic.

The leaders of the group with whom Jenny aligned herself had been working with cancer patients for a long time. When Jenny showed up, she appeared emaciated and readily talked about her chemotherapy and the vomiting it caused as an explanation for her appearance. With such a convincing presentation, why would the group leaders have initially cross-examined Jenny or turned her away? But Jenny backed herself into a corner. She dared to put herself into an environment with genuinely sick women and stay around them for more than a year. Over time there were some deaths in the group, and some women improved while others deteriorated. Yet Jenny was there every week looking the same. Women in the group became suspicious, but none of them wanted to appear insensitive and question Jenny outright, so they voiced their suspicions behind her back.

Although the cases we've talked about here deal with varying patients and different circumstances, the real question to ask about these and all factitial patients is this: Is there an underlying problem, such as depression, in which doctors can intervene? It is important to acknowledge the various psychological or environmental contributions in order to underscore that a factitious disorder is almost never the sole problem.

We don't know all the factors that contribute to the development of these disorders, making certain people react so differently than others in the same traumatic situation. Many women, for example, have broken up with fiancés. Why did Jenny choose her particular course? Is it biological? Is it situational? Is it due to early life experiences? Or is it a combination? All of these factors have contributed to specific cases of factitious disorders.

Hundreds of factitious disorder cases appear in the medical literature, but these reports are almost always incomplete because of the very nature of the factitial patient and the flight reaction that takes over when their hoaxes are discovered. Fortunately, Jenny was different. Perhaps she recognized her illness and wanted to stop the difficult act she had struggled to maintain. Or perhaps, ironically, she *traded* factitious cancer for factitious depression, and her painful admission of her problem was yet another attempt to gain nurturance and shield herself from complete condemnation. The quicker way out—to flee—would have left her with nothing. In any case, Jenny proved the exerciser's creed, "No pain, no gain," in a poignant, albeit pathological, way.

Jenny's case has done more to educate people about factitious disorders than most others in the literature because she stayed around long enough for us to understand her and then treat her.

CHAPTER 2

THE LONGING FOR NURTURANCE

For the mind, like Rome, contains
Catacombs, aqueducts, amphitheatres, palaces,
Churches and equestrian statues, fallen,
broken or soiled.

Delmore Schwartz
*The Mind Is An Ancient And
Famous Capital* (1959)

No one in the emergency room suspected that the 31-year-old hospital security guard was anyone but a run-of-the-mill patient. After all, she held a responsible position and seemed to have legitimate symptoms—chills, fever, and headaches—which she was able to describe persuasively and which she believed required hospitalization. Agitated and fairly demonstrative, as many patients are under emergency circumstances, she complained to the staff that she had spent eight days with the same symptoms in another Kentucky hospital, but doctors there had failed to diagnose her illness. She was a real attention grabber, ranting about how shabbily she had been treated at the other hospital. However, when pressed for specific details about her personal medical history, she became quiet and reluctant to provide them.

While waiting for routine tests to be performed, the guard excused herself to the ladies' room, where nurses found her some time later, dead. Scattered around her body were various drugs including antibiotics, laxatives, alcohol and iodine pads, a package of brewer's yeast, a syringe containing a whitish substance, and a paper bag containing a pale-colored powder.

Given the patient's sudden, unexplained death, all of the articles on the toilet floor were sent to a state police crime laboratory, where chemical analysis revealed that the syringe and bag contained ordinary cornstarch. An autopsy revealed that the guard had been injecting yeast and cornstarch into her veins, some of which had formed clots that traveled to her lungs and killed her. Apart from arteries that were clogged with yeast and starch, this woman showed no other signs of any physical problem.

Staff from the Office of the Chief Medical Examiner in Kentucky described this case in the *American Journal of Emergency Medicine* (May 1990). Through information which emerged after the woman's death, they learned that she had been hospitalized 11 times in three years in Texas and Kentucky for complaints ranging from back pain to bloody urine. She had subjected herself to exploratory operations and, at one point, had been referred to a psychiatrist, but she never kept the appointment. The hospitalization about which she had complained so vehemently shortly before her death had been even more dramatic than she admitted, for doctors there had discovered a needle, syringe, and yeast in her nightstand and confronted her with this evidence. Her ruse discovered, she fled the hospital against doctors' wishes and went straight to the hospital where she died.

Her personal background was as grim as her medical record, overshadowed by a dreary childhood spent in an orphanage, and an adulthood that was marked by divorce and single parenthood. A post-mortem diagnosis of Munchausen syndrome was made. Was her death the result of a desperate longing for nurturance?

In her zeal to be hospitalized and to receive care in a dedicated, stable environment which starkly contrasted her own life, she had found a way to use fairly innocuous substances to create serious-looking symptoms. She lied and misrepresented herself not once, but many times, not only to medical professionals, but to her children, coworkers, and friends as well. It is doubtful that she intended to kill herself; she probably had no idea of what would happen to the yeast and starch after they were pumped into her veins. Initially her physical illness had been a forgery, manufactured for emotional gain. But it turned into something all too real and ended as something all too tragic.

Although her death certificate stated that she died of acute respiratory failure, sadly this woman died from a factitious disorder.

Factitious disorders have been well-described in medical literature for more than 30 years. They typically combine "somatizing" and "dissimulation" elements since they are based on fabricated physical and/or psychological symptoms.

Researchers divide patients with somatic complaints into two general categories. First are those patients who knowingly create symptoms in themselves, either for material gain, as in malingering, or for more subtle benefits such as the gratification of the patient role, as in factitious disorders. Second are those patients who do *not* deliberately produce their symptoms, as illustrated by the somatoform disorders. Somatoform disorders include somatization disorder, which is distinguished by a history of numerous unexplained somatic complaints; somatoform pain disorder, in which psychosocial distress is communicated through complaints of persistent pain; hypochondriasis, which is a conviction, with supporting symptoms, that one is diseased; and conversion disorder, which involves an involuntary loss of or alteration in physical functioning, such as paralysis, blindness, or muteness. Unlike the somatoform disorders, malingering and factitious disorders involve deliberate, willful disease forgeries.

False or dissimulated illness is best described as a continuum (see Figure 1). The continuum ranges from the benign to the pathologic feigning of illness. Factitious disorder is a deliberate act of disease forgery like malingering; however, the goal is intangible and psychologically complex: some form of emotional satisfaction from being a patient.

To illustrate further, prisoners become malingerers when they fake medical disorders to be transferred from a prison to a hospital which has better conditions. A patient who pretends to have cancer to obtain narcotic drugs, saying the drugs are needed to ease the pain, or who fakes a terminal diagnosis to be able to receive Social Security benefits, is also malingering. The malingerer lies for purely material benefits. However, when the gains sought are emotional fulfillment, empowerment over "stumped" health care providers, or simply the attention

DISSIMULATION

CONSCIOUS NONPATHOLOGIC FEIGNING (typical "playing sick")	CONSCIOUS PATHOLOGIC FEIGNING	
Benign Use of Illness	**Malingering**	**Factitious Disorders**
Most common; use of mild symptoms (e.g., stomachaches, headaches) as avoidance or attention-getting tools; no malicious intent; minor material and/or emotional gains are derived.	Intentional use of exaggerated or false symptoms to obtain tangible gains; not a mental disorder, though psychiatric counseling is recommended to determine whether personality disorder exists.	Intentional "disease forgery" for emotional satisfaction through the use of psychological or physical symptoms.

EXTREME VARIANTS OF FACTITIOUS DISORDERS

Munchausen Syndrome	Munchausen by Proxy	Munchausen by Adult Proxy
Chronic factitious disorder in which feigning illness becomes the focus of the person's life; it is carried out until discovered then begun anew elsewhere; characterized by itinerant behavior.	Faking or inducing illness in one's children to elicit sympathy and nurturance as the parent of a "poor sick child."	Like its namesake, but illness is induced in other adults so that the apparent "caretaker" receives sympathy and support.

Figure 1. Continuum of dissimulation.

of others, the diagnosis is probably a factitious disorder or a variation of it, such as Munchausen syndrome.

Researchers urge caution when differentiating between malingering and factitious disorders because human behavior is often motivated by various conscious and unconscious objectives, and a person may feign illness to achieve more than one goal. In other words, the motives for a ruse may be as pitiable as they are criminal. For example, a man might pretend to have chronic pain in order to procure narcotic painkillers and also to get attention from his wife. He may also choose to mimic an illness from which one of his parents suffered, thereby "sharing" their suffering. In such a case, several psychological factors are at work, making the patient much more than "just" a malingerer.

Factitious disorders are also a control mechanism, with patients manipulating the reactions of others by controlling their own symptoms. Just as kleptomania is often stealing for the thrill of the crime rather than for the stolen item, factitious disorders are often disease forgery for the sake of the forgery itself, coupled with the concomitant benefits of being ill (which may include attention, sympathy, and lenience from others). Factitious disorders can occur in children, adolescents, and adults in varying degrees and often coexist with symptoms of some other psychological disorder, such as depression, borderline personality disorder, or antisocial personality disorder. People with factitious disorders often have histories of turbulent and painful childhoods, unsettled adulthoods, and unstable relationships; however, they may well be employed and have roots in the community (except for the chronically itinerant Munchausen patients). Their portrayals of illness are frequently dramatized with lies unrelated to illness, and sometimes in creating symptoms they endanger their own lives. Mental health treatment is *essential* but often refused.

Widely misunderstood even by health professionals, factitious disorders must be considered in a modern perspective instead of the historical view, which erroneously groups all factitial patients under one extreme category—Munchausen syndrome. The term *Munchausen syndrome* was introduced by Dr. Richard Asher in 1951 in a paper he wrote for the British medical journal *Lancet*. Dr. Asher described this illness as "a common syndrome which most doctors have seen, but about which little has been written. Like the famous Baron von Munchausen, the persons affected have always travelled widely; and their stories, like those attributed to him, are both dramatic and untruthful. Accordingly the syndrome is respectfully dedicated to the baron, and named after him." Munchausen syndrome is actually a misnomer. Baron Karl Friedrich Hieronymus von Munchausen (1720–1791) was an honorable man and a famous and colorful war hero. After his retirement from the German cavalry, he spent his time traveling around his homeland, delighting listeners with tales of his military adventures. While he embellished some of his stories for dramatic effect, they were nonetheless essentially true. Historical records bear no evidence of his having feigned illness or duped people into caring for him because of his exploits. It was the manner in which he told his tales, however, which led Asher to associate the great Baron with patients who had a syndrome characterized by itinerancy and sensational lies.

Dr. Asher noted that Munchausen syndrome is distinguished by the patient's fantastic yet plausible description of his or her history (*pseudologia fantastica*), the deliberate use of self-induced symptoms to gain hospitalization, and peregrination, or wandering from place to place. He advised physicians to be alert to the possibility of Munchausen syndrome if a patient had (1) numerous surgical scars, usually in the abdominal area; (2) a truculent and evasive manner; (3) personal and medical histories that were fraught with acute and harrowing adventures that seemed to fall just on the wrong side of truth; and (4) a history of many hospitalizations, malpractice claims, and insurance claims.

Since then doctors have come to recognize, as noted by the eminent psychiatrist Theodore Nadelson, that Munchausen patients make the simulation of disease the center of their lives; they are usually suffering from some concurrent mental disorder such as borderline personality; they have poor job histories and are almost always drifters; and they are relentlessly self-destructive, encouraging and submitting to countless unnecessary surgeries and dangerous diagnostic procedures during their lifetimes. Their joblessness and itinerant natures often put Munchausen patients at odds with the law and push them over the line that separates malingering from factitious disorders; they also use their symptoms to garner room and board and other types of "ill-gotten" gains. Many Munchausen patients also develop drug dependencies, probably because of painkillers administered by well-meaning doctors who are trying to relieve their "symptoms," or because they have self-induced real illness that mandates some form of pharmacologic relief. Yet another motivation for their drug-seeking behavior is the thrill of putting one over on the physician.

With few exceptions in the last 30 years, the terms *factitious disorders* and *Munchausen syndrome* have been used interchangeably, but a distinction must be made between them. Not all patients who suffer from factitious disorders have Munchausen syndrome. Munchausen syndrome is an especially extreme and dangerous form, the pinnacle of a pyramid in which the benign use of illness is the base, factitious disorders are the center, and chronic factitious disorder—or Munchausen syndrome—is the top.

Factitious disorders are not a discovery of modern medicine, even though Asher formally brought them into the realm of medical science and exposed them to scrutiny. As long ago as the second century A.D., Galen, the Roman equivalent of Hippocrates, reported his observations of factitious disorder, listing medical signs and symptoms that some people induced or feigned to simulate disease, including vomiting and rectal bleeding. Attempts to categorize the condition were made in 1834 by Hector Gavin; and one hundred years later, Karl Menninger reported on "polysurgical" or "doctor" addiction, noting that it was marked by intense aggression against oneself and the physician, whom Menninger believed symbolized the "perceived sadistic parent."

In 1968, Spiro took Menninger's theory a step further, observing that the progression of Munchausen syndrome is based upon a person's early development and relationship with his or her parents. Spiro noted that early deprivation, incomplete development of a sense of self, defects in conscience, and abortive attempts at mastery of early trauma set the stage for the behavior to begin, and that hospitals are a natural place for it to unfold because they are equipped to provide caretaking and control. He equated the wanderlust of Munchausen patients with their simultaneous search for and rejection of intimacy. He postulated that these patients turn to the medical profession as part of a sadomasochistic ritual to transfer early hostility toward their parents to the hospital and to place the job of inflicting pain in the hands of a doctor.

Over the next 20 years, as the number of reported cases of factitious disorders increased and doctors had the opportunity to examine and observe some of these patients, researchers added other predisposing factors, including significant physical illness or abuse as a child, anger against doctors for perceived mistreatment, and parents who falsified medical histories or otherwise practiced medical deceit. Recent research has also suggested that the very nature of our fast-paced, indifferent society is fostering the factitious disorders—it just isn't easy to get sympathy, support, and concern in today's world.

Researchers note that *professional patients* (one of the irreverent terms that have been used by the medical community for factitial patients) are men and women of above average intelligence, who (with the exception of Munchausen patients) lead productive lives when they are not in the throes of their disease portrayals. Of these patients, those diagnosed with Munchausen syndrome are usually men in their 20s and 30s, while women (mostly between the ages of 20 and 50) are more often diagnosed with factitious disorders.

People with factitious disorders very often have poor social supports. They have little or no involvement with their families or they may have no relatives nearby, causing them to seek outside nurturance. Their entire purpose is defeated if their deceptions are revealed, so they vehemently deny their ruses, even to the point of threatening lawsuits when confronted. When emotional support begins to wane, the factitial patient often creates a secondary crisis to generate renewed interest and additional emotional support. The person may claim that a beloved relative has died or invoke some other personal tragedy which, when compounded with the alleged illness, mobilizes a new wave of nurturance.

The prevalence of factitious disorders is difficult to determine. After all, only cases in which the deception has not been successful are being recognized and reported! Asher believed that Munchausen syndrome was quite common and, based on the burgeoning number of cases in the medical literature and studies that have been conducted in this country and abroad, we suspect that it is underrecognized and more prevalent than ever. Some researchers suggest that it's difficult to track factitial patients because some of them may feign illness, stop, then return to it years later. The itinerant nature of some of them and the fear of detection experienced by all make it difficult to conduct formal studies; but several have been done with varying results. Studies of prevalence consistently show that many factitial patients work in health care settings, holding jobs as nurses, physical therapists, and nurses' aides. It is thought that their jobs as caregivers may be so emotionally draining that they begin to feel a desperate need for nurturance and use illness as a way of getting it. There may also be a general fascination with medically related matters that leads these people to go into medical fields and ultimately carry out illness portrayals.

In 1991, Dr. F. Patrick McKegney, director of consultation-liaison psychiatry at Montefiore Medical Center in New York City, reported that 1 percent of psychiatric consultation patients seen at his center were diagnosed by his team as having factitious disorders. That statistic is surely an underestimate of the prevalence of the illness since patients with physical complaints alone are rarely referred to psychiatrists. Health care workers often do not recognize or suspect factitious disorders, and even when they do, they may hesitate to confront patients for fear of angry rebuttals. Also, because most factitial patients never follow up on referrals to psychiatrists, many are never formally diagnosed.

In the Fall 1990 issue of *Psychosomatics*, Drs. Amanda J. Sutherland and Gary M. Rodin reported on a Toronto study in which factitious disorders were diagnosed in 10 out of 1,288 patients (or 0.8 percent) who were referred consecutively to a psychiatric consultation-liaison service. Additional psychiatric disorders such as psychogenic pain disorder, borderline personality disorder, and substance abuse were often identified in the factitial patients. Significantly, only two factitial patients agreed to ongoing psychotherapy, and one death which was attributed to factitious behavior occurred in the group. The researchers noted that although most reports of factitious disorders deal with physical symptoms, in another study 0.5 percent of individuals admitted to a psychiatric hospital feigned only psychological symptoms.

Drs. Sutherland and Rodin reported that "since medical practitioners often do not detect psychiatric illness in patients with physical complaints, such referred cases likely represent only a small proportion of all factitious disorders." Thus, as we have already said, the prevalence of factitious disorders is almost certainly far greater than statistics show.

In the Toronto study, factitial patients ranged in age from 19 to 64, with a median age of 26 years. The average age at onset of disease simulation was 21 years, with 80 percent of the factitial patients admitting to having begun their behavior before the age of 28. (Perhaps the onset of adulthood, with its concomitant stresses, causes certain types of people to play sick for sympathy.) The length of time of the factitial behavior averaged 4 years, but ranged from 0 to 11 years. By the time the psychiatric referrals were made, these patients had undergone extensive medical diagnostic testing which included angiography (x-ray examination of the blood vessels), biopsy (removal of body tissue for examination), laparotomy (incision into the abdominal cavity), and lumbar puncture (removal of cerebrospinal fluid from the lower back); and many had received medication. Several of these patients had undergone surgery, including one whose finger was removed because of a self-induced bone marrow infection (or osteomyelitis, caused by the introduction of microorganisms into the blood). Another patient had received electroseizure therapy (electroshock treatments) for factitious depression.

Of nine patients who had been told by their doctors that they were suspected of feigning illness, only one, the woman who had received electroseizure therapy, admitted to playing sick. One of the patients in the study (who was legitimately ill with diabetes but had feigned other illnesses as well) denied inducing her own symptoms and refused ongoing psychotherapy. She was hospitalized four months later for a condition which doctors attributed to her deliberately stopping her insulin to create symptoms. She died three days after her admission.

Drs. Sutherland and Rodin emphasized that factitious disorders are found in greater prevalence by researchers who specifically look for them among high-risk groups. They pointed to a study of factitious disorders among 343 patients who were referred to the National Institute for Allergy and Infectious Disease because of prolonged fever of unknown origin. Factitious disorders were diagnosed in 32 patients, or 9.3 percent!

Some attribute the notable ranks of factitial patients in part to the availability of third-party payments, such as those provided by insurance companies and medical assistance programs. Whether or not this factor contributes to the current prevalence is uncertain, but what is clear is that feigned illness due to factitious disorders is costing a fortune. One individual patient reportedly accrued medical care costs in excess of $6 million. Someone has to pay for these highly specialized services, whether it's federal, state, or local governments (which means that taxpayers assume the bill), insurance companies, individuals, or hospitals which end up absorbing unpaid bills. Concerns over the rising costs of factitious disorders have mounted because these patients consume medical resources in overwhelming volume through their frequent hospitalizations, numerous surgeries, repetitive sophisticated diagnostic studies, and countless hours of care. One report claims that feigned illness absorbs up to $40 million a year from the health care industry because of unpaid bills. And what of those that are paid?

Dr. Dennis Donovan had a rare opportunity to observe firsthand how a single patient can incur a fortune in bills through feigned illness. In 1987 he wrote in the journal *Hospital and Community Psychiatry* about a woman who, in the 12 years between 1968 and 1980, had at least 52 psychiatric admissions. Her known psychiatric hospitalizations alone—which totalled 497 days—cost $20,500 or, at 1992 rates, approximately $185,128. And that just covers her psychiatric care! She had also been hospitalized for intensive medical care on various occasions. Dr. Donovan was unable to trace some other hospitalizations and could not obtain her outpatient or prescription records to determine the cost of her outpatient care and drugs. This amount would have been significant because, according to Donovan, the patient obtained prescriptions from as many as a dozen doctors at one time. This patient also lost 12 years of employment, and received disability pay and $15,000 in damages, which she won from her employer.

The ascertainable cost of this patient's total medical care over a 12-year period was $104,756; conservatively adjusted, this figure is $1,446,601 at 1992 rates. Not one of this patient's bills was paid. Dr. Donovan points out that the "extraordinary cost—both human and economic—of factitious illness might well be avoided through appropriate psychiatric intervention."

Intervention requires a full understanding of the disorder's symptoms. The symptoms within factitious disorders can be classified as follows: (1) *total fabrications*, as in the patient who groans about severe back pain but isn't really having any pain at all; (2) *exaggerations*, as in the patient who claims to have devastating, incapacitating migraines but really has only occasional mild tension headaches; (3) *simulations of disease*, as in the patient who mimics symptoms of a brain tumor or spits up "blood" that was actually concealed in a rubber pouch inside the mouth; or (4) *self-induced disease*, as in the patient who complains of fever and pain after actually inducing an infection by injecting herself with bacteria or dirt. As noted, sometimes the purposeful production of physical symptoms even becomes life-threatening, giving ironic truth to the original lie. The very nature of factitious disorders, with subtle unconscious dynamics and often dramatic physical symptoms, demands that health care providers be dogged investigators, leaving no question unanswered and nothing presupposed.

The extremes to which factitious patients go to create the appearance of illness are often bizarre, and yet so effective that they defy the imagination, let alone medical knowledge. Many patients simulate disease by surreptitiously giving themselves medications. For example, one man displayed symptoms of what appeared to be hypoglycemia, or a low blood sugar; doctors ultimately found out that he was injecting himself with insulin even though he didn't have diabetes. Some patients bleed themselves to simulate anemia; others inject anticoagulants into their systems to cause bleeding disorders; and still others use laxatives to produce chronic diarrhea. Thus, the doctors of such patients must be more than good diagnosticians; they must also be detectives.

The detective work of medical personnel doesn't always involve the factitial patient alone; sometimes the disorder is detected only through the patient's victims. For example, in the stereotypic case of *Munchausen by proxy*, in which a parent or guardian creates symptoms in a child, the parent might at first seem devoted to the "sick" child, admirable and loving—more than worthy of the praise and support of the child's health care providers. The deceptive behavior is not discovered until the child's fake illness is discovered, *if* that ever occurs. Similarly, in an extremely rare variant of Munchausen by proxy, called *Munchausen by adult proxy*, symptoms are created in one adult by another who is seeking the praiseworthy role of the selfless caregiver. Again, the victims' fabricated or induced symptoms provide important clues to the real pathology behind the portrayal.

Victims of factitial patients are not always *primary* victims, as in the Munchausen by proxy cases. In fact, *secondary* victims are much more common and are part of every case. These victims are the family, friends, medical personnel, and others who become engaged in the ruse and devote time and energy to support the pretender. They become, in effect, emotional rape victims, and often they are the ones who expose the deceptions. Duped, then disillusioned, they may need therapy themselves; and, as integral players, they merit our attention in their own section of this book.

The victimization of others should not necessarily be regarded as intentional, however. The havoc factitial patients create for others is more often a by-product of their own masochism than a deliberate goal.

During the perpetration of their factitious illnesses (which sometimes last years), these people live within private hells of their own creation, unable to experience the fullness of life because all their experiences must revolve around sickness. And what makes their plight so sad is that they honestly believe that they must go to such outrageous, desperate extremes to obtain support and attention in their daily lives. Yes, some factitial patients are full of rage, and defeating caregivers is a way to express that rage. They may be especially delighted when the physician finally becomes aware of how badly he or she has been deceived. Others feel they've lost control of their lives, and "outsmarting" doctors allows them to feel "in control." But in any case, playing sick in lieu of communicating one's real needs or emotions is unhealthy, destructive, sometimes dangerous, always pathetic, and almost certainly more common than we know.

CHAPTER 3

A PERSONAL VAMPIRE

Appearances often are deceiving.
Aesop (fl. c. 500 B.C.)
The Wolf In Sheep's Clothing

Jenny's painful gains are our gains as well, for she illustrated how factitious disorders can be treated in some instances with favorable results. This bodes well for the treatment of other cooperative factitial patients. But what about factitial patients who refuse treatment? What happens to those patients who push their bodies beyond their limits and actually create dangerous, even deadly illnesses in themselves, then refuse to let doctors help them? Or to those who continue their self-destructive behaviors in spite of therapeutic efforts to save them?

Dr. Feldman:

I encountered one such patient, a laboratory technician, early in my career. This woman, who was 26 years old, cut a ghastly figure with her ashen skin and alarmingly thin frame. She was hesitant and timid when she entered the clinic of the prominent hospital at which she worked and, in an almost inaudible voice, complained of dizziness and weakness. Because of her appearance and symptoms, I ordered emergency tests on a sample of her blood. Meanwhile, I obtained a medical history from the woman, who insisted that she couldn't offer any reason for her condition. She said that she had been working effectively and that she had come to the clinic only because she had some free time and wanted to talk to someone about how poorly she had been feeling.

Although this woman offered little data, I was stunned by the results of her blood tests. Her blood count was so low that I would have thought it incompatible with life. I performed some additional tests, including one to see if she was losing blood through her intestines. But every test was negative.

The technician did not react to the news of her grave condition as I would have anticipated. Her way of relating struck me and others in the clinic as being odd. She was insincere. Here she was with this dangerously low blood count and she couldn't have been more passive. I thought she was lying when she said that she had no clue as to how her condition had developed.

This woman's anemia was so critical that I wanted to give her an immediate blood transfusion, but she would accept only an injection of iron. While waiting for the injection, she became restless and, as she fidgeted, she told me, "Maybe this was a mistake. I just want to leave." I and other doctors who were present pressed her for more information, and finally she confessed that when she felt agitated she turned into something of a personal vampire to reverse those feelings. With syringes obtained from the lab in which she worked, she would bleed herself, then squirt the blood into a toilet to get rid of it. She drew blood until she felt calm again.

After owning up to her bloodletting and receiving the injection of iron, the technician bolted from the examining room with me in reckless pursuit. When the patient disappeared into a stairwell, I stopped short and asked myself what I would do if I caught her. I realized that there was little I could do. I couldn't detain and force further treatment on her; that action could amount to assault and battery.

I consoled myself with the knowledge that at least she accepted some iron, and we had made her aware that her actions had placed her in real physical danger. But she never returned to the clinic because we knew what she was up to. This woman could have died from what she was doing. For all I know, she did.

Almost all factitial patients who feign blood disorders through self-bleeding or other means are medical professionals. And most of them are women, usually nurses. These patients fall into distinct groups based on the means they use to create their symptoms. For example, some, like the "personal vampire," use a very direct route to anemia, drawing their blood and either throwing it away, ingesting it, or putting it into their urine to create medical signs. Others use more esoteric means to create their symptoms, including injecting themselves with anticoagulants (substances that prevent clotting, such as the drugs heparin or bishydroxycoumarin) or swallowing substances such as rat poison, which contain anticoagulants. The latter are the dicumarol eaters (dicumarol is an anticoagulant drug which can produce bleeding when overdoses are taken). They take anticoagulants until they have all the symptoms of a serious blood disorder—easy bruisability, easy bleeding, and blood that doesn't coagulate—symptoms that look like leukemia or some other severe illness. Some factitial patients have even taken excessive doses of aspirin to cause internal bleeding.

Those who practice bloodletting develop the symptoms of blood loss anemia. What might arouse the suspicions of doctors is that while the total blood count goes down, the reticulocyte (developing red blood cells) count goes up and no site of blood loss is identified. One nurse drew blood out of her arm, then injected it into her bladder through a catheter, urinated blood, and claimed kidney disease. She had already lost one kidney from a variety of manipulations that she had inflicted upon herself. Doctors were able to get her legally committed for treatment, but the state hospital discharged her after one week, stating that she *only* had Munchausen syndrome. Her doctors were very discouraged because they had believed that only through commitment could she be treated.

Several cases of factitious anemia through self-induced phlebotomy (bloodletting) have been reported by researchers. The first such cases to appear in the English language were presented by Drs. W.J.R. Daily, J.M. Coles, and W.P. Creger of Palo Alto, California, and published in *Annals of Internal Medicine* in 1963. One of these cases involved a 30-year-old laboratory technician who complained of heavy menstrual bleeding, but doctors found only an enlarged ovary, which would not have accounted for the substantial bleeding problem she reported. One month later she was hospitalized for weakness and fainting and, without any signs of vaginal or other bleeding, a drastically reduced blood count. Through exploratory surgery, doctors found a ruptured ovarian cyst. This finding would indeed account for some bleeding, so she was treated with a blood transfusion and iron and sent home. Doctors diagnosed her as having iron deficiency anemia secondary to ovarian blood loss.

Over the next few months she complained of nausea and vomiting and was rehospitalized with a host of other symptoms and signs, including muscle pain, sore throat, cough, stomach pain, nosebleeds, and a dangerously low blood count. Test after test proved negative as doctors seemingly checked every possibility for the source of her blood loss. She received iron therapy and four units of whole blood, despite her having had a history of allergic reactions to transfusions. After all this, her blood count fell again and she was hospitalized for reevaluation. While she was in the hospital, her blood count began to rise without therapy. When her doctors pointed this out, instead of being elated, she predicted that it would fall again dramatically. Within 24 hours it did. A battery of new tests still left doctors in a quandary. There was only one other possibility: she was "stealing" her own blood.

Hospital personnel searched the patient's room and found a needle, needle cases, syringe, transfusion tubing, and a copy of *Transfusion* magazine. After obtaining advice from a psychiatrist, doctors confronted her and she admitted to self-bloodletting and agreed to psychotherapy. When her anemia persisted in spite of outpatient treatment, she was institutionalized.

Psychiatric evaluation showed that this woman was depressed and extremely hostile toward medical professionals, feelings which stemmed from a traumatic personal experience. Her fiancé had been in an automobile accident and died after three months of hospitalization. During that time, he had refused to see her and doctors had honored his refusal, so she had been unable to check on his condition or see him one last time before he died. Her factitious disease was probably a way of getting even with doctors by confounding them and making them appear inept but, in so doing, she gave herself a real illness.

Given this woman's background and medical knowledge and the results of early tests, self-bloodletting might have been her doctors' first consideration, but it wasn't. They didn't consider a factitious disorder until they had excluded all other possibilities and had invested months in observation, expensive testing, and medical care.

Another patient allowed major surgery on her intestine (to create an ileostomy) because doctors believed she was losing blood through her colon as a result of ulcerative colitis (ulcerated inflammation of the colon). This 41-year-old homemaker and wife of a Prussian riding instructor had been hospitalized several times with severe leg pain, weakness, and an unsteady gait. Blood tests showed that she was anemic, and barium enemas suggested a moderate form of chronic ulcerative colitis. She was also extremely depressed.

The patient was rushed to a hospital several times for profusely bloody diarrhea. Additional tests confirmed that she had ulcerative colitis and anemia, which doctors thought was being caused by the colitis and related blood loss through her stool. She received transfusions and was discharged, only to be readmitted months later with the same symptoms. She was given more transfusions and iron therapy; however, this time doctors looked askance at her condition because her ulcerative colitis had been responding well to treatment, and she should not have had the other dramatic symptoms, especially the bleeding. Doctors reexamined her and found that a section of her colon was severely lacerated, which led them to suspect that her illness was factitious. When she was confronted, she admitted to having caused profuse rectal bleeding by lacerating her colon with a knitting needle which she had inserted into her rectum on several occasions.

While in therapy, the woman also admitted to having swallowed small amounts of an arsenic-based snail-killing preparation, which had caused her unsteadiness, weakness, and other odd sensations (arsenical neuropathy). Unusually high levels of arsenic had been found in her urine during one of her hospitalizations, but doctors had failed to consider the possibility that it was self-administered.

Psychiatrists learned that she and her husband had viewed their marriage as a business arrangement. When she had exhausted her usefulness as a riding instructor, her husband completely rejected her. Her factitious diseases may have been a way of hurting him while punishing herself for having subjected herself to such a miserable lot.

Cases of factitious anemia have been reported in several countries. Daily, Coles, and Creger noted two cases of factitious anemia in Oslo, Norway, one of which involved a 44-year-old woman who was first hospitalized in 1949 because her urine contained blood and protein (hematuria and proteinuria), which can be signs of kidney disease. During 14 months between late 1953 and early 1955, she received 40 blood transfusions for recurrent anemia even though she showed no external signs of blood loss and tests revealed no evidence of hemolysis (the destruction of red blood cells within the body, which may lead to anemia). Doctors ultimately diagnosed her as having factitious protein-uria (which she had caused by placing egg white, a pure protein, in her bladder through a urethral catheter), and self-induced anemia through bloodletting. This patient denied causing her own illness and was committed for psychological evaluation.

Why would people willingly subject themselves to blood transfusions? Why would they ravage their bodies to the extent that the hoax becomes reality? There are no easy answers to these questions because the underlying motivations and catalysts for factitious disorders are as varied as the patients themselves.

A 29-year-old, married nurse (Dr. Ford's patient) had been seen at a major diagnostic treatment center where doctors accused her of causing a blood disease by unnecessarily taking methotrexate, a chemotherapy agent that kills bone marrow. She denied knowledge of the true uses for the drug (knowledge a nurse would have), saying a friend had given it to her to build up her blood. Feeling that she was being too closely scrutinized, she moved on to a general hospital (at which Dr. Ford worked), where she claimed that doctors at yet another hospital had failed to identify the cause of her illness.

To save her life, this woman had to be transfused with packed red cells and HLA-matched platelets, which are expensive, scarce products. A hematologist (specialist in blood disorders) was assigned to her case and even before her condition stabilized, he began a battery of tests to find the cause of her grave ailment.

She reported a medical history that was rife with blood problems, including the story that at the age of 19 an appendectomy (removal of the appendix) had been delayed so that she could receive a blood transfusion because of anemia. She claimed that two years later she again developed severe anemia, for which she received repetitive transfusions and, she said, at the age of 24 her spleen was removed (a splenectomy, performed because of a ruptured spleen or in the treatment of certain blood disorders). The nurse said that by the age of 27, because of anemia and severe bleeding associated with her menstrual periods, she had received over 500 transfusions of blood products.

She also created a dramatic background for herself that rivaled life at pre–Civil War "Tara," reporting that she had been raised on an elegant farm where life was filled with privileges and frivolity. She said that she had been a high school honor student, had studied at a prestigious university and nursing school, and ultimately achieved the status of head nurse at a medical institution near her home in Montgomery, Alabama.

Dr. Ford:

Her medical history aroused her doctors' curiosity, and they asked me to speak with her to assess whether her illness was self-induced. She elaborated upon her story when she spoke with me, saying that she had been a graduate student and researcher at the University of California at Berkeley. Unbeknownst to her, I am a native of that area, but I pretended not to know anything about Berkeley and the University and questioned her about them. None of her answers were correct, which made me agree with the other doctors that she was likely to be lying about her illness as well. Their suspicions were borne out when tests showed that her blood contained high levels of methotrexate. She did not have, nor had she had, cancer, and she had no reason to be taking such a potent and hazardous drug.

She had self-induced a rare and deadly blood disease called aplastic anemia. In aplastic anemia, there is a simultaneous drop in the number of red and white blood cells and blood platelets (pancytopenia) caused by bone marrow hypoplasia (a disturbance in its development). This type of anemia can be caused by exposure to ionizing radiation, such as x-rays and radioactive elements, or to chemicals such as benzene (a solvent) or drugs used to treat malignant diseases such as cancer.

This patient was a nurse and should have been familiar with the uses of the drug. She was a very sick woman, not only because of her anemia but because she had a number of personality problems, not the least of which was borderline personality disorder. Typical of persons with borderline personality, she created a high degree of discord among the hospital staff, engendering angry feelings and then provoking others to express her anger on her behalf. People on the hospital staff moved into two camps and then started fighting with one another.

Her need for lifesaving measures created the greatest controversy among the nurses, attending physicians, and house staff because these treatments were costly and some caregivers believed that such limited resources were being wasted on a factitious patient. Others were far more sympathetic and argued that the woman was seriously ill, both mentally and physically, and that she couldn't help herself and should receive proper treatment.

She wasn't psychotic (a condition which causes a person to lose touch with reality). As a nurse, part of her fully understood what she was doing and what the implications were. Yet she continued to play the game, which strongly suggested that some kind of disturbed thinking was at work.

We phoned doctors at the other hospital and found that they had made a similar diagnosis and had given her a lecture on methotrexate and told her to stop taking it. They were surprised that she presented the same factitious disease somewhere else. That phone call proved that she knew what methotrexate was and what it was doing to her body and that she had lied to all of us.

When I and other doctors involved with her case confronted her, she told us that we were crazy and that she didn't know anything about the drug. But when we pointed out that her blood level of the drug contradicted what she was saying, she told us what she had told other doctors: that someone had told her it would be good for her.

We let her husband know what she was doing and that she was going to die from it, but he seemed passive. He said weakly, "Oh, my gosh, she is? We've got to do something." Then he went into her room and talked to her. After a while he came out and told us, "Gee, all of you misunderstand her illness." She had completely convinced him that we didn't know what we were talking about.

I tried to assuage the anger of her hematologist, who was furious at having been duped and having wasted time and resources on her. I told him that we had to do whatever we could to save her life because she was about to die. Everyone who had been involved in her care resented what she had done, but in the end they sincerely tried to save her life.

In the midst of this mayhem, the patient demanded additional tests from her hematologist, but he refused to order them. Then she was found to be hoarding an addictive narcotic painkiller called meperidine (Demerol is a brand name of this drug), and because of that, she was discharged from the hospital.

I was able to contact the patient's mother, who told me that the only true part of her story was that the patient really was a nurse. Her mother contradicted most of the other details and painted a grim picture of her daughter's childhood, which was punctuated by her parents' divorce and a financial situation that bordered on poverty. As a girl she had been sickly and had a reputation for being a liar in grade school. Her menstrual periods, which began earlier than most of her peers, were so heavy that her mother occasionally had to bring fresh clothes to school for her. The girl developed a preoccupation with bleeding and blood early in her life.

After she was administratively discharged from the hospital where I met her, this nurse went to another hospital with the same disease, then telephoned the hematologist who had handled her case with me and mockingly told him that she had done it again and this time managed to get the additional tests that he had denied her. That was the last we heard of her. Because of the extent of her illness when we were treating her and her continued factitious behavior, we can only assume that she died not too long after.

Drs. T. Michael Harrington and David G. Folks (with Dr. Ford), at the University of Alabama Hospital in Birmingham, reported another case of a 28-year-old woman who was hospitalized five times by her family doctor for vomiting blood (hematemesis). While doctors looked for the cause, she received 18 units of blood. Contrary to the resistance many people offer to hospitalization, this patient not only sought hospitalization but enjoyed it and spent most of her time in a hospital solarium socializing with other patients. When nurses found cuts over a vein in her leg during three of her hospitalizations, she shrugged off their questions and attributed the cuts to "accidents at home."

During her fifth hospitalization, after diagnostic procedures offered no solution, her doctor told her that he was certain she was drawing off her own blood and swallowing it so that she would vomit blood and give the appearance of gastrointestinal bleeding. She gasped in surprise and challenged him. "Do you really think I would do that?" she asked her doctor. He said he did, and, surprisingly, she seemed to be relieved by his honesty.

Because the physician had known this patient for many years and had a strong relationship with her, he discharged her from the hospital but continued seeing her for the next year for general complaints, such as migraine headaches. Neither of them mentioned the factitious behavior again. Periodic tests showed that she had stopped bleeding herself.

When doctors had the opportunity, later, to review her medical records, they discovered a 10-year history of visits to emergency rooms and acute care centers for cuts and lacerations, eight of which needed a total of 70 stitches. No one ever reported suspecting that her injuries were self-induced. Doctors believed that her factitious disease had been instigated by an "anniversary reaction" (in which holidays intensify feelings of personal grief). They noticed that her hospitalizations and medical emergencies coincided not only with major holidays but also with special occasions such as her child's birthday.

In anniversary phenomena, feelings of loss are reactivated. For example, the feelings may recur on the anniversary of a loved one's death. Reactions tend to be much more severe when they are associated with a holiday, such as Thanksgiving or Christmas.

Psychiatrists speculated that by feigning illness this woman had been trying to cope with unresolved grief caused by her father's death when she was two years old. Her factitious behavior intensified and led to hospitalizations when her marriage began to sour and her husband, the only adult with whom she had a close relationship, threatened her with divorce. Like Jenny, she was unable to cope with this intense domestic anxiety and she resorted to illness as a way of eliciting sympathy from her husband and forestalling the breakup. Doctors believed that she substituted migraines for gastrointestinal bleeding but that the more severe factitious symptoms might well recur whenever she was under extreme stress.

People employ many inventive methods for using blood as a primary agent in faked illness. In one case, a woman drew blood from her armpit with needles, drank it, then complained about blood loss through her colon. When the doctor tested her stools, sure enough, they contained "digested" blood. An 18-year-old Yemeni girl, who suffered from Munchausen syndrome, arrived at a hospital bleeding from several places on her body; she also presented with ulcers on her tongue and air in the skin tissues on her face, around her eyes, and on her upper chest (subcutaneous emphysema). Her disease forgery was uncovered when she was caught injecting air under her skin.

Factitial patients want dramatic symptoms that will cause doctors to take immediate note. Blood is both dramatic and highly accessible. When a person shows up at an emergency room with a very low blood count, doctors will certainly notice. With just a little cut, a person can drop his or her red blood cell count in a matter of minutes. Factitial patients may use this fact to create remarkable abnormalities.

The risk at which factitial patients place themselves is lost to them in their intense quest to achieve their overall goal. They develop a kind of tunnel vision which prevents them from noticing the real dangers of the symptoms they create. As you can see, in a number of these cases people have been given transfusion after transfusion. Death can result from an allergic reaction to blood, not to mention infection with the hepatitis or AIDS viruses (prior to consistent measures for screening blood). What's more, factitial patients endanger others by unnecessarily using blood, a scarce resource. They get transfused and bleed themselves again, and it becomes a cycle.

The cycle can continue (barring the patient's death) until the pretender either is caught and confronted—in which case he or she usually flees—or is gratified by the fulfillment of the needs that drove the ruse in the first place. A woman named Marjorie (Dr. Ford's patient) was hospitalized for severe, bloody diarrhea. She underwent a colonoscopy (study of the interior of the colon and rectum), which revealed what doctors thought were puncture wounds in her colon. The apparent wounds alerted her doctors that she was suffering from a factitious disorder.

Dr. Ford:

I advised the doctors not to confront her directly and suggested instead that I see her as an outpatient. Marjorie readily agreed to see me. Many of these patients are looking for nurturance—for somebody to be interested in them and take care of them and be involved with their lives. That's an important point that is often overlooked in the study of factitious illness. If the doctor can provide that closeness, then the factitious symptoms aren't necessarily so important any-more.

Marjorie didn't have to play the sick game with me because I was seeing her on a regular basis. During therapy she confided that she had been putting a knitting needle up her rectum to cause her own bleeding. She continued her therapy but sabotaged her progress by replacing self-induced symptoms with fantastic lies, as if to ensure that she would remain "interesting." Her disheveled appearance—she was about 100 pounds overweight and unkempt—was indicative of her low self-esteem and the emotional void that characterized her life and thus made her lies her comfort.

In therapy, she told me that she was the lover of a dashing airline pilot who hopscotched around the globe on intercontinental flights. She would come into my office and talk about having seen her boy-friend the night before and that he had flown in from Paris just to have dinner with her. This went on for several weeks, and it was obvious that the stories didn't fit her real personal life. I thought I could help her if I knew more about her, so I finally asked where she lived. She told me that she shared an apartment with her mother, and she gave me permission to call the woman. But there was never any answer, and Marjorie never came back to see me. I had pushed too far in an effort to get beyond her wild stories. Admitting her self-induced bleeding was as much honesty as she could handle; giving up lying altogether would mean facing painful truths about herself.

Researchers note that a number of pregnant women diagnosed with Munchausen syndrome have induced bleeding in themselves. Dr. Robert C. Goodlin of Omaha, Nebraska, reported several such cases, including vaginal bleeding in a 19-year-old girl who was in her third pregnancy. The daughter of a physician, her previous pregnancies had been marked by the same bleeding problem, which had led to long hospital stays. She had an impressive knowledge of medical terms but insisted that she knew nothing of the cause of her bleeding. While she was hospitalized for examination, nurses found blood on her clothing and bed linen. Another patient, not a member of the medical staff, finally uncovered her illness portrayal by catching her rubbing her vulva with such force that skin was missing and it bled to the touch.

In another case reported by Goodlin, a 23-year-old pregnant woman, who had worked as a nurse's aide, went to a hospital with what appeared to be blood-stained underwear and blood running down her legs. Like the 19-year-old woman, she had had painless vaginal bleeding during her two previous pregnancies. She was admitted to the hospital and doctors used ultrasound to confirm that the six-month fetus was normal. She left the hospital of her own accord after two days, only to return a day later covered with what again appeared to be blood. Nurses thought that the color of the "blood" seemed too intense, so it was tested and doctors found that it was an exogenous red liquid. The patient was furious when this was discovered and left the hospital without pressing for admission. This woman had a history of emotional problems, and her children had been placed in foster care because she had physically abused them. Some of the same stressful conditions that contribute to such abusive behavior—strife-torn marriages and the hardships of single parenthood—often foster Munchausen syndrome.

Goodlin says that these pregnant "bleeders" are suffering from more than simple factitious disorders because they repeat the same symptoms in pregnancy after pregnancy, and hospital after hospital, in spite of therapy. He also speculates that some pregnant women feign labor pains, something which is more difficult to prove, especially if a woman is medically knowledgeable. According to Dr. Ford, the apparently high prevalence of Munchausen syndrome in pregnant women may be the result of psychological and emotional turmoil fostered by pregnancy. Some women regress psychologically during pregnancy. At odds with the physical changes in their bodies, they feel more vulnerable because of their inability to maneuver well. Also, pregnancy is a time that stresses a woman's sense of identity and her ego boundaries. If demands are made upon pregnant women to be "superwomen," if they have to run a household and take care of other children, a husband, and their unborn babies, they may look to factitious disorders as an outlet that will allow *them* to be taken care of. Thus, playing sick can be a means of taking control as much as a means of escape and denial.

Pregnancy isn't the only life experience that taxes body and mind and may create a sense of loss of control. Regular daily living often does that. For some, life's challenges seem insurmountable, and they choose feigned illness as their coping mechanism.

CHAPTER 4

TAILSPIN: THE
DEVELOPMENT
OF FACTITIOUS
ILLNESSES

For a moment the lie becomes truth.
Fyodor Dostoyevski
The Brothers Karamazov (1880)

From childhood we are taught that we are responsible for our own actions and that we can steer our lives along any course we choose. Over and over again at home, in school, in song, and in prose the message is reinforced: go where you want to go, do what you want to do, be what you want to be. But all too soon we learn, usually through harsh experiences, that that kind of total control is nothing more than wishful and poetic thinking. Our lives are actually directed to some degree by factors over which we have little or no control, such as people, circumstances, and physical and emotional health. Most of us acquire living skills as we mature that enable us to accept and cope with the perceived and real influences in our lives while maintaining whatever control we can over ourselves, our homes, and other people (such as, our children or subordinates at work).

Some of us, however, are so severely affected by harsh life experiences that we do not become inured over time, but instead plummet into a tailspin when encountering a new challenge. We resort to desperate measures to exercise some control over our lives and to avoid collision. Feigning illness is one such desperate measure. But the control it provides the perpetrator is illusory.

A number of factitial patients use eating disorders to exercise dominance over their bodies and to manipulate others and their environments. We believe that some cases of bulimia are factitious disorders in the traditional sense because bulimia often involves the surreptitious use of laxatives and diuretics to alter weight. The patients continue these practices despite education, and often lie to their physicians about their behavior. The difference between simulated and real illness is the degree of voluntary control a patient has over a particular symptom and the patient's deliberately keeping it secret and attempting to fool other people, including the physician.

A question that often arises is whether or not patients with factitious disorders can control their portrayals of illness. Are these patients aware of their actions? Are they compulsive acts, out of one's personal control? Or are they premeditated?

The best answer is that an episode of factitious illness may reflect any of these possibilities. For example, one patient who has been carefully followed over several years does appear to have genuine "dissociative episodes" in which disease deception occurs. Like a person with multiple personality disorder, this patient will produce simulated illness (e.g., mimic epileptic convulsions) while in a trancelike state. She seems genuinely unaware of the illness productions. At other times, with full awareness, this patient will simulate illnesses such as kidney disease. Her cleverness is such that, despite normal kidneys, she has been able to obtain Social Security Disability payments for end-stage renal disease (this success in obtaining financial gain raises the possibility of malingering). At still other times, she repetitively, in a seemingly compulsive way, gains sympathy and support from other persons by telling them (falsely) that her parents have recently been killed in a car wreck.

But most patients with factitious disorders are fully aware of their behaviors, which often involve considerable skillful planning for their successful execution. Yet, the patients remain unaware of the unconscious factors that motivate the behavior. An analogy can be drawn with behaviors such as compulsive gambling or compulsive shopping: these people know what they are doing and that the behavior is wrong but find the behavior difficult to stop. Certainly a man who does not have diabetes and who injects himself with insulin is aware that he is doing it, but he may not always know exactly why. Regardless of this uncertainty about motives, the majority of psychiatrists consider patients with factitious disorders to be responsible for their behavior.

Because of the way illness is perceived in most societies, it is one of the surest ways to gain the sympathy and support of others, as well as control over them. Using illness or the appearance of illness in this manner is not the sole province of adults. Even as small children we come to understand that with sickness comes TLC. Most of us can recall being told by our mother, grandmother, or some other caregiver when we were children: "You have a bellyache? Poor baby! Rest while I fix some tea for you." Comforting treatment for a simple complaint. And we know that the care is generally commensurate with the gravity of the ailment. Factitial patients—young and old—have learned these lessons all too well.

Twenty-three-year-old Catherine was introduced to the power of illness when she was a very young child. A genuine bout with a life-threatening disease set the stage for the disease simulations she would carry out years later. Just days before her graduation with a degree in psychology from a prestigious West Coast university, she spoke candidly with us about her disease portrayals and how she used two dangerous eating disorders to try to control her life, her body, and the people around her. This is Catherine's story in her own words. Our comments appear throughout in parentheses.

> I was diagnosed as having a cancerous tumor of the spine when I was seven years old, and in the second grade. The thing about having had cancer at such an early age is that I didn't really understand a lot of what was happening to me and my body. I couldn't make heads or tails of the terminology used by the doctors or what they were going to do for me, but I recognized that as soon as my parents and relatives knew that I was sick, I started getting a lot of attention.
>
> *(Today children's hospitals and cancer care centers are aware of a child's need for information when he or she is suffering from a life-threatening illness, and they strive to involve children and their parents as a team in the treatment and recovery process.)*

Before my illness was diagnosed, I was having a lot of pain in my heels and then in my right hip. I suffered so much that at times I could hardly walk, but it was quite some time before doctors were convinced that anything serious was wrong with me. They thought that I was exaggerating some minor problem or just plain faking to get attention because my parents spent so much time working and being involved with my two older sisters. I had always been an active child, and at first my parents thought that I had just sprained a muscle and that I was going to be fine if I would only give it a chance to heal.

In time, instead of improving, I started feeling tired and all I wanted to do was rest my legs. I kept complaining about the pain, which was becoming unbearable, so my mother took me to an orthopedic doctor. During my first visit, this specialist found nothing wrong with me, and my parents were relieved. But the pain persisted. When I was almost paralyzed, the doctor performed elaborate, painful tests and found spots on my lungs, which had been visible on previous x-rays, but had been ignored by the doctor. The tests also showed that I had a large tumor on my spine, which had eaten through bones, and a number of other tumors. I was diagnosed with undifferentiated metastatic sarcoma.

In surgery, which lasted eight hours, doctors removed five vertebrae, but they didn't remove any tumors. The purpose of the surgery was to relieve the pressure on my spinal cord, thus relieving the pain.

When doctors told my parents that I had a 3 percent chance of survival, my father went into the men's room to cry and my mother was afraid to leave the hospital, fearing that I would die before she returned. No one told me that I might die; that possibility was masked by gifts and terms I did not understand. The only thing I did know was that I had cancer.

Information was often withheld from me; the fact that I might have a real life someday was somehow overlooked.

When I asked my mom about this years later, she said her primary concern was with my survival and not my emotions. I understood but did not find it any easier to deal with having been kept in the dark for so long.

Radiation therapy, which I received intermittently for two years, began three days after surgery. It was combined with chemotherapy, which caused me to vomit everything I ate. The chemotherapy lasted two years, with one treatment per month lasting five consecutive days.

When my cancer went into remission, I might have been grateful for the medications had the side effects not been so awful. But, again, my mother worried about the biological effects, while I was concerned with the more superficial ones. My mom became so preoccupied with saving my life that she neglected to warn me of the other side effects—the ones that hurt me most at this self-conscious adolescent point in my life—such as losing my hair, vomiting in public, and looking like a cadaver.

The cure was almost as miserable as the illness.

My doctors had told me that I was going to lose my hair because of the cancer therapy, and they even tried to joke around about it, saying that I would some day get a whole new growth of hair and it might even be a different color than it had been before. All along I had tried to imagine what I would look like without hair, but somehow I couldn't picture it. Somehow I couldn't comprehend the prospect of losing my hair. When it began to happen I was dumbfounded. I cried and was horrified when my hair came out in clumps. I could remember a time when I looked and felt pretty. I was just a little girl, and I was supposed to be able to feel that way. But after all I went through, I didn't even want to look at myself in the mirror. I felt ugly and I was afraid that I was going to look like that for the rest of my life.

I missed more than a year of school during the early part of my therapy, and I had spent so much time in the hospital that my home became the foreign place and the hospital was the familiar place where people took care of me. When I was in the hospital I got lots of presents, and people doted over me day and night. It wasn't that I liked the doctors or that they treated me really well, or anything like that. They didn't treat me particularly well, actually. I was simply more comfortable as a patient than as a survivor reentering normal life.

At first, after returning home, I didn't exaggerate any illness; I didn't need to because it was only too real. But I reached a point when I did exaggerate everything that went along with my illness.

For example, sometimes I would say that I was more tired than I really was just to be able to stay in bed where I felt safe and comfortable and to have my mother wait on me. These were some of the only times I felt free of physical and emotional pain. I was allowed to play the sick role even though I felt okay, which further enhanced my adoption of these hospitalizations as a form of refuge.

A year and a half after I recovered from my first experience with cancer my doctors found another tumor, this time in my lung. I was devastated by the news that I would have to go through the whole process all over again, but I did it, and eventually the cancer was brought under control. Unfortunately, I wasn't prepared to be well. Even though I had been in remission between the cancers, I never lost that label of "the sick girl" and was always treated protectively. At the age of 13 I was afraid to go to school. I was afraid not to be on chemotherapy anymore. I was afraid to grow my hair back and to go back into the real world because I hadn't really lived there and I hadn't learned any of the social skills I needed to make it in that world. In the hospital I didn't need those skills. People sought me out to take care of me and visit me and be nice to me. The nurses and doctors and I always had something to talk about because conversation inevitably focused on my illness and how I was feeling or some special gift that someone had given me. I was absolutely lost and frightened outside of the hospital.

(Chronically ill children such as Catherine would benefit from a therapeutic program of "wellness training," which would make them less apt to fall back on the sick role later, when unmet needs overwhelm them.)

When I went back to school, all of the kids made fun of me because I had to wear leg braces. My spinal surgery had left me with a funny-looking limp (called a "stepping gait"), which made me very self-conscious and drew attention to my appearance. I was so sallow that I looked as if I had "prison pallor," which was accentuated by the faded brown rings under my eyes. The kids pulled my wig off and said that I was wearing a dead rat on my head. Only one or two children stuck by me. Otherwise I was isolated and excluded from all extracurricular activities. If I didn't go home in tears because of the pain, I was in tears because of what the kids did to me. My teachers basically were either unaware or unable to deal with what I was experiencing. That reinforced my belief that the hospital environment was more nurturing, supportive, and safe for me than what was outside of it.

(It is not uncommon for a sick child, or a child who has been ill, to be ostracized by healthier peers. This is detrimental to self-image and the overall recovery process because recovery must simultaneously involve mental and physical components. Because of increased sensitivity and awareness on the part of teachers and school administrators, if Catherine were a child and found herself in this situation today, her illness would more likely be explained to her classmates, who would be involved in communicating with her while she was in the hospital and help with her assimilation into school life once she was reunited with them. Although there will always be cruel children, just as there will always be cruel adults, this kind of involvement greatly reduces peer hostility when a child who was or is sick returns to school. Usually children who are educated this way react more kindly and compassionately toward their sick peers than their parents do, as we have seen with children who are infected with the AIDS virus and have been forced out of school by the parents of other students.)

My parents didn't know what to do for me and couldn't understand why I wasn't glad to be out of the hospital and anxious to go back to school and make friends, and lead what they considered to be a normal life. They constantly lectured me about how grateful I should be that I was alive and repeatedly reminded me that they had saved my life. I had two older sisters who were healthy and attractive and neither of them understood why I was having such difficulty getting along with my parents and the other students at school. They hassled me about it and even ridiculed me. They helped to bring my self-esteem to an all-time low, and never became the allies I needed them to be.

Being around mom felt like the world was coming to an end, but dad looked at everything in an optimistic manner.

In one sense, I understand now that because my mother gave birth to me, she felt it was her mission to save my life. This was a job that required a serious professional attitude. Dad's contrasting optimism conveyed the notion that ignorance is bliss.

My parents tried to nurture me. As I matured, they were excited about my social life. They wanted me to make friends and be asked on lots of dates. However, certain activities were always forbidden by my mother. For example, she wouldn't allow me to go to slumber parties because she feared I wouldn't get enough sleep, or to pierce my ears because she thought they would become infected and I wouldn't heal as well as other girls.

I lied to assert a sense of control over my own life. Sometimes I combined lies with excessive pleading for my mother to allow me to do something that was forbidden. When she gave in I did pay a price for overexerting myself. The problem was that I did not mind the price. I considered any resulting medical complications to be the regimented punishment for my pleasurable sins. If I happened to sneak by once or twice, I was lucky. I became accustomed to expecting the worst. Of course, I did not have to pay hospital bills, nor did I have to take care of me.

My real exaggeration of illness started after my second operation, when my lung cancer went into remission and I was going through puberty and high school. By that time, being sick was like second nature to me. There were times when I lobbied to go back into the hospital and looked forward to it, even if it was just for tests or checkups that did not require hospitalization. When my mother suggested that I go into therapy, I said I would, but only if it meant that I would be hospitalized.

When I was 14 years old, many changes started happening in my life. I was trying to be popular and I didn't know how to be. I wanted to be attractive to the other sex, but I felt awkward and out of sync with the tactics that other girls used to meet boys.

(It was normal for Catherine to be self-conscious under these circumstances and to feel that her new environment was alien. What wasn't normal was the harsh way she was reintroduced to this alternative world, which fostered her negative feelings about herself and everyone around her. A proper support system should have been in place for her, complete with counseling, so that she could have been eased into her new hospital-free environment instead of being cast into it and forced to make a go of it alone. But her parents' actions were dictated more by their past fears of losing her than by their desire to see her assimilate well once

*she was in remission. Catherine and her parents and sisters would proba-
bly have benefited greatly from family counseling.)*

That's when I started looking at how I could control my life, my
body, and the way I looked, and I began my bouts of anorexia and
bulimia.

*(Anorexia nervosa is an eating disorder which occurs most often in
adolescent girls. Persons suffering from this psychiatric illness starve
themselves or use such techniques as vomiting or taking laxatives or
overexercising to lose weight because they have a false sense of their
bodies and believe that they are fat. This can lead to severe weight loss
and, in extreme cases, death. Bulimia nervosa, which sometimes occurs
as a phase of anorexia nervosa, involves cycles of overeating, or binging,
followed by purging.)*

I deliberately created the anorexia and bulimia in myself. I was
cognizant of what I was doing to the extent that I went to the
library and read every book I could find on eating disorders to
learn better and more unique ways of creating them.

*(We hope no readers are using this book as a how-to text, but if you are,
please keep reading.)*

I knew everything there was to know about every eating disorder
on record. I was striving for some sort of independence and control.
No one in my family had ever encouraged me to be independent.
They had fostered my sick role and were overprotective to the point
that I wasn't even allowed to take public transportation. I finally
consciously created my own independence in a negative way.

*(Real anorectics starve themselves as a compulsion, the apparent aim
being the "perfect body." Catherine's feigned anorexia and bulimia had
far more complex origins than a desire for beauty, as she poignantly
explains below. Most people who develop anorexia nervosa and/or bulimia don't consciously plan to have these illnesses. They evolve out of
a distorted attempt at weight loss, which is generally triggered by a poor
self-image and related personality problems. Catherine's eating disorder
was factitious because she intentionally chose the disease.)*

Once I started playing sick I felt as if I had taken control of my
life for the very first time. It was extremely satisfying to pretend

to have an illness that I could command and to deliberately do harmful things to my body because harmful things had happened to me in the past that I couldn't control. I think to some extent I became so accustomed to pain that I thought I deserved it and I missed it and felt that I couldn't live without it. I would do things that were self-destructive, like burning myself or cutting myself to make myself bleed. I wanted to feel the pain, but I don't know if I liked it so much or if I was really comfortable with the dark side, with the pain.

(Self-mutilation can be a manifestation of intolerable anxiety, as it was in Jenny's case. Catherine, however, seems to have used mutilation to reintroduce the familiar element of pain into her life at a time when everything around her was unfamiliar. She was able to inflict pain at will, whereas in the past, as she said, she had no control over it. Her self-mutilation also provided a sort of retribution, as if she were saying, "You did it to me. Now I'm doing it to you, and you can't stop me.")

All of my actions got an immediate response from people around me. And although some of what I did brought negative attention from my parents, the bottom line was that I was still getting their attention. The more my parents fought against me, the more I fought to assert control over them and to keep them in their supportive roles. I got a lot of attention when I didn't eat and, in so doing, I indirectly nurtured myself. Everyone was worried about me. I knew which strings to pull and which buttons to push, and I used them to fulfill my needs. I knew exactly what reactions I would get from playing sick.

I chose to fake eating disorders for several reasons, primarily because I was familiar with them. When I was being given chemotherapy I was nauseated all the time, and whenever I ate I threw up. My mother was very conscious of my eating habits because when I got sick the second time I lost 30 pounds in one month. She was afraid that I would die if I got sick again because I couldn't afford to lose any more weight. I gained it back after the chemotherapy ended, but I deliberately started losing it again because I knew my mother would be upset. I would go into the bathroom and make myself vomit when I knew that she could hear me.

Also, by choosing an illness such as bulimia, I turned an invisible disorder, cancer, into a visible one.

My experience has always been that if I am very ill or limping very badly, I will receive a great deal of remorse or a great deal of fear and disgust. When I appear as a normal person, however, I am generally ignored.

Being self-conscious about my appearance because my sexuality was blooming served as another excuse for my actions. And during the 1980s eating disorders were trendy things, and I was greatly influenced by what I saw in the media. There were a couple of television shows about anorexia and bulimia, and some books at that time, so it was easy to stay on top of things. After a while, the eating disorders became real, and I had trouble controlling the symptoms. I would go through long periods of depression where I would starve all day, then come home from school and eat a light dinner and go to sleep at 7 o'clock. I would do that every day and by Sunday I would be so hungry that I would binge all day. I couldn't stop eating for 24 hours and then the next day I would starve myself or try to make myself vomit.

I once overdosed on 45 Extra Strength Tylenol tablets because I had binged and wanted to vomit. I took all the tablets that were in the bottle, knowing that I was either going to get sick or not wake up the next morning. I was so depressed that I really didn't care which.

(When Catherine was speaking about this episode, a nervous half chuckle gave away her reluctance to use the word die *instead of her more euphemistic choice* not wake up. *In so doing, she displayed an uncomfortable awareness of how serious and potentially lethal her actions had been.)*

Then I reached a point where anorexia and bulimia weren't good enough to control my body, and I started using drugs in addition to continuing with my eating disorders.

I was very good at verbalizing my feelings, but my parents weren't good at understanding them. My mother thought she was helping me by trying to force me to eat, but that didn't work. Bribing and punishing me didn't work either. I saw several therapists and none of them helped me, and I became really frustrated with people trying to influence my life. I could only talk to my friends, and they were primarily the people with whom I was engaging in bad behavior.

(Other psychological problems were at work here, including borderline personality disorder, in which a person experiences identity crises, unstable relationships, and moodiness; becomes manipulative; and undertakes self-injuring acts, such as self-mutilation. Catherine was depressed because she wanted to fit into what she had been told was the "normal" world. She wanted to be attractive to boys and to find a niche among people her own age, but her low self-esteem and other problems, such as an inability to cope effectively with anxiety and stress, prevented her from doing so. She resented having been cast into a hostile world where she was denied the warm, caring environment in which she had actually grown up. She was also extremely angry with her parents because they had not taught her to be independent and had not prepared her for life beyond the hospital.)

When I was 17 I had the notion that if I signed myself into a rehabilitation hospital, I'd be able to prove that my parents were neglecting me, or something crazy like that, and I would become legally emancipated from them. But things got screwed up, and when I signed myself into such a hospital, my parents found out about my drug use and transferred me to a stricter facility. I was there for three months, and it was hell. It was such a terrible environment that I continued to starve and binge and vomit.

Two of the most nurturing and healthy environments I lived in when I was growing up were outside of my parents' home. My environment at home was never authentically supportive, although on the surface anyone would have said that I had been treated like a princess, which I was. I got whatever I wanted, but no one really understood what I was going through. Emotional support was there on some level, but not on the level where it would have helped me.

After I was released from the rehabilitation center, I went home, but nothing was working out so my parents agreed to let me stay at a girls' home, where I was treated with a lot of respect. I didn't have that much more freedom than I had had in rehabilitation, but I really liked the people and, although I don't know why, I was quite healthy there. I signed a contract that I would not do drugs, and I didn't. I also signed a contract that I wouldn't make myself throw up, and I only did that once.

(Catherine was able to stop her disease portrayal and self-destructive behavior because she was in a comfortable, supportive communal environment that mimicked hospital life. Her emotional needs fulfilled, she dropped her symptoms and enjoyed the nurturing and the new, positive kind of control of her body which had been fostered by the contracts she signed.)

I also lived with a friend and her mother for a while, and they helped me to learn many of the living skills that I hadn't learned in the past. They taught me to do things that my mother had always done for me, and I became more independent. I learned to travel on public transportation and got a part-time job so that I could pay for some of my own things. The more real control I got over my life, the more control people outside of my family gave me, and the more I felt nurtured, comfortable, and safe, not threatened.

I can't precisely identify the point at which my life turned around. I remember that the night my parents dropped me off at college, the first thing I did was run to the nearest bathroom so I could stick my finger down my throat and make myself vomit. All during freshman year I worked in the school's dining services. I wouldn't have accepted any other type of work. It was kind of like being offered the forbidden fruit. I was challenging myself: put yourself around food and see if you're going to lose control.

(Catherine's challenge added a new dimension. Being around food made it difficult for her to starve for days at a time, yet she was able to do so, which illustrated how much a part of her life the eating disorders had become and the extent to which they were now in control.)

It wasn't until the summer of my sophomore year that I finally started eating and keeping the food down. I was so busy with other things that I didn't have time to play games. If you're going to live with an eating disorder, whether it's real or not, you have to plan every minute around that disorder. Your whole life revolves around it. I think somehow I got the feeling that it was controlling me more than I was controlling it, and I adjusted my eating habits and reintroduced food—including junk food—into my life in a normal way.

I got good grades in school because I pursued my studies with the same compulsion with which I had pursued the eating disorders. I'm still very compulsive.

(As is the case with many factitial patients, as soon as other interests started to fill her life and meet her needs, Catherine dropped her factitious behavior. Also, in the demanding scholastic environment in which she had placed herself, she couldn't possibly keep up with her studies if her attention was devoted to her sick role. She chose the "fine student" role instead, with the concomitant positive attention. The former outsider became an insider, finding a niche for herself within the close-knit college community.

Although Catherine dropped her factitious behavior, she never received therapy that would have taught her the skills she needs to cope with anxiety and life crises so that in the future she would not feel compelled to reactivate her behavior. Her personality disorder was never appropriately treated, either. This places her at great risk for a repetition of a factitious disorder whenever her emotional resources are taxed to their limit.)

Today my sisters are yuppies and my parents are still trying to control my life. They care more about my physical well-being than whether I'm emotionally happy. They still remind me that I owe them my life, and make it sound as if I should pay them back in some way, which makes me feel very guilty.

(Family therapy would still be useful because Catherine's parents have never fully come to terms with her recovery. As their reward for the pain and worry they experienced when Catherine was sick, and for the financial sacrifices they made, they have turned themselves into martyrs, and apparently perceive Catherine as being indebted to them for their emotional and fiscal investment in her. They are all still deeply affected by what happened more than a decade ago, and it will continue to affect their actions and attitudes.)

I have very poor peer relationships, and I have a hard time socializing in big groups of people. Oddly enough, I'm outgoing and get along well with small groups. I like to keep a few friends rather than a lot of them. I develop stronger relationships with people who are opposites of the kind of people I tried to get along with in high school. I no longer try to be part of the popular group or a jock because, to me, those people are less real than people who have problems and are marginal like myself or who see things from a marginal position.

(Catherine refers to popular people as "less real" when, in fact, she means "intimidating and foreign" to her. She prefers to surround herself with people who are outcasts like herself, who don't challenge her, with whom she doesn't have to feel self-conscious. She functions better within small, more homogeneous groups because she has more control over the interactions. She has no control over the types of people who gather comfortably in large groups, and she is still afraid of opening herself up to the kind of criticism she experienced as a young child returning to school. She is still keeping very close watch over her environment and trying to protect herself.)

I'm comfortable with myself now. My limp is still fairly pronounced when I'm not wearing braces and that makes me self-conscious. But I no longer think that having a disability should be a negative thing, and I'm basically happy.

Catherine's earlier sense of powerlessness and vulnerability was a major catalyst behind her disease simulation and one of the main reasons that eating disorders suited her needs so well. They appeared to give her back some of the control she so desperately wanted over her body and her life, as well as some of the sympathy to which she'd become accustomed. These are the elements which are sought through eating disorders by many factitial patients.

Dr. Ford:

I treated a woman who was absolutely emaciated when she came to see me. She weighed about 80 pounds, and I could actually see the definition of her bones. She told me that her husband wanted a divorce and, with real horror in her voice, she asked me, "How could anybody leave me when I look like this? What would a judge say when he looked at me?" She was using this dreadfully sick appearance to make sure that she could get sympathy from a judge and to put her husband in a position in which it would have been unconscionable for him to leave her. She was killing herself from starvation, and that was factitial in the sense that she was willingly choosing not to eat in order to create this appearance.

Another woman I saw was quietly bulimic and was in and out of physicians' offices a great deal. She was quite angry with her husband because he was spending so much time working and going to school at night, so she induced a very severe electrolyte imbalance in herself through chronic vomiting. Her condition required many hospitalizations, and her husband was in danger of having to leave school because of the time required for her care. I also saw another woman who was 65 years old and used the symptoms of weakness caused by self-induced vomiting to control her husband.

Factitial patients who present with eating disorders as their primary illnesses often engage in self-bleeding as well. We believe the two are related because they are both means of abusing and exercising control over one's body. In one study of factitious anemia done in Switzerland, researchers reported on four women, three of whom also had anorexia nervosa or bulimia nervosa. One woman, a 24-year-old lab technician (who was also diagnosed as having borderline personality disorder), had mild anorexia nervosa. A 28-year-old self-bleeder who had a borderline personality disorder with antisocial traits admitted to taking unwarranted diuretics and laxatives, eventually developing anorexia and bulimia. Even though she received psychotherapy, she never stopped bleeding herself, nor did her eating disorders improve. A third woman in the study (who had narcissistic personality disorder, characterized by grandiosity, self-centeredness, and lack of empathy) also had anorexia nervosa.

Dr. Scott Snyder of Athens, Georgia, wrote about an 18-year-old girl who was institutionalized after cutting her wrists. She told doctors that in the three years prior to her suicide attempt, she had been able to lose 30 to 40 pounds during several bouts with bulimia by resorting to vomiting and the use of laxatives and diuretics. Relatives, however, said that she had never lost large amounts of weight but was fascinated by anorexia nervosa and attracted to people who genuinely suffered from it. Snyder said that this girl, who suffered from borderline personality disorder, might have identified with patients with eating disorders because it gave her a stronger sense of identity, thus boosting her self-esteem, and reduced her sense of boredom. She owned almost a dozen books on eating disorders and was friendly with teenagers who suffered from such illnesses. This patient admitted that she thought anorexia nervosa was an admirable disease and commented on the dedication of true anorectic patients. (That mandatory dedication was what actually helped Catherine turn her life around because her eating habits eventually demanded far more devotion than she was willing to give.)

The ability to lie convincingly, as demonstrated by Dr. Snyder's patient and so many others already reported, is a major part of every successful presentation of a factitious disorder and one of the reasons why so many medical professionals have been duped. Even when test results are negative, when physical appearance belies the presence of illness, and when concrete information is lacking to back up claims of past illnesses and trauma, doctors are so taken in by these patients that they may perform gratuitous tests and unneeded surgery (including the removal of healthy organs), and prescribe unnecessary medications.

One patient who was an extraordinarily prolific liar—having achieved 57 hospital admissions over five years in at least three different countries—was a man named Alistair, whose case was reported in the *British Journal of Psychiatry* in 1986. The ninth of 11 children born to a Scottish family, this classic Munchausen patient was no stranger to illness. His youngest sibling died of a brain tumor, his father had several operations for an ulcer, and his mother suffered from diabetes and cataracts. As a child he endured legitimate ear problems, had an appendectomy when he was 7, and at the age of 16 overdosed on drugs and was introduced to psychotherapy. And as in many other cases which involve members of large families, he learned that the appearance of illness was one way, if not the only way, to get attention from two parents whose emotional and financial resources were stretched to the limit. In an attempt to put his life on the right track, this man joined the Royal Army Medical Corps at the age of 19 and served as an operating room technician until the age of 21, when he was medically discharged following surgery on his knee.

His history of unemployment began after he left the service, as did his Munchausen behavior. After his mother's death when he was 28 years old, he feigned quadriplegia. He learned rapidly, like Catherine, that hospital admission brings quick, if only temporary, relief from emotional problems and stresses and the realities of life. He constantly moved around, staying only a few months in each place, and went from hospital to hospital with a myriad of complaints ranging from renal colic to meningitis. His methods of falsifying symptoms were as varied as the illnesses he portrayed, including putting blood in his urine and pointing out old scars to substantiate claims of illness.

When he was 31 years old, he received treatment for dependency on a mild drug which he acquired legally from hospitals. His demand for drugs escalated from that point on, and each time the medications were denied or cut back, he became increasingly self-destructive. Within a year he was resorting to swallowing razor blades, stitch cutters, and needles to force surgery. Then he began using self-mutilation as a form of blackmail against the doctors who tried to control the amount of drugs he was getting.

He was a quarrelsome loner who had been in trouble with the law and whose only relationships grew out of the hospitals that he frequented. To quell his emotional conflicts and his isolation, he initially claimed falsely to have a drug dependency, but eventually his claim became real. His doctors noted that "drugs became an end to themselves and a tangible symbol of the attention he craved."

We see factitious patients, especially in such drug-related cases, making an effort to prove that they're smarter than doctors, and that's a very important aspect of factitious disorders, regardless of the symptoms that are being feigned. If these patients can prove that they are smarter than doctors, it makes them feel pretty clever and boosts their sense of self-esteem and power.

Another patient with factitious disease, Dave (described in greater detail in Chapter 6), was truly an important patient from our own experience who helped us understand the specific triggers for factitial behavior. Whenever Dave's mother would leave town, Dave would have an enormous feeling of helplessness (infantile anxiety similar to an infant's being abandoned). He would then head for an emergency room and put on a display. What did that do? First, instead of feeling impotent and abandoned, he suddenly felt that he was pulling the strings. Second, he was able to have himself taken care of because his charades put him into the hospital. He met both of his needs simultaneously. Which was the greater? It's almost impossible to determine which need is more important to someone like this.

Researchers have said that for many factitial patients there's an almost orgasmic feeling associated with seeing the look on physicians' faces as they start to realize that they've been fooled. We believe that's one of the things factitious patients are after. There's almost a "high" associated with it. We saw this firsthand in Dave.

A false identity enlarges beyond illness per se when compounded by lies about the faker's whole life. When these lies are carried to outrageous proportions to build fabulous personal histories, they add a new dimension to factitious disorders called pseudologia fantastica—the telling of fantastic stories as if they were true.

CHAPTER 5

TALLER TALES
WERE NEVER
SPOKEN

Oh, what a tangled web we weave,
When first we practice to deceive!
Sir Walter Scott
Marmion (1808)

Few involved with factitial patients are spared entanglement in the sticky web they spin. They deliver their tales of woe and derring-do so glibly that they often rival the most silken-tongued con artist, and take in all willing parties, usually starting with doctors. Factitial patients then allow the hoax to assume a life of its own, growing and seeking out new participants until finally someone who is caught up in it catches on.

Ironically, the very nature of medical care, with ever-present concerns about patients' rights and malpractice claims, actually facilitates disease portrayals. The implicit obligation of physicians to their patients is the persistent pursuit of a definitive diagnosis and treatment, even when symptoms defy logic. Vague or confusing descriptions of symptoms are not unusual. Most men and women want to be well and, if they can afford it, expect to see their doctors once a year for a checkup and—they hope—a clean bill of health. Unless a person has a known history of a factitious disorder, no physician anticipates that a patient is presenting for any reason other than a routine physical exam or valid medical complaint. The general assumption, as the Bible says, is that "they that be whole need not a physician, but they that are sick" (Matthew 9:12).

Physicians expect their patients to be honest about their complaints and to try to verbalize them as clearly as possible so that they may be correctly treated. And, generally, the more complete and accurate a patient's descriptions of symptoms, the easier it is to make a proper diagnosis. A self-aware and articulate patient is thus appreciated as an active participant in his or her own health care.

While solid information is necessary for optimal care, the old adage about too much of a good thing may apply at times. An abundance of information, fraught with detailed medical terminology, should be a warning sign to medical professionals. Even if that patient is a health care professional with a working knowledge of the body and certain illnesses, the patient's comments usually will not sound as if they have been lifted straight from a textbook. If they do, it may suggest that the patient has done an extraordinary amount of homework. Like Catherine in her study of eating disorders, factitial patients often hit the books and study about their diseases of choice. Doctors, dentists, other health care professionals, and even laypersons should proceed with caution when this red flag is up and at least consider the possibility that the patient is misleading the listener.

Other red flags for factitious illness include excessive drama in the presentation of symptoms, and a captivating story about the patient's life accompanied by either a scanty medical history or a fantastic one (pseudologia fantastica).

Dr. Ford:

My first patient with a factitious disorder was a young man named Billy, who was admitted to the neurosurgery unit of a hospital from its emergency room. There, a chief resident diagnosed him as having a brain tumor on the basis of the physical examination. Billy's complaints were very specific and convincing: left parietal headaches (the parietal bones form the top and sides of the skull), memory loss, and an unsteady gait due to weakness on the right side of his body, especially in his right leg. He even manifested a slight inequality of reflexes between his right and left sides.

The attending neurosurgeon ordered a battery of expensive and sophisticated diagnostic studies, some of which were painful and dangerous for Billy, including bilateral carotid angiograms (injections of dye or radioactive fluid into the carotid artery—the chief artery that passes up the neck and carries blood to the head—followed by x-rays) and a pneumoencephalogram (injections of air into the cavities of the brain followed by x-rays).

While awaiting the test results, 23-year-old Billy evoked a great deal of sympathy from the medical staff when he humbly revealed that he was a football player on the brink of a brilliant professional career which now stood to be destroyed by his illness. He said that he had tried out for the Los Angeles Rams and made the team, but he realized that something was seriously amiss when his performance on the field drastically declined over a period of only weeks. "Something was going really wrong," Billy told doctors. "My leg was getting weaker and I couldn't figure out why." Everyone on the medical staff who had ever dreamed of becoming a professional football player was rooting for Billy, who stiffened his lip, curled his mouth, and humbly thanked them for their encouragement.

All of the tests proved negative for a brain tumor. The neurosurgeon assigned to Billy's case said that the only other possible explanation for his condition was multiple sclerosis (a chronic disease of the nervous system, which may have symptoms similar to those Billy displayed and for which there is no known cure). "Oh, my God," Billy cried when he heard the news. He covered his face with his hands and wept. Billy gradually began to appear extremely depressed and started talking about suicide. His doctors suggested that he see a psychiatrist, and he was transferred to the psychiatric unit and placed under my care.

He told me the story with great emotion about how he had worked very hard to become a place-kicker and he had tried out for the Los Angeles Rams and made the team. He said he could kick a field goal 50 yards away every time at practice. And then all of a sudden, during spring training, he couldn't make it at 50 yards any more. He could only make it from 45, then somehow it slipped down to 40, and before long he had trouble making it at 30 yards. It was terrible because he couldn't stay on the team that way.

During the early stages of his hospitalization, Billy had refused to let social workers notify his family, but eventually he permitted them to contact his sister. When his sister showed up at the hospital, she asked me, "Is he doing this stuff again?" Then she added snidely, "He's always sick with one thing or another. When he was in high school he was on the football team but spent an entire season on the bench with a cast on his leg. I'm still not sure if it was really broken."

I liked Billy and I felt sorry for him. He seemed to be a nice, easygoing person and I wanted to try to help him so I phoned his parents to find out as much as I could about his background. I discovered that ours was the seventh hospital in one year that he had been admitted to for a brain tumor and that he had had carotid angiograms at every one of them, all of which were normal.

Billy came from a horrible, dysfunctional family in which abuse was a way of life and included severe corporal punishment. He was the sixth of 11 children and the family subsisted on welfare. His eldest sibling had been given up for adoption in infancy, and his other brothers and sisters competed madly for their parents' attention. His father carried the diagnosis of paranoid schizophrenia, and this illness made him both unpredictable and the object of disdain by neighbors. Billy's father spent much of his adult life in hospitals and was once institutionalized for two years. His mother was a resentful, exhausted woman who showed only indifference toward her children. Described by her daughter as a hypochondriac, she too had been hospitalized a number of times and was given to outbursts of temper.

Billy had wet the bed until the age of 10, and his mother used to push his face into the wet sheets as part of his punishment. He told me that once, as she gripped the back of his neck and forced his head down toward the wet sheets, she shouted, "You piss on your bed, you piss on me, and I guess you'll grow up pissing on the world."

Billy was really a pathetic man. When he was a young boy he had been hospitalized for several weeks for a legitimate medical problem. During that stay, the nurses treated him with kindness and love, the sheets were clean, and the food was good. The hospital was so different from his home life that a very positive learning experience was attached to being sick and being the focus of caring from medical people. The longing for this type of nurturance fostered his disease simulations, and he brilliantly feigned an illness that was sure to get him hospitalized every time.

Billy's family told me that he had repeatedly played sick throughout school and his early adult life. He had never been gainfully employed and had not functioned well in any capacity other than the sick role. After he got out of school, Billy became a traveling shoe salesman; he then enlisted in the U.S. Air Force, but that career was cut short by an administrative discharge. Billy then alternated between trips to the hospital and trips back home. His sister believed that Billy's most recent spate of hospitalizations had been precipitated by his parents' preoccupation with their own illnesses—his father had pancreatic cancer and his mother had diabetes. Nothing had changed in Billy's life since he was a little boy; it was still true that the only way he could get any attention from anybody, including his siblings, was by playing sick.

Billy had been an unremarkable student in school, yet he had obviously studied so much about the symptoms of brain tumors that he was not only able to discuss them but to act out some of them. The more often he was hospitalized, the more information Billy acquired and the more believable his presentation became.

Billy was on our ward for three months. We did extensive psychological testing with him and tried to help him, but we didn't see any progress. Then we found that he was hoarding Darvon (a nonnarcotic painkiller). Every time he knew he was going to have a test, he'd pop a bunch of Darvon capsules in his mouth, which would make him impaired and create symptoms until the drug was metabolized.

We knew Billy pretty well by then and told him that he had to be discharged. But Billy had really settled in and he panicked when told that he had to leave. I told him that he had to find a place to live because I didn't think he would benefit from living with his family, and that he had to build a life for himself. One afternoon he asked for a pass to look for a job. He was brought back by fire department paramedics after he had a "seizure" on the sidewalk along Rodeo Drive. He was willing to do almost anything to remain hospitalized.

When I told Billy that he was suffering from a factitious disorder, he penitently said, "I guess if you say so, it must be something like that. I'm terribly sorry." But within moments he added, "Look, doctor, I know there is something wrong with me. I just know there is. I may exaggerate a little bit to get these tests, but I really am sick." Billy would have stayed with us forever if we had allowed it. He finally had to be put out of the hospital bodily by security guards. He returned several days later complaining of his same old symptoms plus respiratory difficulties, but he was turned away.

Billy was diagnosed with inadequate personality and Munchausen syndrome. After being released from my care, he moved on to another hospital, where he once again became the gifted, yet doomed athlete with a terrible disease. What Billy hadn't seemed to grasp was that he truly was plagued by a terrible problem, one from which he would most likely be compromised his entire life. Like his career fantasies, it was all in his mind.

How was Billy able to convince so many doctors that he had a serious illness, persuading them that his symptoms were genuine even when the tests were negative? A person like Billy with pseudologia fantastica is usually very facile verbally, while the members of his audience are comparatively passive. Factitial patients sound and act so believable that other persons just soak it up.

Pseudologia fantastica is almost always associated with Munchausen syndrome but is not part of every factitious illness. Jenny, for example, told only those lies that were essential to get her portrayal of a cancer patient going and to give it a boost when sympathy started to fade. She never lied about her background or position in life or any other part of her previous medical history. Billy could have simply shown up at a hospital with the symptoms of a brain tumor, sans the elaborate background, and he would have received prompt medical attention. However, the enveloping nurturance that he craved, and the boost in his self-worth, were best served by pseudologia fantastica. Simply being a patient with a serious illness would not have been colorful enough for Billy.

Sometimes factitial patients have had some actual physiologic abnormality on which they capitalize. Recall that Catherine had experienced chemotherapy-induced eating difficulties when she was a youngster and, because of that, she knew exactly how her portrayal should appear to others. Similarly, one man (Dr. Ford's patient) was genuinely afflicted with congenital nystagmus (rhythmic involuntary eye movements), which does not hinder vision and is not a symptom of underlying neurologic problems. As part of his disease simulation, this man would go to emergency rooms and say that he had just been in an accident in which he had hit his head and had been rendered unconscious. A neurologic examination would inevitably follow, and doctors would notice the nystagmus, believe it was a new finding, and immediately admit him to the hospital for a possible brain stem contusion (or bruise). Knowing that his real but benign condition could be construed as something more serious under the right circumstances, this man used his nystagmus as his "symptom" and further exaggerated his situation with tall tales about his professional and social life in Miami, where he claimed to live.

His medical condition appeared so interesting that his physicians presented him to their peers at a neurology conference. To the patient's dismay, one doctor attending the conference recognized the patient as having been at another local hospital only weeks before, where he had received the same diagnosis and had been discharged.

This spontaneous discovery led to the patient's being referred for psychiatric evaluation, which revealed that he had not only been faking illness but faking his background as well—he was a local resident who had never even visited Florida!

Pseudologia fantastica is one of the most intriguing elements of factitious disorders, and especially of Munchausen syndrome. Also known as mythomania, pseudologia fantastica has such well-defined characteristics that some researchers believe it is a sickness unto itself, deserving of further specific study. Typified by enduring stories that are often built upon some element of truth and which become self-aggrandizing, pseudologia fantastica is seldom used for profit or material gain, but for the kind of intangible benefits which underlie factitious illnesses.

As intense and outlandish as pseudologia fantastica is, these stories don't cross the line into the realm of delusions because the tellers of these tales understand the difference between fact and fiction and know when they are lying. They believe their own lies only to the extent necessary to be totally convincing, and upon confrontation they will acknowledge, at least in part, what they have lied about.

Since before the turn of the century, pseudologia fantastica was recognized as a unique disorder, and people who employed it were dubbed "pseudologues." It usually begins during adolescence, and the ranks are evenly distributed between men and women. Like many factitial patients, they often manifest frequent career or job changes, vanity, facile and eloquent use of language, and a low tolerance for frustration.

A medical paper written in 1909 by Dr. E. Dupre itemized three criteria for pseudologia fantastica: the story must be probable and maintain a reference to reality; the fanciful adventures must be able to be applied to any number of circumstances in a reasonable manner; and, while the theme of the adventures may vary, the distinctive role of hero, heroine, or victim is almost always reserved for the storyteller.

One-fourth of all pseudologues, male and female, simulate illness in addition to lying, and one-fifth of them not only feign sickness but also take it on the road (as in Munchausen syndrome). In some Munchausen patients, pseudologia fantastica may be the primary disorder, with disease simulation but a secondary behavioral manifestation.

One of the most elaborate and effective uses of pseudologia fantastica by a factitial patient was credited to a 41-year-old divorced woman who went to a California hospital complaining of pains in her joints and fluctuating fevers. She became the star patient of the entire hospital within 24 hours—the amount of time it took for word of her heroic deeds and thrilling life to spread among the medical staff. Convincing in every way, she claimed that she was a Sabra (a native Israeli woman) and an active freedom fighter in the Israeli War for Independence in 1948. She said she had been arrested and tortured by the Arabs. According to her account, after regaining her freedom, she became an integral player in the formation of the government of Israel. When her political usefulness tapered off, she immigrated to the United States, where her selfless work continued at the World Health Organization (WHO) in New York City. She said that as an official of WHO she was charged with overseeing the distribution of food to starving children in Asia and the Middle East, with caring for Arab children in Israel, and with rescuing orphaned children in Southeast Asia.

Resident physicians and other members of the medical staff were awed by this woman, and they lingered in her room during daily rounds, listening to her exciting stories and lauding her heroism and dedication to such noble causes. She was a woman of above-average intelligence, able to use the English language effectively. She could also tell colorful anecdotes about regions around the world where she had supposedly worked or visited in an official capacity. She did not try to hide the pleasure she derived from "holding court," and she enhanced these mini-dramas by occasionally wincing with "pain" and rubbing her knees, drawing an immediate ripple of sympathy. What a shame, members of the medical staff observed among themselves, that such a wonderful woman should be so afflicted.

Doctors told her that, on the merits of her symptoms, they suspected she had a collagen vascular disease (which involves destruction of collagen, the principal component of connective tissue, and can affect any part of the body in which collagen is found). She cried aloud that her illness and prolonged hospitalization were curbing her humanitarian activities and, even worse, might force her to give up her duties with WHO altogether. While awaiting the results of her diagnostic studies, she became so visibly distressed that she was referred (to Dr. Ford) for psychiatric treatment for her anxiety and depression.

Dr. Ford:

As a new member of her audience, I was treated during our first meeting to expanded versions of her original tales. She spoke of her continued involvement with the Israeli government as an advisor and ambassador of goodwill and, to illustrate how close her ties with that government were, she related that she was engaged to marry the Israeli ambassador to the United Nations. She expressed regret that her fiancé couldn't be by her side, even though he wanted to, because of his own pressing duties. Still, she took consolation in the fact that she had seen him only weeks before when she and her three children had been flown to New York City in the private jet of a legendary recording artist and actor, whom she said was one of their friends.

When I asked about her early years, she told me that she was born to an Orthodox Jewish family and that her father insisted that the women in his family assume subservient roles. She overcame that facet of her upbringing, she said, after both of her parents died when she was a teenager. Short of this thin information, which may or may not have been accurate, she volunteered little about her childhood.

This woman's calm, almost subdued demeanor when she was with me contrasted with the exuberance she exhibited before the rest of the medical staff. This mood change, combined with her boast that she was to wed an ambassador, put me on my guard. Although I didn't verbalize my suspicions, I promised that I would stop in to see her again.

I returned to see her the next day and found her weeping profusely. When I asked what could possibly have happened overnight to catapult her into such a dreadful state, she dramatically whipped a telegram from the drawer of her nightstand and shoved it into my hands, too distraught to read it to me. As she dabbed at her tear-stained eyes, she peered above her handkerchief to watch me read silently: "We regret to inform you that his Excellency, the Israeli ambassador, was killed in an automobile accident in New York City this morning."

I quickly scanned the rest of the telegram before she had a chance to snatch it back, and noticed that the dateline read: Inglewood, California. I knew then that she had sent the telegram to herself and, in so doing, she had outsmarted herself. When I checked with her attending physician and learned that all of her tests were negative, I challenged the patient. I told her that I believed she was faking her illness and had probably lied about everything else, just as she had lied about her relationship with the ambassador. She furiously denied these allegations and threatened to sue the hospital and everyone who had been involved with her treatment. When I asked for permission to contact her daughter, she signed herself out.

A doctor from a local hospital who heard about her case told me that he knew her to be an optical technician who worked at the same hospital complex as he and that she had recently been divorced. She had been seen at that hospital numerous times for poorly substantiated physical complaints, most often after she'd argued with her husband. She was born and raised in Los Angeles and had never traveled any farther than its borders.

This patient's alleged pains and recurrent fevers alone were not overly dramatic. They had been intense enough to imply something serious, while being vague enough to be feigned effortlessly, and they provided her with a platform from which she could deliver her fantastic stories. After she checked out of the hospital, no one who had been involved in her care heard from her again.

One of the things that was most interesting to me about this woman in terms of the pseudologia fantastica was the capacity she had to judge her audience and play to that audience. The first time I went into her room, she was sitting on the bed and the house staff had literally formed a circle around her as she was telling her stories. She locked into a group of young people who were fascinated by her heroics in the 1948 war and wanted to be associated with her, and she soaked up everything they had to give. It was relatively easy for me to pick up the inconsistencies in her story because I was totally unimpressed by her. Still, it took a week and a lot of medical resources before we were able to prove that she had a factitious disorder.

CHAPTER 6

MANIPULATING MERCURY: FAKE FEVERS

A wise man should consider that health
is the greatest of human blessings, and
learn how by his own thought to derive
benefit from his illnesses.

Hippocrates (c. 460–400 B.C.)
Regimen In Health

The phony Sabra relied on fever as one of her symptoms. As uninspired as that may seem because of its simplicity, it was truly a clever choice.

When patients have fevers and other symptoms for more than two weeks and all test results are negative, they are diagnosed with "fever of unknown origin" (FUO) and must be carefully evaluated. FUO may indicate a number of underlying illnesses, including at least four inherited diseases. The most common of these particular diseases is familial Mediterranean fever, which occurs almost exclusively in Armenians, Sephardic Jews, and Arabs, and is also characterized by arthritis. Whether or not the "Sabra" knew of this disease and hoped to suggest its possibility through her tall tales, we will never know.

Fever, researchers say, is certainly one of the most popular of all factitious symptoms because it is among the easiest to feign and because it can also be a harbinger of grave illness (for example, Hodgkin's disease or malaria), depending upon its apparent duration and severity. In a study of 343 patients with prolonged FUO conducted by the National Institute for Allergy and Infectious Disease, 9.3 percent were diagnosed with factitious disorder. Fever may not sound like a big deal, and in most patients it isn't; usually it is a sign of a minor viral infection and, as such, is short-lived and requires minimal treatment. But early in their training, doctors are taught to take careful histories, perform thorough physical examinations, and observe closely when working with febrile patients. This makes fever an effective tool for the factitial patient because it guarantees attention when presented in the proper context. Fever is rarely the only sign of an illness, and so factitial patients usually couple it with some other carefully chosen feature (just as the "Sabra" coupled it with joint pains). The combination is sure to elicit plenty of attention and set doctors on a mad search.

Most of the factitial patients who seek assistance for FUO are young women, often in health-related professions. They generally fall into two groups: patients who manipulate thermometers and have had a bona fide febrile illness in the past, and slightly older patients who usually have serious psychiatric problems and frequently induce real disease in themselves to engage caregivers. Unless a rapid-reading electronic thermometer is used or the temperature of the urine is determined, a person can easily cause the appearance of fever simply by vigorously rubbing a thermometer on bed sheets, placing it in hot liquid, or drinking a hot liquid before a temperature reading is taken. But maintaining apparent fever by manipulating temperature-taking devices can be difficult in a hospital where personnel are hovering about. Patients who want to leave nothing to chance go for the real thing and cause authentic fevers by injecting themselves with foreign substances such as drugs, dirt, or feces.

Temperatures above 105.8 degrees Fahrenheit were labeled "hyperthermic fever" in 1889 by French physiologist Charles Richet. While a patient can experience genuine hyperthermia, ridiculously high phony fevers have been recorded by doctors since 1891, when Dr. H. Jones reported a 14-year-old patient with temperature readings of 108, 115, 135, 150, and 156 degrees Fahrenheit. Modern researchers caution that whenever hyperthermia exists (even if someone's temperature doesn't reach 156), a factitious disorder is among the diagnostic possibilities.

Morven S. Edwards, M.D., and Karina M. Butler reported on a 15-year-old girl who was admitted to the Texas Children's Hospital with symptoms that included fever, cough, and nausea. She was diagnosed as having strep throat, given oral penicillin, and sent home. Despite the antibiotic, her fever and cough persisted, so she was referred to the Infectious Disease Service and hospitalized for extensive testing. Numerous diagnostic studies—including a chest x-ray, upper gastrointestinal tract study, abdominal ultrasound study, bone marrow aspiration (withdrawal of bone marrow for examination), and bronchoscopy (insertion of an instrument down the throat for examination of the trachea and bronchial system, also allowing removal of tissue samples or foreign bodies)—were unremarkable. Her blood was screened for infectious agents such as hepatitis and Epstein-Barr viruses, but there was no evidence that she had had any recent infection. She was once again sent home, but her fevers persisted.

After seven months, the teenager continued to complain of fevers and added reports of ankle pain. Tests for juvenile rheumatoid arthritis were negative, and she was given an antipyretic (medication intended to control the fevers). She experienced side effects to the medicine and was given a different prescription drug; but still, after eight months, her fevers seemed to persist.

She claimed to be having daily temperatures of 101 to 105 degrees Fahrenheit; but when she was readmitted to the hospital, her readings were sometimes normal, and this fact began to make doctors suspicious. In addition, her fevers would rapidly disappear whenever she was closely scrutinized by caregivers and she lacked the sweating, hot skin, and rapid heart rate that accompany high fever. Her doctors stopped all medications and ordered that her temperature now be taken rectally and only in the presence of a nurse. That evening the girl's temperature was 99.6, and the nurse noticed that her anus was irritated. Less than two hours later, the patient asked for her temperature to be taken again and this time it was up to 101 degrees. Her rectum was now far more irritated and extremely painful to the touch. A resident physician documented in the patient's chart that he believed she was using some sort of device to increase her temperature readings.

The next day, nurses tried taking the girl's temperature orally with four different thermometers, including three electronic and one mercury, but the readings were chaotic, ranging from 105.4 to 99.2 degrees.

They again instituted rectal readings, this time with simultaneous documentation of her heart rate. The nurses were also instructed to check the temperature of the girl's urine if a thermometer registered a high temperature. When her doctor proceeded with a request for psychiatric consultation as well, the girl's fevers suddenly ended and she tried to play them down.

When she was interviewed and confronted by the psychiatrist, the teenager admitted to having faked her fevers by using a heating pad and a hot water warmer, which accounted for the irritated and tender condition of her rectum. She confessed that her factitious behavior was initially intended to allow her to miss classes; she had previously been performing so poorly in school that she needed an "excuse" for not meeting the expectations of her father. Then the behavior got out of hand and she felt unable to stop.

Although this girl's background wasn't as dysfunctional as Billy's had been, she certainly wasn't living or feeling like Rebecca of Sunnybrook Farm. Her parents divorced when she was six years old, and she lived with her mother for seven years until her mother's poor health forced her and her brother to move in with their father, his girlfriend, and her 13-year-old son. The girl had been a loner who had difficulty making friends. Her family tree was dotted with depression; indeed, one of her cousins was hospitalized for depression at the same time this patient had been hospitalized.

Researchers have found that many adolescents respond well to treatment, and their fraudulent fevers may be pleas for help. Factitious disorders in general are ways of expressing dire emotional needs. Adults, however, may be more resistive to change than teenagers, who are in a constant state of flux and whose frames of reference change continually. This resistance partially explains why so many adults who suffer from factitious disorders can become swept up in them, focusing their lives on them and dramatically altering their portrayals as needed, often incorporating apparent fever.

For example, one 35-year-old Munchausen patient feigned signs ranging from fever to bloody urine, subjecting herself to multiple exploratory surgeries for suspected peritonitis (inflammation of the membrane of the abdominal cavity). As her presentations changed, she was tested for diverse disorders, including diabetes and tumors of the lymphatic system. This woman's adeptness at switching illnesses was facilitated by her employer's profession—she was the housekeeper for a doctor and drew on his textbooks and professional literature to maintain the illusion of genuine illness.

Another seemingly well-read factitial patient, a 24-year-old man named Dave (Dr. Ford's patient), initially feigned a bowel obstruction, which had resulted only in negative test results and a psychiatric referral for a possible factitious disorder.

Dr. Ford:

I listened to a hard luck yarn about Dave's depression over having been laid off from his job; about his subsequent inability to look for work because he was so sick; about his mounting medical bills, which had depleted his savings; and about his declaration of bankruptcy. To top it all off, Dave was also on probation for forging prescriptions for painkillers, which he claimed to need for regional enteritis, also known as Crohn's disease, a serious disorder of the alimentary tract. I thought that he was faking illness and recommended group therapy. Dave agreed to such therapy but dropped out of the group after only two sessions. He soon discovered the power of fever as a medical sign when he claimed to have Mediterranean fever and was rushed to the hospital in an ambulance with a skyrocketing temperature.

The one hitch with Dave's new portrayal was that while he had fever in the emergency room, it vanished as soon as he was hospitalized. After a short time, Dave's hoax failed when tests for Mediterranean fever proved negative.

Dave was in and out of the hospital several more times before doctors convinced him that his real focus should be on getting onto the psychiatric ward. Surprisingly, Dave suddenly agreed. The two months he spent on that ward gave us a chance to gather Dave's records from other hospitals and to track down his family. It wasn't until I spoke with Dave's mother that I understood the heartache that was underlying Dave's persistent disease portrayals.

Dave was the only child of a southern couple. He had suffered humiliation and ridicule as a child because of congenital ankylosis of the jaw (the fusion of bones of the jaw). This condition made it difficult for him to eat and gave him a speech impediment that led to mockery from other children. Dave's father, a clerk, was a kind and indulgent man and, although often sick with abdominal problems that kept him home from work, he took care of Dave while his wife pursued her own career. Dave's mother showed relatively little interest in him and had no compunction about brushing him off whenever he tried to get close to her. She worked as an auditor and would frequently leave home for jobs out of state, being gone for long periods. Dave was thus subjected to two traumatic elements: the long, severe illnesses of his father and the repetitive absences of his mother.

When Dave was only 8 years old, he was placed in a home for emotionally disturbed children because of his increasingly bizarre behaviors, which included dressing peculiarly to attract attention, telling lies, and shying away from most other children. These behaviors, as well as his speech problem, made him the object of extreme cruelty from his fellow students. Dave's father died six months later, and his mother went to live in another state while Dave remained in institutions, eventually including reform school. Dave found his way into a foster home when he was 15 years old, but was never able to put himself on firm footing as he grew older. He barely graduated from high school and flunked out of college after only three semesters.

It is not uncommon for men and women to find themselves sometimes in love-hate relationships with one or both of their parents, especially as each new generation finds itself in conflict with the social mores and life-styles of the preceding generation. In Dave's case, however, the love-hate relationship with his mother was exaggerated: after years of his only contact with her being an occasional gift, he relocated to Tennessee and went to live with her.

Because he was unemployed, Dave's mother provided for his basic needs; however, she continued to be extremely critical of him and, finally unable or unwilling to fill the emotional void in Dave's life, tried unsuccessfully to have him permanently committed to a state institution. Despite the deplorable way in which his mother treated him, each time she went away on business Dave experienced horrendous anxiety and what he described as "unbearable loneliness, an enormous sense of emptiness and abandonment and fear of the world." His disease portrayals were precipitated by these desperate periods of separation from his mother. Several times Dave even flew to other states where his complaints of abdominal pain (no doubt vividly recalled and mimicked from his father's illness) led to surgical procedures. On two occasions while he was flying from his home to other cities where he intended to get treatment, his symptoms appeared so acute that the airliners were forced to make emergency landings with ambulances waiting so that Dave could be rushed to hospitals.

Between bouts of "illness," Dave said that he found time to fly to Israel, where he had been wounded by shrapnel during the Six Day War. This was never proved, however, and almost certainly represented a dash of pseudologia fantastica. Even on the psychiatric ward Dave's role-playing continued. True to the character of a factitial patient, Dave managed to be the focus of attention while hospitalized. He was an absolute master actor. His mannerisms were perfectly suited to whatever personality he chose to portray on a particular day. One day, for example, he would dress in a three-piece suit and look for all the world like the white-collar executive that he described himself to be. On another day he would put on tennis whites and shoes and adopt the look and mannerisms of a socialite walking off the court in Palm Beach. The next day he'd be "Joe College," outfitted in a university sweatshirt, pleated pants, and oxfords, and you'd swear he was a student at any college in town. He even admitted that when he assumed these different identities he almost believed them himself.

Dave's mother was useless in his treatment. She once visited him while he was hospitalized under my care and told me, "I want you to take this kid, lock him up, and throw away the key." What she really meant was "throw away the kid." Dave had some endearing qualities, and we really tried to help him and get him involved in psychotherapy, but he just couldn't tolerate that kind of intimacy.

We were able to follow Dave over a period of several years because every once in a while he'd come back to our hospital, but we couldn't hold him long enough to help him. During that time he often flew around the country, getting himself admitted to hospitals and charging it all to a credit card. Once when we saw him, he had had all his teeth pulled. He had convinced an oral surgeon to pull his teeth for something related to the problem he had with his jaw. His belly looked like a road map because of his numerous operations. After a while, we no longer heard from Dave and we conjectured that he had died from complications of multiple operations. He was a pathetic character, and none of his caregivers could remain angry with him. We all felt sorry for Dave.

Dave's story was made sadder still by the fact that he had a superior intelligence and creativity, as proved by psychological tests, yet he was only able to display them in the most ineffectual ways. While he elicited a great deal of genuine concern from the medical staff, his personality deficits rendered him unable to establish close relationships, even with his doctor. After Dave was discharged from the hospital, he entered outpatient therapy but gradually established a pattern of missing sessions until he disappeared back into his factitious world; once again, he dashed around the country, seeking and receiving care and nurturance from strangers. Dave, unfortunately, was a Munchausen patient who was so caught up in his portrayals that, by his own admission, they eventually threatened to become his total reality.

CHAPTER 7

SENSATIONAL
SYMPTOMS

Are you the new person drawn toward me?
To begin with take warning, I am surely far different from what you
  suppose;
. . . Have you no thought O dreamer that it may be all maya, illusion?
            Walt Whitman
            Are You The New Person Drawn Toward Me?
            (1860)

We recall the story of a 21-year-old United States Navy enlisted man (Dr. Ford's patient) who had orders to go to Vietnam at the height of America's involvement in Southeast Asia. While flying on board a commercial airliner from the East Coast to California, where he was supposed to report for duty and ship out to Vietnam, he "developed" the agonizing symptoms of acute renal colic and simulated the frightening appearance of passing a kidney stone. (One of the symptoms of renal colic is excruciating spastic pain.) The crew was incapable of comforting him, and his apparent distress was exceedingly disquieting to other passengers. The plane was forced to set down in Phoenix, Arizona, so the young man could receive emergency treatment.

Like Dave, this fellow understood the value of using sensational symptoms in eliciting equally dramatic responses from others. What could be more dramatic than a transcontinental jetliner making an unscheduled emergency stop on behalf of a sick passenger? How about an ambulance idling on the runway, its red lights flashing as it awaits its suffering passenger?

The sailor was taken off the plane on a stretcher and rushed to the nearest hospital, a private institution rather than a government hospital. Because he was a serviceman, the government was nonetheless responsible for his bills. After several days, when doctors at the hospital could not identify the source of his discomfort, he was sent to another private hospital where the bills continued to mount.

Dr. Ford:

When all tests proved negative, the Navy transferred the sailor to a military hospital where he was placed in a psychiatric ward under my care (I was a Navy psychiatrist at the time) because he was suspected of feigning his illness and the Navy needed to control his movements.

The Navy learned more about this young man by the trail of bills that he had left around the country. I was able to get medical records from every hospital to which he had been admitted. From these emerged a story of a yearlong flurry of emergency hospital visits, followed by hospitalizations, with each evaluation ending in a failure to diagnose his ailment.

Through psychological testing and his medical records, I became so suspicious that I finally told him that I thought he was faking his illness. He denied it, and several days later I received a letter which had supposedly been written by his attorney in his home state of Florida, warning me not to make allegations against his client because if I did I would be in big trouble. The problem with the letter was that several words were misspelled and the typing was extraordinarily sloppy. I phoned Florida and established that there was no such attorney, confirming my belief that the sailor had written the letter himself. However, he did get out of going to Vietnam and, instead received an administrative discharge from the Navy on the basis of having a severe personality disorder.

Although other military personnel might have called this a case of malingering, I diagnosed it as factitious disorder because of the young man's apparent delight in the patient role and the pseudologia fantastica which consistently characterized his stories.

He was a histrionic kid who was very good at playing roles and acting out things that most of us wouldn't be able to pull off. I believe that the primary reason for his false illnesses was his need for highly focused attention and support. These set him apart from someone who was purely interested in malingering his way out of going to Vietnam. The itinerant nature of his portrayals, and elaborate lies associated with them, put this young man in the class of Munchausen patients.

Another Navy corpsman was referred to me because he was thought to be depressed and, he argued, with good reason. "I was a pre-med student, working hard and getting good grades," he explained to me, "and just before I was able to matriculate into medical school full-time, I was drafted into the Navy." Instead of looking to grandiose events such as emergency plane landings to provide his drama, this man relied almost entirely on telling lies to enrapture his audience. He spent an hour telling me how his whole life had turned topsy-turvy after he left school. Teary-eyed, he said that he only hoped that he would be able to return to school someday and that his career hopes hadn't been entirely dashed by Uncle Sam's poorly timed intrusion into his life.

I determined that the corpsman had mild reactive depression (which is not uncommon among inductees who are trying to adjust to military life), and sent him back to his unit. But several days later a chief petty officer volunteered some eye-opening information about his young charge in a telephone call to my office. "Did you know, Dr. Ford, that he shows up at Corps School wearing campaign ribbons, but he's never been overseas?" the CPO asked. "And he tells fantastic stories about his exploits in Vietnam. Why, I don't believe for one minute that he was a pre-medical student."

The patient had withheld significant information about himself from me, but the men in his unit were wise to him because they had the opportunity to observe him every day. I called the corpsman back to my office and this time I asked pointed questions about his education and background. The corpsman was at such a loss to discuss the specifics of his studies that it was clear that he had fabricated his entire story.

When I confronted him about his pseudologia fantastica and what he had been doing, I discovered that he was just a frightened, immature boy who was trying to appear to be a lot more in control of his situation than he actually was. He felt powerless and lost in the Navy and wanted to feel that he was important. He made up stories about his education and heroics in U.S. military actions in an effort to be admired. Factitious disorder entered into my reevaluation of him because he had presented himself as being ill for reasons that weren't valid. He was not looking for any kind of material gain. And, in fact, he had carried more than his fair share of responsibility in his unit because he wanted to create the appearance of someone who was exceedingly diligent and who was willing to do more than what was expected of him. That was part of his heroic image.

Unlike his military counterpart whom I had also treated, this young man had not feigned any physical symptoms. It was easier (less acting and less research were needed) to let language and emotion foster attention. Also, feigned depression could not be quickly disproved by tests and examinations as feigned physical ailments sometimes can.

Most factitial patients still seem to need the reinforcement that physical symptoms provide; indeed, they view the acting and the research as a challenge rather than a problem.

Although fever is said to be the easiest sign to feign, the symptoms of renal and urinary ailments are also relatively simple to produce while generating a great deal of concern and need for diagnostic studies, as we saw with the sailor who fancied the drama of kidney stones and emergency jet landings. Renal and urinary ailments also keep doctors guessing long after tests are found to be negative because the features of genuine renal disease can often be erratic. Researchers say that feigned illness of this kind may be more common than is generally appreciated; they underscore the high number of hospitalizations and examinations that may be required before a precise diagnosis can be established. Some people with actual renal problems bleed for a while and then stop, so it's not unusual for a genuine patient to show signs which suddenly disappear. Sometimes objective renal and urinary findings don't even have to be demonstrated to draw a strong reaction. The pain of renal colic, for example, is so distinctive that most doctors only have to hear a person describe it to start treating him or her for it.

Factitial patients know how to manipulate renal and urinary symptoms, many of which are indeed accompanied by bloody urine. For example, if a person wants to do something simple yet anxiety provoking for doctors, he or she just has to put a few drops of blood into a urine sample, not even enough to make it look red. This will almost inevitably trigger an entire diagnostic workup. It's also not unusual for people to manipulate their urethras to cause bloody urine.

A related sign involving the urinary tract is the passing of calculi, commonly called stones, out of the body. A Canadian study of 3,300 specimens of calculi submitted to doctors by patients showed that 116, or 3.5 percent, had not been produced in the body. Yet the appearance of all of the stones was so convincing that medical professionals could not differentiate between the fake and genuine stones with the naked eye; the stones were examined with laboratory diagnostic methods including infrared and wet chemical analysis and x-ray diffraction. Eighty-eight of the phony calculi were minerals such as quartz and feldspar (calculi in the urinary tract are commonly composed of calcium oxalate or uric acid) which people had literally picked up somewhere and then presented to their doctors as substitutes for genuine calculi. Researchers found that the majority of the imitation stones were submitted for some sort of tangible secondary gain (as in malingering) or for psychiatric reasons, such as a factitious disorder.

Drs. Neal J. Meropol and Richard M. Zaner (with Dr. Ford) reported on a 25-year-old woman who gave her doctor a container full of calculi which she claimed were kidney stones she had passed in her urine. Laboratory analysis showed that the stones were made of cholesterol, indicating that they were not likely to have come from this young patient's body. It turned out that her mother's gallbladder, which contained gallstones, had previously been surgically removed (a cholecystectomy), and the elderly woman had eccentrically chosen to display the recovered stones on her mantlepiece. Her daughter then claimed them for her own.

Quite a few people have tried to pass off spurious stones as kidney stones. But the wildest case we're aware of is a Munchausen by proxy case in which a woman was so literal when she thought of trying to pass her son off as having kidney stones that she put pebbles from a nearby creek in his urine sample. That obviously was not a crafty deception, and it displayed the kind of ignorance about a disease that is seldom seen among factitial patients.

As noted, urine samples deliberately contaminated with blood are usually more successful in duping doctors. Because no one witnesses the giving of urine samples—except in cases of suspected drug abuse or suspected factitious disorder—patients can pass off bloody specimens relatively easily. Two patients in India presented bloody urine (hematuria) and even underwent extensive surgical diagnostic procedures, including kidney biopsies (the extraction of tissue samples for examination), before doctors caught them putting blood into their urine from cuts they had made on their skin.

Biochemists at Manchester Royal Infirmary in Great Britain dealt with a man who had signs of kidney disease, including protein in his urine. Their suspicions about the authenticity of his condition were aroused by his medical history, which was fraught with emergency visits to hospitals; his negative results on other tests; and the continued presence of an unusual protein in his urine, which they believed to be exogenous (not produced by the body) but could not immediately identify. Electrophoresis, a test used to analyze the different proteins in a patient's serum and urine, confirmed the presence of the unusual protein. Then, with sophisticated isoelectric focusing, a procedure for checking the composition of a substance by examining its electrons, they identified the protein as egg white. For confirmation, the doctors used the antiserum for egg protein. (Now stop to consider the valuable time, money, and materials spent on this one case alone and you will have an inkling of the waste generated by factitious disorders.)

Normally there should be no protein in the urine, and doctors routinely test for its presence when a urinalysis is performed. When protein is in the urine, it generally indicates some kind of kidney damage, and doctors are immediately concerned about it. The very fact that this man knew that by putting egg white in his urine he would create the appearance of kidney disease is a testimonial to the cleverness displayed by almost all factitial patients. We don't always know how they acquire that sort of knowledge. We would not have known to do what this man did. And although his choice of hoax was unusual and very specific, it was not unique. It has occurred in other cases. One can't help but think that if factitial patients took the creativity they put into their deceptions and applied it in more constructive ways, they could probably do and be anything. The mind reels at the variety of techniques people have used to feign illness. When reading the medical literature on factitious disorders, you sometimes find yourself angry, sometimes titillated, and sometimes awestruck at what these patients have been able to come up with. The egg white is a wonderful example of that.

Some ideas for medical signs and symptoms are based on ailments factitial patients have heard about—such as putting stones in a sample of urine. Many people with factitious disorders may be getting their medical information from lay publications. Others obviously do a fair amount of research, as we saw with Catherine, who studied about eating disorders at a library.

Like Catherine, many factitial patients don't have to go much further than their everyday environments to find the bases for their illness portrayals. In most cases, the means to create their hoaxes are readily available. It is the lab technician who has access to syringes and pathologic specimens. Or the maid who works for a doctor and is surrounded with medical books and supplies. It may be a person whose grandmother takes insulin for diabetes, inspiring him to inject himself with the insulin and create severe hypoglycemia. Jenny knew someone with cancer and copied what she had observed. Had she known someone with myasthenia gravis, perhaps that disease would have been what she chose to portray. Catherine's reactions to chemotherapy laid the foundation for her creation of an eating disorder.

A microbiology technician with the requisite access and knowledge ate rat poison containing warfarin (an anticoagulant used to treat certain clotting disorders and contained in many rodenticides) to create blood in his urine. (Eating rat poison has proved to be surprisingly common.) He also injected himself with contaminated material to cause a blood infection. He was able to control the amount of warfarin he ingested to get the desired effect; however, he added a dangerous element to his portrayal by simultaneously inducing a raging infection in his body— a real, serious illness which he could not control.

Because the technician was knowledgeable in the lab, he would have been able to calculate carefully the amount of rat poison he had to eat to make blood show up in his urine. But most people only know that they are aiming for a clear-cut reaction, and they proceed until they get some obvious effect. In doing so, they probably err on the side of overdosing and sometimes go way too far. The female lab technician who endangered her life through bloodletting probably did not intend to take her hemoglobin down to a near fatal level; after all, she did seek treatment in the clinic that one time. But how many previous times had she bled herself? Probably a hundred, but that time she had obviously gone too far and it was apparent even to her.

As illustrated in the case of the warfarin-eating technician, many factitial patients create multiple deceptions to confound doctors and keep them searching for causes. Some patients shift constantly from one phony illness to another, especially in Munchausen cases. But doing this is like playing Russian roulette, because presenting multiple symptoms can be exponentially more dangerous than presenting the symptoms of a single illness. In many cases, the numbers of diagnostic tests and lengths of hospitalizations increase many-fold, carrying with them the risks inherent in testing and surgery.

Another way in which factitial patients display their bizarre disregard for their bodies is by creating dermatoses, medical signs on the surface of the skin. Dermatoses are especially common because the skin is the most accessible and most visible organ. Patients create skin lesions by picking, gouging, or scratching themselves with their fingernails, as we saw in Jenny's case. Or they cause wounds by burning themselves with hot objects or chemicals. Factitial lesions almost always appear within reach of a person's dominant hand, which should be a tip-off to doctors that they may be self-induced.

A 48-year-old registered nurse who showed up at a hospital with nodules on her thighs and trunk and a slight fever was suspected of faking because of the location of the lesions. A muscle biopsy determined that the lesions contained talc, which she had been injecting under her skin. When doctors told her and her husband that they knew she was making herself sick, she glowered at them, then ranted about their incompetency and left the hospital. This woman, who as a nurse should have realized how life-threatening her hoax could be, refused follow-up mental health treatment. She died a year later when some talc entered her blood stream, formed a clot, and killed her.

Some people inject themselves with everything conceivable—and some things that are inconceivable—to induce infections. In one case, a 35-year-old nurse got hold of 11 different bacterial specimens, put them all together in a kind of laboratory cocktail, and injected her leg with the concoction. She developed a blood infection and an ulcer that wouldn't heal in spite of surgery and assorted treatments. Her infection was finally cured with antibiotics, and a psychiatrist was called in to treat her for borderline personality disorder and factitious disorder. Her plastic surgeon and psychiatrist collaborated on her treatment, which was a good idea, and effectively cut back on her hospital admissions and the lengths of her hospital stays.

Medical reports teem with tales of people who found their ticket to the hospital in self-infection. In two separate cases in British Columbia, Canada, patients actually developed septic arthritis of their knees (in which tissues deteriorate) after injecting bacteria into their knee joints. In another case, a woman who authentically had hypogammaglobulinemia (a deficiency in the blood protein gamma globulin, which helps the body fight off infection) induced an infection in herself knowing that her body was ill prepared to deal with it. In another highly unusual case a young man was hospitalized for lead poisoning. After extended treatment, he still had his original symptoms, which included stomach pains, diarrhea, and vomiting; in addition, he showed signs of a blood infection which had been caused by several rare bacteria. Doctors ultimately discovered that he was injecting himself with lead and the infection-causing bacteria. Fortunately, he accepted and responded to psychiatric treatment, which enabled him to end his factitious illnesses and cope with a myriad of personal problems which he had been unable to deal with effectively in the past.

Although saliva has been used in the general population of factitial patients as an agent of infection, it is thought by some researchers to be especially common among prison inmates. The Stough Dermatology and Dermatologic Plastic Surgery Clinic in Hot Springs, Arkansas, has reported three cases in which prisoners used saliva to induce infection. (The body reacts to the bacteria in saliva by producing infection.) When this kind of hoax is perpetrated by inmates, the possibility of malingering cannot be overlooked; but because prisons offer a depressing existence, it is also possible—even probable—that factitious disorders affect many inmates.

Saliva served as the agent of self-infection for a 40-year-old woman who spent 44 days in a hospital undergoing diagnostic tests and treatment for a fever of unknown origin and a persistent infection. When all possible cures failed, her doctors saw only one answer: factitious disorder. They searched her belongings while she was out of her room and turned up syringes and a spittle cup. With this damaging evidence in hand, they confronted her and she admitted that she had been injecting herself with saliva. The search and seizure carried out by her doctors posed legal questions, which we'll address later on, but they brought an end to her dangerous and costly factitious illness. Caregivers were then able to offer her psychological treatment.

Sometimes the costs of factitious illnesses do not end when the ruse does. Such is the case when people continually infect and reinfect their skin grafts. By the time their self-destructive behavior is discovered, the skin may have been mutilated and scarred beyond repair. That's what happened to a 44-year-old microbiologist in New England who had to be hospitalized three times for repair of a skin graft to her buttocks because the graft repeatedly became infected. In a last ditch effort to isolate the source of her infection, doctors performed lab tests on the discharge from the graft, revealing pure *Staphylococcus aureus*. This evidence strongly suggested a factitious disorder, as it is rare to find the pure form of this bacteria in the body. A nurse then found a needle and a syringe containing the pure bacteria stashed in the patient's room. Doctors believed that she had taken the bacteria from laboratory plates to which she had daily access at work. This patient had been treated at a nearby hospital for undulant fever, a bacterial disease uncommon in New England. Curiously, the patient acknowledged only part of her disease portrayal by admitting to causing her undulant fever, but she denied infecting her graft.

Perhaps the most horrendous means of self-infection exercised by factitial patients is the use of feces as the infecting agent. As anyone can imagine, this has substantial shock value among medical professionals, and compounds the feelings of disdain and hostility they often experience toward factitial patients. Nurses and doctors are so repulsed by this act that they often reject the notion that persons could be so desperate for care and attention that they would infect their bodies in this way. Because the literature is replete with cases in which factitial patients do go to such lengths to induce symptoms, health care professionals must be willing to consider this very real possibility as part of their assessments.

The thought of injecting oneself with feces is equally incredible to laypersons because handling feces is taboo in developed societies. From the time we are old enough to recognize that some of our bodily functions produce physical waste, it is drummed into our heads that we are not to touch or ingest excreta because doing so can make us sick. Yet some adults with factitious disorders exhibit total disregard for this taboo. We know of a woman who infected her breast with feces to create stubborn lesions and ulcers that had to be corrected surgically.

We all do things that we know are bad for us. A man may know, for example, that he has high blood pressure but he eats the salty potato chips anyway. Having information isn't necessarily enough to make our behavior fall in line. The other factor contributing to this alarming behavior is that sometimes the things that are the most forbidden are simultaneously the most appealing. We all get a potent message early in life that feces and urine are off limits, but that doesn't mean that people just accept it and move on. Some people get fixated on bodily waste, and the interest never ends. It can still seem abhorrent to us, but it's not as unintelligible as it may appear.

It's also not so irrational as it may appear. Body waste and saliva are not only the most accessible sources of bacteria, they are also two of the most potent and fast-acting sources for self-induced infections.

People with factitious disorders are not thinking that in two years or even two months they may get caught, so they had better not do this. They're thinking: "I'm in emotional pain. What can I do right now to make that better and to get attention?" An infection is an effective tool for getting immediate medical care and nursing, and the easiest way to create it is with materials produced by one's own body.

Related to the problem of self-infection are self-inflicted wound-healing disorders. Here, people who have wounds, almost always from legitimate surgery, refuse to let them heal. Most of these patients impair the healing process by infecting their wounds. In contrast to cases mentioned earlier, the object of a patient's attention in self-inflicted wound-healing disorders is a preexisting wound, not one created through means such as injecting bacteria under the skin. In a German study of 10 patients (8 women and 2 men, all in their twenties) with self-inflicted disorders of wound healing, 9 of them had previously required major surgeries to correct a variety of conditions. However, they then repeatedly infected their surgical incisions and their resultant need for care lasted from 18 to 84 months and involved a total of 85 surgical interventions.

Like virtually all factitial patients, these people suffered from a myriad of problems. One woman was anorexic, 2 others had psychogenic seizures (seizures that originate in the mind instead of the body), and 3 had marital or intimate partner problems. One man had self-inflicted skin emphysema and committed suicide two years after the study was conducted. One of the women died of blood poisoning (septicemia) as a result of her self-induced wound-healing disorder. Wounds were ultimately healed in 7 patients, but psychotherapy was considered truly successful in only 2.

One of us (C.V.F.) served as a consultant to attorneys in litigation involving an unmarried ambulance attendant from southern Mississippi who was hospitalized for the better part of a year because of persistent nonhealing of surgical incisions. This 22-year-old woman underwent a successful heart operation and became inordinately attached to her cardiac surgeon, whose charm, good looks, and obvious concern about his patients fed her hunger for nurturance and care. Only days after her discharge, she turned up at the emergency room with an infection in her surgical wound. The infection seemed to heal while she was hospitalized, but it returned as soon as she was discharged. A host of treatments had disappointing results, and she was repeatedly admitted to the hospital for what was becoming an increasingly serious condition. Her doctor was baffled by the persistent infection, but he stayed with the case, showing his characteristic concern. He called in other specialists as consultants but no matter what any of them recommended her incision always became reinfected.

On the ward this woman was less than a model patient, and she displayed characteristics of Munchausen syndrome. She often became disruptive and boisterous, complaining to hospital administrators about the staff and demanding what seemed to nurses to be undue amounts of narcotics for her pain. Her attitude and conduct toward her surgeon, however, was exactly opposite. She showered him with cards, gifts, and flowers while boasting to hospital personnel about how competent and caring he was and how very much she trusted him. The doctor, not recognizing her infatuation with him, was all too willing to believe that she was simply grateful for his attentiveness. Feeling sorry for her because she had spent so much time in the hospital, he often reminded her that he was doing everything in his power to send her home speedily. He honestly couldn't understand why this sweet woman was so unpopular among the hospital staff. When he spoke to her about it, she said that the staff was hostile toward her because her condition required so much of their attention. She added that she was only trying to get the nurses and residents to give her proper care.

Her infections worsened; and even though she was being treated with antibiotics, her kidneys failed. Her doctor became increasingly frustrated by her condition and decided to transfer her to another hospital. Over her protests, he told her, "I can't help you and I'm afraid that you will die here."

Despite the change of doctors and hospital, every time her discharge was planned, she would develop another infection. Weeks slipped by, with her seesawing between improvement and deterioration. After several months it was obvious that every time discharge was attempted, she relapsed. By now her physicians were certain that she was infecting her own incision. They only needed proof. The essential evidence finally came when fecal material was found in her wound during a test designed to pinpoint the source of her infections.

Her doctors told her that they believed she was infecting her wound with her own feces; she vehemently denied their allegations and arrogantly said that she was going to go back to her original surgeon because he was the only one who knew what he was talking about. Before she had a chance to see the surgeon again, however, he was notified of the other doctors' suspicions of factitious disorder. When the patient called for an appointment, he refused to treat her. Her infection resolved and her wound healed, but she filed suit against the surgeon claiming now that the postsurgical complications had been caused by his malpractice.

Dr. Ford:

I believe that this woman took legal action not because she was attempting to get money, but because her relationship with her surgeon had clearly come to an end. In her mind, she hadn't been discharged by a doctor; she had been spurned by her man. Having suffered a narcissistic injury, a burning indignity to her sense of self, her reaction was to try to redeem herself and get even by creating the misimpression that her infections had been the result of malpractice.

During the trial she sat in the courtroom looking perfectly normal, calm, and ladylike. The trial ended in a hung jury rather than outright acquittal because many of the jurors couldn't believe that anyone who appeared sane would put feces in her own wound to cause an infection.

In the aftermath of her treatments, doctors learned that this woman had endured extremely troubled interpersonal relationships throughout her life and that her work history was spotty at best. She had been fired from a number of jobs because of frequent absences from work due to illness and a tendency to sudden emotional outbursts with threats of suicide. Her doctors believed that she was suffering from borderline personality disorder in addition to a factitious disorder.

Most medical professionals are as unsuspecting of factitial patients as this litigious patient's surgeon had been, and that kind of ingenuous attitude constitutes one of the biggest problems surrounding factitious disorders. Although factitious disorders are uncommon in some medical disciplines, no one is really safe from its tangled web; and although many doctors don't bother to report factitious disorder cases, almost all of them can recall dealing with at least one patient who they believe was suffering from it. Our message is simple: caregivers within all specialties must be aware!

Dentists and eye doctors may be as apt to encounter factitial patients as internists and general surgeons. One dentist spoke candidly about a patient referred to him for evaluation of cancer of the mouth (oral squamous cell carcinoma). She had a lesion on her palate that was almost identical to one pictured in an oncology textbook that the dentist had consulted in preparing to handle her case. In the hospital, she said that she neither drank nor smoked (risk factors for oral cancer), which so surprised the dentist that he mentioned it to a nurse who was assigned to her room. The nurse abruptly contradicted the doctor. "Either you're wrong or she lied to you," the nurse said. "I've seen her smoking on several occasions."

Once questions were raised about the validity of the patient's report (at least as it related to her smoking history), the nurse decided to be more watchful around this woman. When the patient thought she was unobserved, she took a lighted cigarette and, with the help of a mirror, carefully pressed it into her palate at the site of the "carcinoma." The nurse caught her in the act and alerted the rest of the staff and the dentist, thereby preventing unnecessary treatment and saving a great deal of time and effort . . . at least at that facility.

Some feigned dental illnesses are not discovered so quickly and the patient can keep up the wild goose chase for months. For example, a 23-year-old woman went to a dentist with irritated white patches inside her mouth which had variously been attributed to cheek biting, a potentially malignant condition called leukoplakia, and a skin disease called lichen planus. For 18 months dentists had unsuccessfully treated her condition with topical compounds and steroid injections (which have many potentially serious side effects).

A new dentist stated she might have oral leukoderma, a condition in which the skin turns white and the discoloration spreads until it overtakes an entire area of the body. However, because the condition had been so resistant to treatment, a factitious disorder was considered as well. She was hospitalized and under the watchful eyes of the staff the patient was found to be putting a caustic, over-the-counter corn-removal preparation on the inside of her cheek. It bleached and burned the skin, causing the appearance of a serious disease.

Sometimes the medical treatments endured by these great pretenders are as harmful to them as their own manufactured symptoms. A woman who had undergone numerous ear surgeries at East Coast hospitals sustained profound hearing loss as a postsurgical complication. Still, she sought further care, ending up at the New York University Medical Center with self-induced inflammation of the ear canal (otitis externa, an infection occurring between the eardrum and external opening of the ear, frequently found in swimmers). When the infection resisted treatment, doctors suspected a factitious disorder and referred her for psychotherapy. The patient, who actually had Munchausen syndrome, refused psychological treatment and took her act back on the road, seeking medical assistance at other hospitals. Her case led otolaryngologists to warn fellows in their field that any time a thorough evaluation does not result in a "reasonable organic diagnosis," a factitious disorder should be suspected.

As we have seen, multiple operations are not uncommon among factitial patients, and they are most prevalent among sufferers of Munchausen syndrome. A case reported in Europe in 1990 involved a 35-year-old female Munchausen patient who had undergone six operations to examine her abdominal cavity (laparotomies) for suspected peritonitis (inflammation of an abdominal membrane caused by bacteria in the bloodstream). She had also had a venesection (surgical opening in a vein to remove blood) and lymphography (x-rays designed to locate tumors in the lymphatic system). Obviously, she had created believable symptoms if so many doctors had been fooled, and she was aided by the fact that she, like some other factitial patients, worked for a doctor and had access to his textbooks. Ironically, one who works for a doctor should know better than most the risks involved in every operation; however, that knowledge seems rarely to deter individuals with factitious disorders.

Risk taking seems to be part of the attraction for these patients. A 32-year-old man in Brandenburg, Germany, feigned head injuries, seizures, paralysis of one side of his body, and paralysis of both legs. Diagnosed with caudal syndrome, a problem involving a bundle of nerve roots that run vertically from the spinal column to openings in the vertebral column, he underwent four operations, each time risking paralysis as a complication. The thought of a person's sacrificing the uninhibited movement of a healthy body in exchange for torturous diagnostic studies, perilous surgery, and the austerity and sterility of a hospital environment boggles the mind. How emotionally bankrupt, how desperate can these people be that the means don't matter as long as their goals are achieved? That is the question we, as psychiatrists, explore and we, as authors, implore you to consider before judging the faker of illness.

CHAPTER 8

IF I SHOULD LIE
BEFORE I WAKE

Truth exists, only falsehood has to
be invented.
Georges Braque (1882–1963)
Pensees sur l'Art

Factitial patients are among the most arduous patients to diagnose
and treat. They may be pathetic though likable, like Billy (who
displayed his factitial behavior on Rodeo Drive), and doctors feel
terrible if they end up having to turn them away. On the other hand,
factitial patients may be downright despicable, like many Munchausen
patients, making physicians loath to offer them the kind of compassion
that medical professionals are expected to extend. Nowhere are the
troubling characteristics of these patients better illustrated than in an
unprecedented case involving a 39-year-old man who feigned a rare
disorder called cyclic hypersomnia, characterized by recurrent episodes
of excessive sleep.

Like many factitial patients who have an authentic medical problem
that serves as a basis for elaboration or that they actively make worse,
this man, whom we shall call Harry (Dr. Feldman's patient), actually
suffered from sleep apnea (a temporary cessation of breathing which
interrupts sleep, causing a person to feel perpetually tired). Harry had
never heard about apnea until a specialist diagnosed his condition and
began treating him for it. He became frightened when he learned that
while he slept there were intervals in which he stopped breathing, and

that the condition, if left untreated, could worsen. Once his apnea was brought under control and Harry was asymptomatic from it, he felt much more at ease, having learned much about apnea and related sleep disorders from his doctor.

Harry was an average, middle-class man in his fifties. He had served in the Army as a medic, but opted not to pursue a medical career in civilian life. He labored as an autoworker in his native Michigan to provide a comfortable life-style for his wife and two sons.

Because he never asked for much for himself, Harry believed that he was justified when he occasionally played king of the roost, demanding a little more conformity from his children than was actually necessary, a bit more submission from his wife than is considered acceptable in our liberated times. He fancied himself a kind of Ralph Kramden character—not completely dictatorial, just wanting to keep things in their proper perspective, or at least in his perspective, so that he would get the credit he felt he deserved for being a solid husband, father, and provider. No one in his family denied that Harry was all three.

Harry's wife held a college degree, but she had never put it to direct use, choosing instead to have children and be a homemaker while they were growing up. But like many middle-aged women who have raised children, she reached a point at which she wanted to pursue more individual interests. While her children were still in high school, she decided to attend graduate school, get her master's degree, and establish herself in a second career. Harry never objected to her continuing her education because she attended school during the day and it didn't cut into the time she spent carrying out tasks for him and their children.

When their elder son graduated from high school he accepted a good-paying technical job with an out-of-state firm, which would begin in the fall and help pay for his college education. Within days of the older son's graduation, Harry's wife received her master's degree and lined up a position with a computer manufacturer, which she would begin as soon as both sons were back in school. The younger son found a summer job as a lifeguard, working seven days a week.

The members of Harry's family had grown and become independent seemingly overnight. Harry was at once confused and overwhelmed by the prospect of these changes, which had long been coming but had been virtually invisible to him, and he started feeling old. At first, common sense prevailed over Harry's thinking. He didn't want to deny his older son the opportunity of getting a higher education (Harry couldn't afford to pay college tuition), and he reasoned that the younger boy should learn the value of a dollar earned instead of fooling around all summer with sports and his friends. And, Harry told himself, his wife's exciting new career was tantamount to her being rewarded for having successfully raised their children.

Harry tried to convince himself that he wasn't losing his family but rather that they were simply doing the things that he had always figured they would do when the time was right. But as the end of summer neared and his older son started preparing to leave home, as his wife changed her wardrobe from casual slacks to business suits, Harry started believing that the time wasn't right for any of these changes. He felt that he had lost his grip on his family and with it their respect and love, which he equated with how attentive they were to him and how much time they spent at home.

Harry became sullen and filled with self-pity and feelings of inadequacy. He tormented himself with thoughts of how inconsiderate his family had become. He had reversed his thinking, telling himself now that his son could get a job and put himself through night school closer to home; he didn't have to live 500 miles away. And he believed that his wife didn't really need to work outside their home. He had supported his family all these years without any spousal assistance, and he was still capable of doing just that. As for Harry's other son, well, he could make do with his allowance and spend more time at home. Harry was missing his boys, even though he had never spent much private time with them or actively participated in any of their activities; he wanted them around just the same. He reckoned that no one in his family had thought about what he was going to do while they were off pursuing their interests, and he decided that their choices were patently unfair to him. He felt abandoned and left out.

Harry's sense of separation had actually begun several years earlier, when his wife returned to school, but he had not been fully affected at that time because her classes were limited to a few hours several days a week, and his children were still young enough to be governed. Now that his wife and children had matured and were moving on, Harry set out to regain control over them by playing sick for attention. At first, he complained of vague symptoms that could be related to apnea, such as fatigue and light-headedness. When his wife suggested that he had just been working too hard and that he should take a couple of days off from work to rest and recover, Harry said that absenteeism could jeopardize his job. Within weeks, however, he slowly escalated his "illness" to the point where he indeed began missing work, at times spending 20 to 24 hours per day in bed, appearing to sleep. Harry's exhaustion and bouts of sleep lasted for days at a time, then they would clear up and he would seem energized and return to work. Then he would become symptomatic again. This pattern continued until his wife and children became deeply concerned.

In conversations with his family, Harry wondered whether his condition might be due to a serious flare-up of his apnea. At first his wife doubted that because she hadn't noticed a return of the overt signs of apnea, such as horrendously loud snoring punctuated by brief intervals of silence in which Harry actually stopped breathing. She was also perplexed because Harry's apnea had been manifested nightly and this new illness had a transient nature.

Regardless, there was no question that Harry's family believed he was ill, and they doted on him as if he were an invalid. He was extraordinarily convincing, but Harry could not have been so effective had his family not been enabling. His illness portrayal had an element of codependency to it; his behavior was calculated to keep his children and his wife from moving too far away from him, literally and figuratively, and they readily accepted the constraints. If he said, "I'm too tired to get up. I have to stay in bed and sleep, and you have to bring meals to me," they were willing to do that. The message he received was that his behavior was going to succeed.

His wife and children finally prevailed upon Harry to see his doctor. Even though he was not seeking the attention of outside caregivers, he had to visit the doctor to show his family that he was really ill and was trying to get help. When his otolaryngologist, who had treated his apnea, was unable to pinpoint the cause of Harry's symptoms, he referred him to a neurologist, and Harry went to the appointment to keep up appearances. Harry told the neurologist that his problem involved disabling, unexplained "sleep cycles." During these "cycles" he would experience a week of alertness and good energy, followed by several days of increasing daytime fatigue. This fatigue would progress to severe hypersomnia. Then the cycle would repeat. Harry's primary complaint remained these inexplicable, extended periods of sleep. He didn't add to those symptoms, and he even denied having other symptoms or any substance abuse problem that might have pointed the way to a diagnosis.

The neurologist was intrigued by Harry's case both because pronounced hypersomnia is unusual and because Harry's illness had a cyclic element (that is, it came and went). The neurologist insisted that Harry be hospitalized for an evaluation, but this had not been part of Harry's plan. Although he complied with admission, Harry was a markedly reluctant inpatient. In many ways Harry behaved as so many Munchausen patients do, bucking the system constantly, disapproving of the tests that were done, and insisting that the care was inappropriate. Sometimes he would refuse tests entirely, saying that he would allow blood to be drawn or some other procedure to be performed only if his neurologist were present; Harry knew full well that the tests would have to be cancelled because his doctor couldn't attend exclusively to him all day. He was disparaging of an endocrinologist who found no abnormalities in the functioning of his glands. A computed tomography (CT) scan of the brain was normal and Harry dismissed the results.

Harry's wife and children were overly attentive to their grumbling patient during their daily and nightly visits. His younger son adjusted his work schedule so that his afternoons were free to spend at the hospital or to pitch in and do his dad's chores at home. His wife was at the hospital at the start of visiting hours and remained there until her elder son met her in the evening. He had taken a minimum-wage job at a grocery store until the gravity of his father's illness could be determined. When Harry learned of this, he marveled at how effective his ruse really was. Harry had successfully reversed his family's plans and once again had their total attention, devotion, and respect—but that wasn't enough. He believed that they would "forget" him again as soon as he was declared well. He had no choice but to remain ill, so he continued to feign incapacitating hypersomnia.

At his family's insistence, Harry finally agreed to undergo sophisticated tests recommended by his doctors. They monitored his brain wave activity around the clock, observing and testing him during periods of apparent sleep lasting up to 18 hours. To their surprise, they found that the bulk of Harry's sleep was feigned: even though his eyes were closed as in sleep, the character of his brain waves never changed as it would during actual sleep. This was the tip-off that explained why doctors had failed so miserably to diagnose Harry's "illness." His "cyclic hypersomnia" actually was nothing more than prolonged bedrest and contrived sleep.

Harry's neurologist was furious when he confronted him with his findings, after which Harry became equally enraged. Harry insisted that the findings of the tests were the result of his "cycling out of the hypersomnia and getting better," and that the neurologist was incompetent. Harry told his family that as a former medic he knew the doctors had screwed up the tests and that all of the results were invalid. At times he would "swoon" into sleep as if to prove his point. His wife and children were bewildered by the accusations that Harry's illness was feigned, and they tried to convince the doctors to repeat the various studies. Despite the protests, Harry's neurologist insisted that he receive a psychiatric examination, and a psychiatric consultant from the hospital staff was assigned to Harry's case. Harry reluctantly agreed to see the psychiatrist "if for no other reason," he told his neurologist, "than to prove that you're wrong."

Dr. Feldman:

After the first meeting with Harry, the consultant confided to me (I was one of her supervisors) that she knew Harry was lying to her about his condition and that frankly she couldn't stand him. She asked me to take over his care.

Harry was still trying to salvage the idea that he had a rather esoteric sleep disorder even though the consultant knew that he didn't. Similarly, she found no evidence for a mood disorder such as depression, and his bluster and belligerence contrasted with his depiction of himself as helpless. I agreed to see him until the other doctor was able to set aside her personal feelings, but she never felt comfortable treating Harry, and neither did I. I, too, could never be sure if he had told me the truth about anything, and I felt sorry for his family because they were still so worried that he had a "sleeping sickness."

Harry had a number of personality problems, evident in his fragile self-image and hostility. After going for several days without diagnostic tests, he realized that psychiatric intervention was taking the place of medical studies. A frustrated Harry checked out of the hospital in a huff, his wife alongside him, vowing to find doctors who could provide competent care. Because his family viewed his case as "unresolved," he could call on the same symptoms in the future whenever he felt the need to regain control over his wife and sons.

We had offered Harry behavioral therapy focused on sleep as well as supportive individual and group psychotherapy, but he rarely agreed to attend. Furious about being defined as needing psychiatric care, he signed himself out of the hospital and refused offers of outpatient follow-up. We believed that we could have helped Harry if he had let us, but just like the anemic lab technician who ran from me in the clinic, we couldn't force Harry to accept treatment. Admittedly, it would have been protracted and difficult regardless. We hope that if we can engage factitial patients in some kind of ongoing psychotherapeutic relationship, they will learn that they don't have to use the appearance of medical illness to elicit interest from others. They will always have a supportive, actively listening person involved with them in the form of the therapist.

Harry's family could have been invaluable in his treatment because they were so important to him and they loved him so much. Unfortunately, they couldn't see past his hoax, but then neither could the husbands of the nurse who was killing herself with a chemotherapy drug and the nurse who killed herself with a talc embolism.

Certainly Harry is not the only factitial patient who has used illness to manipulate family members. A 27-year-old nurse injected herself with epinephrine (or adrenaline, the hormone which prepares our bodies for flight, fright, or fight reactions) as a way of inducing medical signs that would get the attention of her workaholic veterinarian husband. She began her deception soon after marriage, when her husband opened a practice in a rural area, leaving her with nothing to do. She believed that the only way to get his attention was to play sick. To some extent, it worked, just as it had in Harry's case, and her husband was forced to divide his attention and time between sick animals and his "sick" wife.

As reprehensible as the actions of this woman and Harry were, they were driven in part by their lack of insight. Had Harry accepted psychiatric treatment, his caregivers would have felt more sympathetic toward him and also better about themselves. Even though many health care professionals had already been duped, they could have felt more confident that he wouldn't pull such a hoax on other earnest caregivers. They could have trusted that he would learn healthier ways of expressing his needs. But Harry's story didn't have a happy ending for him or his caregivers. When he left the hospital, everyone who had had anything to do with his care, including food service and maintenance employees, was glad to see him go. They openly expressed their wish that he would never return, and hoped he would be turned away if he did. But what if Harry had reappeared at that hospital with a legitimate ailment and no one believed that he was really sick? Suppose they just brushed Harry off as a faker?

The chances of a factitial patient being refused treatment are substantial once he or she has established a reputation at a medical institution. Billy (Dr. Ford's patient) was later turned away by the same hospital at which he had been treated because his reputation preceded him, and doctors thought that they would once again find themselves entangled in his web. Although this is an understandable reaction, it is not necessarily appropriate because virtually all human beings legitimately need medical attention at some time in their lives. Thus, like the boy who cried "Wolf!" just to manipulate others, factitial patients might someday encounter a real wolf of an illness only to find themselves alone in fending off the attack.

CHAPTER 9

FALSE
ACCUSATIONS

He who would distinguish the true
from the false must have an adequate
idea of what is true and false.
                    Benedict Spinoza
                    Ethics (1677)

We know that confirmed factitial patients have been denied hospi-tal treatment, but what happens to someone who is legitimately sick but is suspected of having a factitious disorder?

Dr. Feldman:

I recall just such an unsettling case. I worked at a hospital where staff members who were assigned to a ward for difficult-to-diagnose patients were given a weekly opportunity to discuss with a psychiatrist their patients and any special problems they might be having. During one of these group sessions, the nurses complained vehemently about a patient who they believed was faking his illness.

They said that this man had been admitted to the hospital with complaints of crippling pains all over his body, fever, headaches, and weakness. When the nurses went into his room to treat him, he could hardly move, and even the most simple procedures became quite difficult to carry out. The nurses had to shift his body from one side of the bed to the other to change the linen, and he generally couldn't even feed himself. Yet, the nurses said, it seemed that when he wanted his cigarettes, he rarely had any particular trouble reaching for them, lighting one, and smoking it. Tests were being conducted to determine the cause of this man's complaints, but several of the nurses resented his presence because they felt that costly medical resources were being "wasted" when they could better serve someone who was genuinely sick. They felt strongly about this because they had some very sick patients under their care.

The office in which we held these sessions was directly across from this patient's room, and the nurses would voice their objections in barely audible whispers so that he wouldn't hear them. The man's doctors knew about their suspicions and, as a result of the meeting, the staff agreed that they had to do whatever was necessary to make the patient comfortable, to follow his doctors' instructions, and to maintain their professional attitude while a conclusive diagnosis was being established.

This bitter staff was extremely shaken when the patient suddenly died on the fifth day of his hospitalization. Some people cried, and everyone on the ward felt guilty about not having believed him. Some of the nurses felt they had been gruff with him, and some had given priority to other patients who were more "seriously ill" when they had to choose among patients to respond to first. Everyone was devastated by the experience, and they were relieved that this patient's doctors had not directly accused him of a factitious disorder. Although I reminded them that they had done everything that was expected of them professionally, it was an event that none of them would ever forget. It would certainly color their actions in the future, and they would be far less willing to accuse someone of faking an illness, even when that really *was* the case.

An autopsy revealed that this patient had suffered and died from meningitis, an inflammation of the membranes lining the skull, vertebral column, and brain, which causes a variety of symptoms including headaches, fever, and stiffening of the muscles. His death raised a host of questions about whether or not malpractice had been involved in his treatment because his illness had not been taken seriously by some caregivers. His medical records, however, indicated that doctors had followed an acceptable course toward diagnosis, though they had failed to pinpoint the nature of his illness before it claimed his life. Had the staff openly accused him of faking, or withdrawn care, other legal questions might have arisen—especially if the suspicions of factitious disorder were documented in his medical chart.

Fifty-two-year-old Joan Nelson of London, England, knows firsthand what it's like to be unjustly accused of fakery and then to suffer the consequences. Joan is a registered nurse whose years as a young bride and mother were spent traveling with her husband during his service in the Royal Air Force. After his discharge, they settled down to family life in a quiet London suburb, and Joan found herself well-suited to her roles as wife, mother, and nurse, working for a doctor in general practice. An easygoing woman with an even temperament and gentle manner, Joan had struggled through her teenage years with difficult menstrual periods which were precursors of serious legitimate health problems she would have later in life. Here, in her own words, is her account of how she came to be falsely accused of having Munchausen syndrome:

I'd been a particularly healthy child until my periods began when I was 13. I had problems with menstruation right from the start, and my periods were not as much heavy as they were excruciatingly painful. I was told by our family doctor that what I was experiencing was normal and to get on with life and not to worry about it. Even when I was training to become a nurse, when I passed out from the pain one day in class, I was just picked up and given iron tablets and nobody really looked into what was happening to me. I was simply told that it was part of being a woman and I was expected to learn to live with the pain.

I was a nurse before I got married, and I had my first baby at the age of 23 by caesarean section. I was in Singapore at that time because that's where my husband was stationed, and that first birth was a horror story. I had a hemorrhage when I was almost eight months pregnant and was rushed to a hospital, but doctors waited a week before they delivered the baby even though I had lost all the fluid. I had a dry caesarean birth, which was followed by a quite severe uterine infection. The wound had a lot of problems healing up and I was ill for some time. A couple of years later I had a miscarriage at about 16 weeks, but I was able to become pregnant again and had another baby, who was also delivered by caesarean because my uterus actually burst open where the scar from my first pregnancy was. The doctors who delivered this baby said that my insides were "falling to pieces" and, had they known how bad my condition was, they would have put me on total bed rest during that pregnancy. Instead, I'd actually been walking around, doing chores, and trying to lead a normal life. I had been telling doctors about my problems for years by then, but it just seems that they didn't listen to anything I told them.

After the birth of my second child, the obstetrician told me and my husband that my abdomen was in an awful mess, but he didn't tell us what was wrong. He simply said that he would discuss it with me when I went back to see him for my six-week checkup. But he did issue a stern warning that under no circumstances was I to have any more children. People moved around frequently in the service, and when I went back for my postnatal visit, the obstetrician who had delivered my son was gone, and I saw a different doctor, who happened to be a Catholic. I told him what the other doctor had said about not having any more children, and he assured me that no matter where I was in the world, he would supervise my future pregnancies because he didn't believe in sterilizing a young, healthy woman.

I felt that this man was letting his personal opinions get in the way of giving me proper health care, so I tried to get birth control pills, but nobody would give them to me because of my medical history. Our family doctor finally referred me to a gynecologist in the town where I live now who, after reviewing my medical records from my second pregnancy and birth, said that I should be sterilized; instead, he removed my appendix! After the surgery he told me and my husband that he'd "done some tidying up," but what the tidying up was I don't know because he never explained any further. The wound from my second birth required constant care because it kept breaking down. Following that, I had year after year of horrendous period problems, which worsened with time.

I was 27 at that time and kept going back to our general practitioner about the problems that I was having after my second son's birth. I couldn't even walk the length of our driveway without being in severe pain. I couldn't go down to the toilet at night without putting on a maternity girdle because I felt like everything inside me was coming undone. One of the worst problems my husband and I had was painful intercourse, and I was fortunate to have a husband who was patient and greatly concerned about my health. Still, no matter what I told the doctor, it got me nowhere. He just said that the pain was caused by the scar stretching and curtly added that all women have period problems and I just had to put up with it.

Finally, when I was 39 years old, this doctor, whom I had stayed with all those years since the time of my second baby because he had assured me that I was just having common woman problems, sent me to hospital to have a scraping. The doctor who performed it said they found nothing abnormal. But by that time I was really feeling quite poorly and was in so much pain that I wasn't sleeping well. One morning I went to sleep at the steering wheel while driving to work. The general practitioner with whom I worked could see how ill I was and he said, "You can't carry on like this. I'll ring your doctor and see if he'll consider sending you elsewhere for a second opinion."

Knowing full well that I was in the office with the doctor for whom I work, my doctor told him bluntly: "I don't consider that there's anything wrong with her, and she won't be happy until she's had a hysterectomy anyway. If you want to refer her you can." My employer referred me to a gynecologist in another area, and I was seen within a week, which was then coming up to Christmas, when I was just 40 years old.

The gynecologist said he thought that he knew what was wrong with me and asked me if I could stand it until after Christmas and go into hospital January 3, 1980. He said I was going to have to have a hysterectomy. In January I had the operation, which took more than four hours. The doctor only removed half of my uterus at that time. The rest had to be left on my bladder because it couldn't be divided since it had too many adhesions to be separated. They couldn't remove my ovaries because they were bound down by scar tissue, and they couldn't take the cervix because they couldn't get low enough onto where the cervix joins the uterus to get it out. So they only did a partial hysterectomy.

I came home feeling reasonable straight away, but within a few weeks I was having periods again. I went back to see my general practitioner and he basically said: "Tough. If you feel there's a problem, refer yourself back to the gynecologist." I'm certain that he resented my having sought a second opinion and having had surgery against his wishes. I returned to the gynecologist and he then told me that he'd found endometriosis; that's when he explained it all to me and how bad things were.

Endometriosis is a disease in which tissue similar to the mucous membrane that lines the uterus grows elsewhere in the pelvic area, causing pain, especially during menstruation. Endometriosis has only recently been recognized as a serious problem affecting countless women, and education programs for health care professionals and women have been introduced so that the scope and nature of endometriosis can be understood; the aim is to ensure that women receive accurate diagnoses and proper treatment. The formation of adhesions is a common problem in endometriosis, and removal of the uterus, fallopian tubes, and ovaries is sometimes necessary to alleviate symptoms.

As a nurse I understand a lot about my body, but endometriosis hadn't even crossed my mind. I had no idea that that was what was wrong with me. I just knew that I had pain and was getting very heavy periods with clotting. At times I couldn't get off the toilet because I was losing so much blood, and it was the only comfortable place to sit because I couldn't bear the pressure of sitting on anything solid. With all of this, my general practitioner still decided that there was nothing wrong with me.

Now I found myself with a gynecologist who said that I had such extensive endometriosis that it was in the cervix, and I also had fibroid tumors. I was hospitalized six months later and my cervix was removed vaginally. I continued to have a lot of abdominal pain, and each time I went back to my general practitioner he told me to get in touch with the gynecologist myself. This is contrary to our system of health care in England, where one's general practitioner or family doctor is supposed to refer patients to specialists. I then was given a medication which is used for treating endometriosis, but I had a very bad reaction to it and had to stop taking it. I had abdominal surgery so that more endometriosis tissue could be burned off, and I had a cystoscopy [a means of examining the bladder and removing growths or tissue samples] because they found endometriosis tissue on my bladder as well.

During one of my hospitalizations I was found to have thyroid antibodies, which create symptoms of an underactive thyroid—weight gain, hair loss, lethargy, cold—all of which I'd complained about. One of the doctors who had been researching endometriosis at St. Thomas Hospital discovered that I had this condition, which required that I be treated with thyroxine [a hormone synthesized and secreted by the thyroid gland].

In the middle of all this, I had to go into the hospital to have an impacted wisdom tooth removed. During the oral surgery, the dentist dislocated my jaw, and I had a lot of bleeding afterwards. Subsequently, I got an infected hematoma on the side of my mouth from which my tooth had been removed, which ended up damaging both temporomandibular joints [the hinge joints of the jaw]. After a number of visits with my general practitioner, I was finally sent to a specialist who wired my jaw to give the joints a rest, and I could only drink through a straw. I couldn't eat solid food. I was wired for several months, but the joints had not progressed at all. Then metal strengths were put on my teeth which had to be hooked up with rubber bands, and for several months I could only eat soft foods.

The professor who wired my jaw then sent me to another professor who performed 5½ hours of microsurgery to repair my temporomandibular joints. He had just been to the United States where he learned this new technique, which enabled him to correct my problem. Although I still have restricted movement I can eat and talk now.

After all this, I was still having a lot of problems with the endometriosis, and my ovaries had to be removed. Reports on these findings had been sent to my general practitioner to be included in my permanent medical records. I also began having problems with my bowel. The doctor who'd done my hysterectomy said that I should get my general practitioner to refer me to a gastroenterologist to have a look at the bowel situation. He said I might have endometriosis or adhesions in my bowel. I asked my general practitioner to refer me to such a specialist; and not long afterwards I was also advised by a friend that I should seek compensation for the damage that had been done to my jaw.

This is how I ended up seeing my medical records. My lawyer asked the hospital for copies of the notes pertaining to my jaw. When he received those records, the referral letter from my general practitioner to the gastroenterologist was among them and it should not have been. My lawyer asked if I had seen that letter. I hadn't. The letter stated that I had manipulated my way into getting a hysterectomy against medical advice, which led to my opening a pandora's box of problems and, consequently, I was having bowel problems and had asked for a referral. At the bottom he had written: "In my opinion, this woman suffers with Munchausen syndrome."

As a nurse I basically knew what that meant. But this letter was sent without my knowledge. Suddenly the callous and cold treatment I had received from the gastroenterologist made sense. When I had seen him, he simply said to me: "You've had your ovaries out. You can't possibly have any more trouble with endometriosis." And that was it. And yet I know, especially now that I've learned so much about endometriosis, that it's quite possible to continue to have problems even after the ovaries have been removed because the tissue can turn up in any part of the pelvic area.

When I saw this in my medical records I felt, to put it bluntly, gut struck. I just couldn't believe that he had written this about me. I knew that I had problems communicating with this man, but considering the fact that I had a diagnosis of endometriosis, he should have recognized that I was authentically ill. And I certainly couldn't pull wool over anybody's eyes about my temporomandibular joint problems. I was treated by professors who were experts in their fields. My case with my jaw was illustrated in a medical magazine because it was such an unusual case, and it was the first one this doctor had done involving two joints. It was a new operation over here in the U.K., so he had asked for my permission to write about it. There was no way that my general practitioner had any excuse to write in my medical records that I had Munchausen syndrome and, sadly, there is no possible way to get it removed from my records.

I work in the health service, and I think all patients should know what is being written about them. I tell my patients what I write about them. My husband and I confronted this doctor, and I said, "How dare you put something like this in my notes!" He said, "I don't understand endometriosis, and I don't understand anything about temporomandibular joints." I said, "Don't you think it's time you learned?" I also told him that I was changing doctors, and he said, "Well, this will be in your medical notes. The new doctor will see it." I said, "He already knows about it. I've explained it all to him." He just didn't know what to say. But the damage was done and I have no redress. I couldn't sue for malpractice because I didn't have the finances to pay attorneys. I couldn't even pursue the suit for compensation on my jaw because I ran out of money.

To think that somebody who has worked as I have for so many years in the health service and coped with so many problems should be unjustly accused of something like this! To further call this doctor's actions into question, I want to point out that at the time I had my ovaries removed, I gave up my job on health grounds, and I received invalid benefits for 2½ years because my health was so poor. The same doctor who wrote that I had Munchausen syndrome signed the certificate for me to receive benefits. If he thought I had Munchausen syndrome, he shouldn't have signed any such certificate.

In the end, the doctor with whom I had worked as a district nurse contacted me and said that he knew that my work was good and asked me to consider returning to work with him part-time. I began by working 6 hours a week and I'm now up to 26 hours. Although I still have some problems, I cope with them. I think back to the day when I learned that I had been accused of having Munchausen syndrome, and I can still recall how totally devastated I felt. I was in tears. I just could not believe that that would be written about me. Although I thought that I knew what it meant, I had to look it up in a library. I was even more devastated when I read the medical literature on it, and I was extremely angry because if that doctor really thought that I had Munchausen syndrome, I should have been seen by a psychiatrist. It's an illness! No matter what people think about the condition, it's an illness, and anybody with that illness needs help. My husband was totally upset by what our doctor had written because he has witnessed what I've been through over the years and what we've coped with. Both of my sons had seen what I had gone through, and they were devastated.

By the time I learned of the letter, I knew more about endometriosis. I'd contacted the Endometriosis Society in desperate need of help, and they supported me through a lot. But nobody can support you through something like being accused of faking serious illness by a doctor whom you trusted for years. This is something you have to come to terms with yourself. It took my confidence totally away to think that somebody thought that of me. Even now I get shaky if I see that man around town. He's retired now but I still don't like to see him. The bottom line is that if this had been properly diagnosed, I'd have received earlier treatment. I think I've had endometriosis right from the start of my periods because they've always been such a problem.

When I told my new doctor about what had been written about me, he was very sympathetic because he's a close friend of the doctor with whom I now work, who had vouched for my honesty and integrity. Looking back, I don't know how I got through all this. I think it's only since I've started to feel better generally that I realize how poorly I did feel and what a struggle it was to cope. I think I just took each day as it came. My husband was wonderful and remarkably patient and kind. I've had 15 surgeries and anesthetics since I was 23.

I'm very sympathetic toward people who are ill, probably because I have suffered so much myself. I feel that anybody who comes to a doctor or nurse with a problem or perceived problem needs help. Even if somebody's suffering with true Munchausen syndrome, he or she needs help. I've had the feeling at times during my career that some patients' ailments weren't legitimate, but if you talk to them and talk around things, you find that they quite often have another worry. They've come to you saying they've got a pain somewhere, when in fact their problems are probably something quite different and they're just looking for support and maybe some guidance and answers. Loneliness has a lot to do with this sort of thing. If they know you've got a sympathetic ear, they will come to you, and I always thought that was part of the caring profession—to listen.

Why do people think that individuals with real Munchausen syndrome are repulsive? Those people are sick, and no matter what they have done, they need help, particularly with something like Munchausen. There's got to be an underlying reason why these people are presenting with signs and symptoms that aren't really there. I worked in a psychiatry division for 5½ years, and I believe that there's got to be something underneath that's driving them to do that. It's a cry for help when you look at it.

CHAPTER 10

PAIN FOR GAIN: THE MOTIVES BEHIND THE ACTS

Never . . . be mean in anything;
never be false; never be cruel.
Charles Dickens
David Copperfield (1849–1850)

Identifying the motivations behind disease portrayals can help to answer questions about the types of people apt to carry out such hoaxes. But motivations can be multifold and vary from case to case; thus, it is difficult to make generalizations about all factitial patients. Doctors are trained to follow specific paths toward diagnosis and to scrutinize small pieces of information in reaching conclusions. But when dealing with factitious disorders, medical professionals must look at these patients in the broadest terms and overlook nothing, no matter how farfetched it may seem, that might contribute to answering the questions, Who would do something like this, and why? This perspective must include the surprising possibility that some people believe that pain has spiritually redeeming qualities and that, for them, factitious disorders may be the equivalent of what a stone in the shoe and self-flagellation were for followers of some ascetic religious movements.

We assume that suffering is always a terrible thing, and wonder why anybody would want to self-inflict pain; we come up with complex psychological formulations that often include childhood deprivation and abuse. But in certain subcultures and religions, there is an explicit admiration for the solemn endurance of suffering that might lead some people volitionally to deprive themselves of good health. These people may perceive the pain and punishment they are inflicting on themselves as an admirable goal. Doctors are missing this moral component in some cases because, although we try not to, we always approach patients with preconceptions, one of which is that people would never want to be in pain.

Dr. Feldman:

I'm reminded of a woman who plunged a knife into her chest, barely missing her heart. She claimed to be a member of a religious group which didn't believe in any demarcation between life and death, so she couldn't understand why the doctors were anxious about her well-being and why we were talking about protracted hospitalization for psychiatric care. She really believed that her action was insignificant, and yet we, as a group of professionals, were dismayed. Even if patients earnestly say things like "Suffering is good for the soul," most doctors would dismiss that explanation instantly. Yet self-piety for tolerating pain may be an unconscious factor in some cases of factitious disorder. People do things all the time for reasons of which they are not aware, and their actions may be highly influenced by religious beliefs, even unconventional ones.

Given sufficient time with a factitial patient, which is rare because these patients typically flee, doctors may be able to pinpoint motivation, even if a person is unaware of the forces driving his or her own false illness. For example, doctors were able to spend enough time with Billy to observe him and learn about his background of neglect and his childhood fears that persisted into adulthood; they could then unearth his motivation for hospitalization: Billy was actually looking for a safe haven. Protective environments, such as hospitals, are hard to give up if a person is not used to feeling safe in life.

Other disease portrayals are fraught with elements of sadomasochism. In a sadomasochistic relationship, we sometimes identify with those who mistreat us. The relationship becomes symbiotic, and an identification occurs between captive and captor. Similarly, in factitious disorders, grown-ups may perpetuate through self-induced illness the physical abuse they experienced as children. They may accept the idea that abuse is a part of living. They may also engineer for doctors to contribute to the abuse through unnecessary tests and surgeries. Through this behavior, the patient may feel in control: in childhood he or she could do nothing about the physical punishment; now the patient can intensify or curtail it at will.

Sexual abuse also provides a foundation for self-inflicted physical disorders. We point to the case of a young girl who stuck her eyes with pins to escape continual rape by her father. Once she became ill she was extricated from her painful environment. That was obviously an extraordinarily desperate way of ending the abuse. Sometimes feigned illnesses have symbolic aspects that also suggest a background of sexual violation. Munchausen by proxy, for example, has some sexual overtones because instrumentation being applied to the body in some ways is a sexual act. And tampering with and handling another person's genitals, urine, and feces, and injecting substances into the body all have sexual connotations.

Sometimes factitious disorder and Munchausen patients appear *not* to have had troubling backgrounds, instead coming from apparently healthy families. A number of researchers believe that underlying brain dysfunction may be partly responsible in these cases. Some patients have abnormal findings on imaging studies of the brain or cognitive tests, and this area of investigation has exciting potential.

Being knowledgeable about factitious disorders in general and the various factors underlying them is central to any hope of treating these patients. Often, however, such knowledge isn't enough to snag a great pretender. The keen detective work that we spoke about earlier, perseverance, and the ability to approach a patient correctly once feigned illness is suspected are essential because factitial patients are so very good at what they do. This is well illustrated by cases of factitious endocrine disorders (such as phony diabetes and thyroid disease), which occur with alarming frequency among factitial patients.

Fakers of endocrine disorders may actually have diabetes, and purposely stop taking their insulin to raise their blood sugar levels, sometimes to the extent that they go into coma. Or they may not have diabetes and take insulin to lower their blood sugars, which can also result in coma or in problems such as seizures. Factitial patients have been known to steal insulin from friends and relatives. In some states, insulin can even be purchased without a prescription. Hospitalized fakers commonly hide insulin in their hospital rooms. One patient hid the insulin in the toilet reservoir in his hospital bathroom; another suspended some on a string outside the hospital room window; and a nursing sister hid her insulin and syringe in the hem of her habit. They hoard their precious "creator of symptoms" the way addicts hoard drugs. The bottle of insulin actually becomes a so-called "transitional object"— a kind of security blanket that has a connection with comforting childhood memories. This transitional object also reflects the motivations underlying the portrayal.

For example, factitial patients seeking control might place special value on the secrecy of their transitional object because they alone have the power to keep it concealed. They also have the power to use it to manipulate others whom they then control in a paradoxical way: even while those others are entirely ignorant of the "faker's little helper," they become thoroughly involved in the havoc wreaked by the abused substance. Similarly, people who self-mutilate often revere and protect their own transitional objects, the tools for deliberate self-harm. Be it a razor blade, a piece of glass from a broken thermometer, or even a nail file, the value often lies more in its concealment than in its capacity for inflicting damage.

Self-mutilation sometimes coexists with factitious disorder and, as we saw in Jenny's case, it is difficult to treat. A person who self-mutilates often has borderline personality disorder and, therefore, a poor sense of self. At times, such a person may feel lost because of a certain weakness inherent in her personality which makes it unclear to her where she ends and other people begin. Cutting her skin, experiencing pain, and seeing blood help to delimit in her mind her physical presence.

Blood itself may function as a transitional object. It is soft, warm, and enveloping, and people will cut themselves to access this virtually literal "security blanket." Blood also sobers those who experience "derealization" in which reality is only loosely grasped and their lives become like extended déjà vu experiences, vaguely familiar to them but without any sense of certainty. The sight of blood and its concomitant pain are very real sensations that help such individuals focus, thereby reminding them of their humanity and of their realness. Many bloodletters say that cutting themselves also alleviates tension. It may be that by self-mutilating, they reduce their anxiety over whether they have control over their own bodies; as we've pointed out, a need for that kind of control is often seen in factitious disorders.

Control was a key element in the rare and extremely self-destructive case of a woman who made herself appear to have pheochromocytoma (an adrenal-cell tumor that releases excessive adrenaline and associated products to cause recurrent episodes in which a person feels exceptionally anxious, sweats profusely, and has headaches, nausea, and a rapid heart rate). The 35-year-old nurse had all of the classic symptoms which, unbeknownst to doctors, she developed after injecting herself with procaine hydrochloride (a local anesthetic) and epinephrine (or adrenaline). Because of the uncommon nature of her "illness," doctors performed an extraordinary array of complex, expensive tests on her for six months as they tried to locate tumors that they believed were causing her problem. Tests such as magnetic resonance imaging (MRI) showed that her adrenal glands were normal, and a computed tomography (CT) scan of her chest was normal. But her symptoms persisted. When doctors isolated high levels of epinephrine in the blood in her left renal vein, they believed that the left adrenal gland was the culprit.

The patient's left adrenal gland was removed (adrenalectomy), and her symptoms vanished for several days. But then they returned and persisted in spite of various costly treatments. This prompted more tests. In the interim, the adrenal gland that had been removed was examined by pathologists and declared healthy!

Because a healthy gland had been lost and the patient displayed renewed symptoms, she was referred to the National Institutes of Health in Bethesda, Maryland, where tests either proved to be normal or showed signs of only moderate irregularities in her system. Her episodes of symptoms continued in the hospital however. Although she initially responded well to medication, later on the episodes resisted ever larger doses of drugs. With dramatic displays of frustration and anger, she left the hospital of her own accord. Doctors, still uncertain about the cause of her illness, speculated that she might have adrenal hyperplasia (increased growth of normal cells in the adrenal gland).

The woman's symptoms worsened at home, and nine months after she began her disease portrayal her right adrenal gland was removed at another hospital. Now she developed a real disease as a result of losing both adrenal glands. When she showed up at an emergency room with tremors, she underwent tests that showed she now had Addison's disease, a syndrome caused by low levels of corticosteroid hormones from the adrenal glands, requiring treatment with steroid replacement therapy. As expected, because of her missing adrenal glands, her plasma epinephrine concentration was low. The amount of epinephrine in her urine, however, was close to 20 times higher than the upper limit of the normal range. Her doctors were baffled.

In the months that followed, she complained of poor appetite, weight loss, fatigue, and diarrhea and was treated with steroids. Her episodes of anxiety, tremors, and sweating continued as well. Retesting showed that once again her urinary epinephrine level was extremely high. Thinking that her continuing episodes simply must be caused by an undetected tumor, her doctors had her readmitted to the National Institutes of Health. There, additional sophisticated tests were performed, including a special test which is highly accurate in locating tumors.

When the test results were found to be normal, doctors finally suspected factitious disorder. They proceeded to devise a scheme to confirm their suspicions through a staged test. As the test was being performed, the patient experienced another "episode," and doctors faked giving her medication designed to relieve real symptoms quickly. Although she'd been given no drug, her symptoms promptly subsided.

The following day, she was seen going into a bathroom carrying a small purse, and soon afterward, she had another attack of tremors, rapid heart rate, and high blood pressure. When the episode passed and she left her room, a clinical associate searched her belongings and found needles, syringes, and a bottle of epinephrine marked "for veterinary use," which she had apparently pirated from her veterinarian husband. When confronted by her doctors, she denied having injected herself, but when they refused to believe her, she said that she had injected herself only during that hospitalization to keep doctors looking for the tumor which she believed she had. Because she was so insistent that she was genuinely ill, doctors struck a deal with her: they would keep searching for the elusive tumor if she agreed to continuous observation and searches until she experienced another spontaneous episode. She agreed, and after another search, which failed to uncover any hidden medications, she was moved to a different room.

A psychiatrist then interviewed her, but she refused psychiatric help.

Because she nonetheless seemed uncharacteristically calm, her doctors believed that she had plans to dupe them again, so they searched her room the following day. Under the mattress they found another purse with needles, syringes, and epinephrine. They were then certain that she was causing her own "episodes."

A second confrontation led to more denials, and she left the hospital. She later spent two weeks in a psychiatric hospital, but then signed out. Doctors learned that she had created her illness in an effort to curtail her husband's work hours and get more attention from him. She eventually left her husband and moved to Washington, D.C., where she was seen for her Addison's disease at the National Institute of Health and Human Development. Doctors there found that her main problem was her failure to follow physicians' instructions for the treatment of Addison's disease. She continued to be her own worst enemy even while attempting to be "in control."

We have to wonder if she literally set out to mimic pheochromocytoma, or if she simply grabbed whatever drug she could most easily get her hands on. We don't know how well planned her disease portrayal was because she didn't stay in treatment long enough for her entire story to unravel. She moved from place to place, presenting with untreatable symptoms and behaving with extreme hostility everywhere she went, which made her seem like a Munchausen patient. What is so interesting, and troubling, is that she developed an authentic medical illness as a result of the intervention for a factitious illness. This also presents the potential for a malpractice suit, because healthy organs were removed from her body.

Most factitial patients who feign endocrine disease are medical professionals or have other ways to access insulin, thyroid hormone, androgens, or other hormones. At least three other patients have simulated the signs and symptoms of pheochromocytoma by using drugs. A 27-year-old nurse, who acknowledged that she enjoyed and sought out medical care, added epinephrine to her urine specimens, submitted to numerous x-rays, but then refused to undergo exploratory surgery as her doctor recommended. Later, when real abdominal pain made her believe she actually did have the adrenal tumor she was faking, she requested surgery. Doctors operated because x-rays had indeed shown a mass, but it proved to be an ovarian cyst. One 41-year-old woman, who was a paramedic, created the appearance of pheochromocytoma by using a drug called isoproterenol, which is used to dilate air passages in asthma and bronchial conditions and which also stimulates the heart. And a 22-year-old medical student injected herself with metaraminol (which raises blood pressure), tampered with her urine samples, and subjected herself to a unilateral adrenalectomy. Their access to drugs not available to the general public enabled these women to create extraordinarily realistic features of a specific disorder, and it also enabled their doctors to prove they were fakers.

Proving that a patient had access to the medication is but one step in confirming the presence of a factitious disorder. Medical professionals often must also show through conclusive tests that the condition cannot be otherwise explained. In other words, one is presumed ill until proved guilty of faking. That's sound medical ethics, not to mention good legal advice. Had Joan Nelson, the Englishwoman falsely accused of having Munchausen syndrome, been in the United States, some sharp lawyer would undoubtedly have counseled her to sue her doctor for negligence, libel, and pain and suffering. But this burden of proof can be costly— and not just in terms of the time and money spent on medical care. The time spent by factitial patients in inducing dangerous symptoms, while fending off medical "detectives," can result in the greatest cost of all— a life.

In one case of factitious thyroid disease reported by Drs. E. Rose, T. P. Sanders, W. L. Webbs, Jr., and R. C. Hines (*Annals of Internal Medicine*, August 1969), a 34-year-old single woman incurred that very high cost. Her portrayals began after the death of her father. At that time she had suffered diarrhea and heat intolerance and lost 30 pounds. Years slipped by, and her symptoms continued to suggest thyroid disease, yet doctors could find no organic cause for her illness. She denied that she was taking thyroid medication but surreptitious use seemed certain. Fifteen years after her first symptoms appeared, she was admitted to a hospital for an overdose of digitalis. Afterwards, when she was seen by doctors to be evaluated for reemployment, she showed signs of thyroid disease, but now she denied all of her symptoms. She was hospitalized for further tests and transferred to a psychiatric unit for three weeks of evaluation.

Searches of her belongings failed to turn up any damaging evidence, but through therapy sessions doctors learned that she had been especially close to her father. After his death, she had lapsed into depression for which she was given electroseizure therapy. She lived with her mother and brother, who were both alcoholic and, apart from her job of 29 years as a clerical supervisor, her life was empty. Loath to tolerate personal weakness, she set high standards and was extremely hard on herself. She put up a good front, but beneath the pleasantries were anger and denial of her hardships. She handled her feelings by keeping busy—in her case, by being hospitalized, having tests run, and engaging doctors and caregivers. She eventually returned to work and nine months later was found dead in her bed, the victim of a probable barbiturate overdose.

Unable to prove that she had taken thyroid medication to cause her own symptoms, her doctors diagnosed her as having *occult thyrotoxicosis*, a term used when indisputable evidence of factitious thyroid disease cannot be uncovered. Doctors noted that she was excessively emotional and attention seeking, immature, and dependent. She was secretive about her true feelings and background, which is characteristic of factitial patients, and denied taking thyroid medication although it seems certain that she did. The increased energy she derived from thyroid medication (which can act as a stimulant) may actually have facilitated the ruse, jolting her from her depression and motivating her continued use of the medication. Thyroid medication appeared to be her means of coping.

Drs. Rose, Sanders, Webbs, and Hines note that factitial patients who abuse thyroid medications "have a serious psychiatric problem, often underlying depression, requiring definitive treatment. They should be carried in a supportive relationship until they will accept full psychiatric therapy. They should be treated as in suicidal attempts, watched for continued use of thyroid medication, worsening of depression, or suicidal gestures." And they warn that in such cases, confrontation between patient and doctor is not so important as a supportive relationship. If confrontation becomes necessary, it should be carried out only after the doctor-patient relationship has been cemented.

Although feigned thyroid disease makes for fascinating and unusual case histories, the most common form of factitious endocrine disease is surreptitious injection of hypoglycemic agents such as insulin. What ensues after they inject themselves—the coma and other signs and symptoms—is not simulated, it's real. There's a blackmail aspect to factitious disorders which is highlighted in a number of cases of factitious endocrine disease. Because insulin is so effective at getting quick, dramatic results, patients can induce symptoms right away and use them as leverage against caregivers. For example, one factitial patient who indeed had diabetes was hospitalized 15 times in five cities from January 1967 to July 1969 for hypoglycemic episodes and coma. This 18-year-old girl would inject herself with insulin and put herself into a coma to get herself hospitalized. When she stabilized and her doctor tried to discharge her, she'd inject herself again so that the doctor ended up with a woman in a coma who couldn't go anywhere.

When doctors were convinced that this patient had factitious hypoglycemia, they searched her hospital room in her absence and found six vials of insulin, syringes, needles, and alcohol swabs in her purse. Because of her past denials that she was injecting herself with insulin, doctors secretly added a radioactive chemical to each bottle of insulin. That evening she had a serious hypoglycemic reaction, and the next day she was taken to a low-level irradiation laboratory where tests proved that she had injected some of the radioactive insulin. Her caregivers also discovered that the level of insulin in one of her hidden vials had dropped.

Before bringing their findings to the patient, doctors consulted a psychiatrist who urged them to talk to her in a nonaccusatory way and to propose that she allow them to help her manage her diabetes. The patient admitted her deception and, although she couldn't offer an explanation for her actions, she agreed to psychiatric evaluation and treatment and to regulation of her insulin dosage by her doctors. Her diet and insulin intake were thus controlled and she was followed for several years, with no relapses of her illness portrayal.

Therapists learned that this girl was racked with self-pity and frustration after learning that she had diabetes. She came from a dysfunctional family, where her father worked away from home during the week, and on weekends ruled their home like a dictator. Her mother had surrendered to this unhappy life and did nothing to try to change it. Of the four children in the family, this girl and one of her younger brothers were the main objects of their father's rules and restrictions. She wasn't allowed to date, and her feelings of being trapped turned into anger and tension which had to be suppressed lest she incur more of her father's wrath. Doctors learned that her factitial illness was an unconscious way of striking back at her parents for the life they had imposed on her and at her doctors for not being able to treat her "whole" problem. She took pleasure in keeping her caregivers confounded over her illness and spending time in the hospital away from home.

The extremes to which some of these patients will go are unbelievable, and patients who were self-injecting insulin have even allowed the removal of their pancreas (pancreatectomy) in the search for a supposed insulinoma (an insulin-secreting tumor which produces symptoms ranging from faintness and sweating to loss of consciousness). Sometimes when a doctor gets wise to them and they fear discovery and abandonment, these patients put themselves at the threshold of death, and the doctor then ends up still having to take care of them rather than let them die.

The first case of factitious hypoglycemia was reported in 1946. Since then, it has become one of the diseases of choice among factitial patients. Some researchers have speculated that the number of factitious cases of hypoglycemia may be equal to the number of authentic cases of insulin-secreting tumors in the United States. The diabetes branch of the National Institute of Diabetes and Digestive and Kidney Diseases in Bethesda, Maryland, tracked 10 patients with factitious hypoglycemia for an average of five years, but some were followed for as long as 15 years. Two patients committed suicide, and only three of the patients abandoned their hoaxes and went on to lead lives that did not center around fraudulent illness.

Another group of doctors who studied 12 cases of factitious hypoglycemia found that the average age of the patients was 26 years. Six of the patients worked in medical or paramedical fields, which gave them easy access to insulin. Nine of the patients genuinely had diabetes mellitus. Eight of them subjected themselves to exploratory surgery because doctors believed they were suffering from insulinoma. One patient had two exploratory abdominal operations, and another had seven. In two cases, a doctor's suspicions averted exploratory surgery. In yet another study of factitious hypoglycemia, doctors found that 12 patients underwent a total of 22 abdominal operations.

Nearly all of the patients reported to have feigned diabetes have been women, quite a few of whom were nurses, health care workers, and/or actual diabetics. Many of them had personality problems and troubled sexual relationships, and they all had symptoms of other mental disorders, such as depression. Like factitial patients in general, they were familiar with and had access to medications that would create their symptoms; they had a keen interest in medicine and doctors; and many of them witnessed illness in friends and relatives and used them as models. Also, a significant number of them had been deprived of parental love and support through the death of parents or through their parents' indifference or immaturity.

We underscore the fact that health care professionals make up a large percentage of all factitial patients, perhaps a third to a half of them. Others acquire their knowledge by reading. Some of them have better knowledge of the disease they are simulating than the hospital staff members who take care of them. These are clever people.

CHAPTER 11

PLAYING THE
MADMAN

Do not veil the truth with falsehood,
nor conceal the truth knowingly.
Koran, chap. 2, v. 42

T he marked cleverness of factitial patients has piqued the interest of virtually every clinician or researcher who has dealt with or studied factitious disorders. And although this distinctive resourcefulness is seen in a majority of factitious disorder cases, it is perhaps most powerfully represented in factitious disorder with psychological symptoms.

The bulk of the published cases of factitious disorders involve only physical symptoms; however, enough of the remaining cases combine both physical and psychological symptoms to be classified officially as "factitious disorder not otherwise specified" and to lead some researchers to suggest that there should be a category called "factitious disorder with mixed physical and psychological features."

While reports of factitious disorder with psychological symptoms *alone* are infrequent, when such cases do arise, the traits that are manifested typically resemble those seen in Munchausen syndrome. Those traits include itinerancy, lawlessness, self-destructiveness, problems with developing and maintaining relationships, difficulties with sexual intimacy, open hostility, a worsening of symptoms during observation, and pseudologia fantastica. Factitial patients who display psychological symptoms are generally men with serious personality disorders, such as borderline personality, and their prognosis for recovery is considered poor. The diagnostic criteria for factitious disorder with psychological symptoms are identical to the criteria for factitious disorder with physical symptoms, except that the symptoms must be only psychological or emotional.

References to feigned insanity date back to ancient times and are found in the Bible, 1 Sam. 21:11–15, which describes King David's feigning madness before Achis, the king of Geth:

> And the servants of Achis, when they saw David, said to him: Is not this David the king of the land? Did they not sing to him in their dances, saying: Saul hath slain his thousands, and David his ten thousands?
>
> But David laid up these words in his heart, and was exceedingly afraid at the face of Achis the king of Geth.
>
> And he changed his countenance before them, and slipt down between their hands. And he stumbled against the doors of the gate; and his spittle ran down upon his beard.
>
> And Achis said to his servants: You saw the man was mad. Why have you brought him to me?
>
> Have we need of madmen, that you have brought in this fellow to play the madman in my presence? Shall this fellow come into my house?

Although a number of cases of factitious disorder with psychological symptoms have been reported, some researchers believe that because the motivational basis in these cases is often unknown or uncertain, its diagnostic legitimacy is compromised. In a 1989 paper published in the *American Journal of Psychiatry*, Dr. Richard Rogers proposes that the diagnosis of factitious disorder with psychological symptoms be abandoned altogether because of the difficulty in determining whether or not psychological symptoms are intentional. Rogers and others contend that patients who are diagnosed with factitious psychosis (pseudopsychosis) tend to have family histories of mental illness and often seem over time to develop true, undeniable psychoses such as schizophrenia. One researcher reported on six patients who were thought to be feigning schizophrenic psychosis, but ultimately only one case proved to be factitious.

We think that the main reason for the insistence of some people in the medical professions that factitious disorder with psychological symptoms does not exist is that it has not been scientifically studied and robustly evaluated. Actually, it might be easier to portray a psychological illness than most physical illnesses because psychological phenomena can be entirely subjective and thus harder to confirm. But some authors suggest that what we're diagnosing as factitious disorder with psychological symptoms is actually the initial warning sign of what is going to emerge as an authentic psychosis, and that we may be doing these patients a disservice by giving them a factitious disorder label.

A sufficient number of cases exist, however, to fuel this debate and justify the contention of some researchers that factitious disorder with psychological symptoms is a valid diagnosis. There are parallels between factitious disorder with physical symptoms and factitious disorder with psychological symptoms. We consider factitious disorder with psychological symptoms to have the same psychodynamic origins. In essence, the goal is the same—the sick role. Also, factitial patients pick different symptoms at different times. Many of the patients who engage in factitious behavior with physical symptoms will use psychological symptoms at another time. While we suspect that many patients with physical symptoms never have psychological complaints, most patients with psychological symptoms at some time report physical symptoms.

Two cases described in the *British Journal of Psychiatry* in 1978 point out the commonalities between factitious disorders with physical and psychological features. The doctors who reported the cases noted, just as we have, that because circumstances and experiences dictate a factitial patient's choice of symptoms, it is to be expected that some of those choices will be psychological. One case involved a 27-year-old man in Canada who had 25 known psychiatric hospitalizations and other hospital admissions in 11 years. During his hospital stays, which lasted from a few days to more than a year, he was most often treated for acute psychosis (a mental illness, such as schizophrenia, characterized by a loss of contact with reality). Yet his caregivers noticed that he was coherent when he interacted with other patients. Doctors' suspicions were aroused because he did not respond to antipsychotic medication, nor did his condition worsen when medication was withheld. When confronted with charges that he feigned his illness, he would predictably discharge himself and go to another hospital, sometimes within the hour.

In the second case, a 49-year-old man had 20 psychiatric admissions (usually for complaints of depression), 40 known general hospital admissions, and numerous operations. A number of his admissions were gained on the pretense of wanting to detoxify himself from alcohol, which he had supposedly abused for 14 years, but he never demonstrated withdrawal symptoms and alcohol dependence seemed highly unlikely. An irascible, demanding patient who had once worked as a hospital attendant, this man blamed his ostensible alcohol abuse as well as his itinerancy and unemployment on his divorce.

A 1986 study in England revealed that out of 775 patients under the age of 65 who were admitted to a psychiatric hospital, 4 had Munchausen syndrome. The researcher believed that figure was an underestimate because factitious disorders may have been overlooked in a number of cases. One of the confirmed Munchausen patients, a 28-year-old man, was admitted after supposedly taking an overdose of drugs because he was suicidally depressed after having been diagnosed with AIDS. Blood tests for the AIDS virus, however, were negative. He told doctors that he was alcoholic and a homosexual prostitute. Although he denied having had psychological problems in the past, his caregivers learned that he had received psychiatric treatment in England, Scotland, and elsewhere in Europe for a variety of diagnoses including personality disorder, alcohol abuse, sexual deviancy, and Munchausen syndrome. The oldest of eight children of alcoholic parents, he was raised in foster care. By the time he was 20 years old, he was facing an 18-month prison term for gross indecency. Like other Munchausen patients, he did not stay in any place long enough to benefit from therapy, and he continued his behavior.

A sordid childhood served as the background for another case report, which had a happy ending. In 1987, in the journal *Hospital and Community Psychiatry*, Dr. David Greenfeld reported on a 14-year-old New England girl who was 8½ months pregnant and nearly mute when she was admitted to a psychiatric hospital for seclusiveness and severe confusion. She had been in psychiatric institutions twice before for those symptoms as well as for hallucinations in which voices told her to kill herself. During her first hospitalization, she was diagnosed with schizophreniform disorder (early schizophrenia) and discharged after three weeks. During her second hospitalization, she was said to have full-blown schizophrenia. Antipsychotic medications were prescribed for her, but she never returned for follow-up treatments.

This girl had been abandoned by her father in infancy, and was raised by a mother who was unemployed and supported five foster children and four natural children through public assistance programs. A social worker for a state agency had placed the foster children in other homes and referred the woman's 14-year-old daughter for her current hospitalization, during which she gave birth to a baby girl who was quickly placed in foster care. When the teenaged mother realized that she would lose her child, she made a startling recovery and declared that nothing had ever been wrong with her. She confessed to her doctors that she had learned to mimic psychosis by watching her cousin who suffered from real psychiatric illness. She feigned symptoms whenever her situation at home became intolerable, and she resorted to withdrawal, in the form of silence and staying in bed, as her means of escape.

Her worsening symptoms, such as hearing voices, and her first two hospitalizations coincided with family problems such as sexual harassment from her mother's alcoholic boyfriend. Elements of malingering crept into her illness portrayals during her third hospitalization, when she admitted to doctors that she had pressed for that admission so that her baby would be born under the best possible conditions; this represented an act of desperation as well as an ingenious survival tactic. She asked her doctors to help make it possible for her and her child to stay with the baby's father.

Psychological tests proved that she wasn't psychotic, and she and her baby went to live with the child's father and his family. Doctors thought that she had carefully selected the man who fathered her child because he lived in a more secure and nurturing environment than her own, a belief that was substantiated by follow-up two years later which showed that mother and daughter were thriving and that the mother had had no further psychiatric hospitalizations.

Dr. Greenfeld notes that feigned psychosis may be common among extremely poor and homeless youngsters and adults, who could view mental illness as a way of escaping intolerable conditions. In that regard, there is marked overlap between factitious disorder and malingering.

We have seen cases of pure malingering in which psychological symptoms were used. For example, one man said he was going to kill himself because his business was going very poorly, he felt guilty because there was no hope that he could salvage things, and he was very depressed. He forbade the staff to talk to his family because he didn't want to upset them. After a couple of weeks, however, his wife contacted the ward staff and informed them that this man was a compulsive gambler who was always running up debts that he couldn't pay. He was afraid that the police were going to get him or that someone he owed money to was going to take it out of his skin so he was hiding out in a psychiatric hospital, pretending to be suicidally depressed!

One of us (C.V.F.) has seen another man who becomes "suicidal" and has to be hospitalized anytime he gets into trouble. His last hospitalization coincided with his court date to be sentenced for drunk driving. He didn't have the money to pay the fine and keep himself out of jail, so he came to the hospital pretending to be suicidally depressed, missed the court date, and asked that the judge be informed that he couldn't attend because he was in a psychiatric facility.

Psychiatrists frequently see people who fake illness simply to dodge the law or avoid court appearances—classic cases of malingering. They generally ask for a letter stating that though they were supposed to go to court on a specific day, they couldn't because they were hospitalized. They act as if this were pure coincidence and the supposed illness wasn't related to the court date.

As noted, malingering and factitious disorders sometimes overlap and doctors may have difficulty determining which diagnosis is correct. Those are the cases that become subjective calls. Supposedly, if you can identify a clear external motivation, then it becomes malingering; if you can't, it's factitious disorder. But those are pretty soft territories, and a lot of cases are right in the middle.

The symptoms most commonly associated with factitious disorder with psychological symptoms—such as depression, visual and auditory hallucinations, memory loss, and suicidal thinking—are frequently tied to claims of bereavement. In a 1983 paper in the *American Journal of Psychiatry*, Dr. M. R. Phillips and colleagues reported on 20 factitial patients who dramatized or fabricated the deaths of loved ones to assume the sick role. In addition to exhibiting psychological symptoms that included threats of self-destruction, 15 of them had also feigned physical symptoms at one time or another. Our own experiences with patients

who fake or exaggerate psychological symptoms due to bereavement
have shown that these pretenders often claim that numerous family
members have died; however, when doctors check out their stories, they
find that nobody close to them has passed away at all.

In 1978, in the *British Journal of Psychiatry*, Drs. John Snowdon,
Richard Solomons, and Howard Druce reported on 12 cases of false
bereavement to point out the high prevalence of such behavior. Of the
12 patients, all of whom were observed at a London teaching hospital,
6 had hurt themselves or reported acts of self-destruction, 1 had threatened suicide, and 5 had also been admitted for feigned nonpsychiatric
reasons. These patients ranged in age from 20 to 62, with the median
age being 35. All but one of these patients were men. Nine of them said
that they were grieving for more than one dead family member.

One of the 12 patients, a 41-year-old man, was admitted after complaining that he had lost consciousness after a fall, but he was transferred to a psychiatric ward when he told his caregivers that he was
deeply depressed because he had lost his wife and two children in an
auto accident two years earlier. When doctors contacted his private
physician, they learned that this man had never been married. He
discharged himself without warning.

In another of the cases, a 28-year-old man sought admission to the
hospital after he supposedly took an aspirin overdose. He told doctors
that he had been depressed and suicidal since witnessing the gruesome
death of his mother three weeks earlier when she fell down a flight of
stairs and was impaled on a railing. He seemed so sincere that he was
admitted to the psychiatric unit, where he attacked a female patient,
then discharged himself. Doctors, who were unable to substantiate his
story, later learned that he had been previously admitted to three mental
hospitals using aliases.

Dr. Snowdon and his associates note that the telltale signs of feigned
grief include lack of corroborating witnesses or difficulty in reaching
them; patient referrals from nonpsychiatric wards, where ingenuous
caregivers may be sympathetic to such sad tales; and grief that is unusual
in that it appears delayed, inhibited, extended, or especially intense.
Most of the deaths described are dramatic and especially violent and are
usually reported to have happened to a child or adolescent.

Just as some factitious patients rely on their own or someone else's actual experiences to lend credence to their portrayals of physical illness, some patients tap into real life events to add drama and true emotion to their feigned psychological symptoms.

Dr. Ford:

With some of these patients, the bereavement is real from prior losses, but they may lie about the time and circumstances of someone's death. In most cases there's nothing really factitious about the grief these people have experienced. What's factitious is the story about how and when the loved one died and the fact that they are able to call it up when they need it.

The patient who stands out most clearly in my mind as having factitious disorder with psychological symptoms was a man who was hospitalized for factitial chest pains but also feigned bereavement. He said that he had had coronary bypass surgery at another hospital, and he did have a scar on his chest. However, angiography (x-ray examination of the blood vessels) failed to show evidence of the coronary artery disease that would have accounted for a bypass. We wanted to learn more about his background so we invited him to one of our psychiatry conferences. There he told us that he was a physical therapist and that he had worked at a variety of hospitals in the Northwest, particularly one in a tiny town in Washington state. He said that at the time he was working in that town he became engaged to a young woman who had been previously married and had two small children. One night while he was working he heard sirens, and two ambulances raced up to the emergency room. He wandered out to see what was going on, and there were the bodies of his fiancée and her two children, killed in an auto accident.

As he told this, tears ran down his face. He talked about his suffering and feelings about the tragedy and the loss of these children. There were a few teary eyes in the audience, too. He was pretty convincing, so we contacted his family because we were trying to decide on follow-up psychotherapy for him. His family said that he had never been engaged to be married and that he went from hospital to hospital with complaints of chest pain. Once we knew the truth, we gently suggested that he receive private psychiatric treatment back in his hometown and he left the hospital.

Bereavement is the easiest psychological condition to feign because most of us have experienced losses in our lives and others readily empathize when they meet bereaved people. It's tough to feign schizophrenia for a long period of time, and we're not sure that anybody could do it without being caught eventually: a person couldn't artificially manufacture and sustain the changes in thought processes that occur in true schizophrenia. Similarly, dementia also seems to be pretty hard to feign. (Dementia is caused by organic factors and is marked most prominently by difficulties with memory.) Still, it should be a little easier to catch someone who is feigning dementia because during cognitive testing the pattern of answers is not characteristic.

Someone is probably feigning dementia when the person remembers what you said near the beginning of one interview and later incorporates it into another where it is pertinent. The memory of a person with genuine dementia wouldn't be that accurate. For example, a woman was asked a number of questions by a resident doctor, but she repeatedly complained of severe memory loss. When she was examined again the next day, she said, "As I said yesterday, I can't remember anything." Obviously, a person with advanced dementia would have had difficulty remembering the previous day's questioning.

A patient who was seen by one of us (C.V.F.) appeared to have factitious schizophrenia. He came to the hospital late one night with the story that he had been diagnosed as having schizophrenia at another institution and that his main symptoms were bizarre delusions of people following him and looking at him. Then he described hallucinations in which voices were telling him to do things like injure or kill his family (called command hallucinations). One common sign in schizophrenia is an alteration in emotions, with patients often showing blunted or inappropriate emotional responses. There's a dissociation between the emotions being expressed and the words the patient is saying. Also, the answers the patient gives are kind of odd, and the interviewer can't quite follow the thought processes behind the answers. When you've finished talking to a person with acute schizophrenia, you tend to get the strange feeling that you didn't quite make contact. You're always left wondering what's really going on inside that person's mind.

When the more experienced staff on the ward talked with the man, however, they found that his thoughts were just too well organized, too well directed, and so he received psychological testing. Even though he endorsed some of the obviously psychotic items, such as saying yes when asked if he heard voices, the psychological testing suggested antisocial or sociopathic personality rather than thought disorder or psychosis. He was not able to fake the more subtle items within the psychological tests that would indicate real distortions in perception and the way he thought.

Factitious disorder has been recorded as existing simultaneously with apparently real multiple personality disorder (MPD). In 1991, Dr. Ellen Toth and therapist Andrea Baggaley of Alberta, Canada, reported in the journal *Psychiatry* on a girl who developed five different personalities as a way of dealing with years of parental indifference and sexual abuse by her brother and a male baby-sitter. In addition to psychiatric treatment for MPD, she had 58 nonpsychiatric hospitalizations for symptoms that included shortness of breath, head injuries, nosebleeds, chronic anemia, blood clots, gastrointestinal bleeding, urinary tract problems, and self-induced hypoglycemia. She also reported fever and vomiting, but these signs were never documented by caregivers. Through disease portrayals, she subjected herself to 13 operations and received 76 units of packed red blood cells. She was officially diagnosed as having Munchausen syndrome only once after a syringe and vial of suspected fecal material were found in her hospital room, and only once did the suspicion of factitious disorder appear on an emergency room record. This patient still seeks and gains hospitalization, and discharges herself whenever she hears talk of factitious disorder among her caregivers.

In a bizarre variation, authors from Massachusetts reported in the journal *Psychotherapy* (Summer 1991) the feigning of MPD itself in a 15-year-old girl. They traced this girl's problems back to elementary school where she had had poor relationships and had been considered a pathological liar. (People who genuinely suffer from MPD are often accused of lying because one personality doesn't know what another personality has done, and so they deny some of their words and deeds. In authentic MPD cases, lies are also designed to trap or embarrass another personality.) This girl displayed signs of self-mutilation and once blamed her innocent father for burning her with cigarettes. During an early hospitalization, the patient described four other personalities in addition to her own, including three girls, aged 4, 8, and 12, and a 10-year-old boy. Later, before beginning therapy, she presented two others: a 78-year-old woman and another young boy.

This girl's portrayal was so convincing that she was diagnosed as having MPD and referred for hospitalization and then outpatient therapy. Her hoax began to unravel during therapy when she told lies about events that had never occurred and which seemed designed to get attention from adults. The other red flag was the detailed biography the patient provided about her 78-year-old personality, which was totally out of character for even the most creative MPD patient.

Instead of confronting the patient, therapy was continued and caregivers learned that the patient had previously read all she could about sexual abuse after meeting a girl who had experienced this trauma (such abuse is said to be a contributing factor to MPD). She read the book *Sybil*, saw the movie of the same title, and even mimicked some of the sketches that Sybil drew. After weeks of treatment, the patient told her therapist that she kept a journal, which the girl was asked to bring to her next session. By that time, another personality had emerged, this one a paraplegic who turned up on the floor outside the therapist's office, crawled inside, and presented the therapist with the journal. Entries intimated that the patient was feigning MPD. When confronted by her therapist, the patient seemed relieved that the truth was finally known. After a further year of therapy, she no longer showed signs of MPD.

Drug and alcohol abuse are common among factitial patients with psychological symptoms, who may secretly use psychoactive substances to produce signs that suggest a mental disorder. Stimulants such as amphetamines, cocaine, or caffeine may be used to produce restlessness or insomnia. Hallucinogens such as LSD (lysergic acid diethylamide), mescaline and cannabis (marijuana), or THC (tetrahydrocannabinol) might be used to induce altered levels of consciousness and perception. Heroin and morphine, which are analgesics (painkillers), may be used to induce euphoria, and hypnotics such as barbiturates may be used to produce lethargy. Combinations of these substances can produce extraordinarily bizarre presentations. The main difference between drug abusers with factitious disorders and authentic drug abusers is that the factitial patient induces an altered state not as an end in itself but to mislead caregivers and others.

Many phony drug abusers are working the system as part of the game of factitious disorder. For them, the issue is not whether they have truly become addicted but whether they can get the drugs under false pretenses and thereby stay connected with health care professionals.

The motivations underlying factitious disorders may be unconscious even though the choice of symptoms is deliberate. Lying, by definition, is a conscious behavior. People know when they are lying, but unconscious mechanisms drive the need to lie. Some patients who feign psychosis really do fear that they are "falling apart." But they don't have the particular disorder they are trying to feign. Because there may be some overlap between what they are really suffering from, such as depression, and what they are feigning, it takes a lot of work by mental health professionals to sort out the true illness from the fake one.

The medical literature shows that not all patients with factitious disorder with psychological symptoms are looking fearfully over their shoulders at invisible men or openly talking to themselves. Factitial patients can be far more subtle than that and have, for instance, faked bad results on IQ tests and similar measures designed to assess for brain impairment. Unlike IQ tests, personality tests don't necessarily have correct and incorrect answers, but through the patterns of answers doctors can gain a sense of whether people are minimizing or exaggerating symptoms. Certain questions are easy, and a clever patient can readily figure out what to say to appear emotionally compromised. But most of the questions are much more subtle, and an average person wouldn't know how a sick person would respond. In general, though, to see if the results are being faked, a doctor must look not only at the results of the tests but more broadly at the whole clinical picture.

Dr. Feldman:

I recall a case of factitious transsexualism involving a young man who traveled from hospital to hospital trying to get psychiatric clearance to have a sex change operation. He had been denied a transsexual procedure at a major medical institution and was looking to be recommended to another hospital where that type of surgery was being performed. The patient was elaborately groomed and in some ways was the stereotype of a Southern belle, with a soft, high-pitched drawl, very heavy makeup, and brightly painted lips. But at the same time, he had short hair and his overall appearance struck us as parodied and insincere. He appeared to be a man with borderline personality disorder who was seeking some sort of self-definition, and this claim was a dramatic way for him to feel a little bit special. As he was turned away from one facility after another, it made him more "complex," and his "transsexualism" became more of a mission for him. Obviously, physicians at other institutions had felt the same way. We were so thoroughly convinced that he wasn't transsexual that we urged him to table the notion of getting any surgery and to get psychotherapy instead. That wasn't what he was after, so we never heard from him again.

Dr. Ford:

I saw a patient who resorted to a ruse of transsexualism because he thought it would bring him security and special care. This man was 68 years old and owned a small ice cream cart which gave him a modest income. His most genuine medical problem was that he had varicose veins, yet he repeatedly came to me asking to be changed into a woman. He even showed me photos of himself dressed as a woman and wearing a wig. I never believed that he was transsexual, and finally, one day he confessed the real reason for wanting the operation. "Listen," he said, "nobody cares about old men, but they take care of old women." He had it in his head that he couldn't get any sympathy or care as he really was, but that as an old woman those things would be available to him. I presented him to a transsexual program for evaluation and that gave him a lot of attention. He still contended that he was transsexual, but when I said that I would continue to see him, though I doubted his transsexualism, it took a lot of his fear away and he stopped pressing for the operation. If he got the nurturance, he didn't need the surgery.

When looking at the "broader picture" to determine if a patient has factitious disorder with psychological symptoms, examiners must take social climates and world events into consideration. With AIDS being a major health concern, psychiatrists are starting to see factitious AIDS cases. Likewise, with each new military conflict, we see factitious post-traumatic stress disorder (also known as PTSD), which is characterized by symptoms such as high anxiety and "flashbacks" of the traumatic situation that emerge after shattering events like participation in combat. After a military conflict, doctors always see cases of factitious PTSD in which the individuals are ultimately found not to have served in the military at the time.

The first known cases of factitious PTSD relating to Vietnam emerged years ago. Doctors have also reported on patients who feigned illnesses related to alleged action in Korea and even in Grenada. One doctor saw a 30-year-old woman with factitious PTSD and factitious seizures who claimed to have been captured on the Ho Chi Minh Trail in Vietnam and held as a prisoner of war. The doctor discovered that although she had served two tours of duty in the military, she had been stationed in Korea and never went to Vietnam or experienced any of the horrifying events that she described. The same doctor reported on a Navy veteran who claimed that his traumatic experiences happened aboard ship during the Korean war. He made his way into two PTSD therapy programs before a psychiatrist who had served in the Navy during that time checked the records of the ship on which the patient had been stationed and exposed his stories as lies.

Researchers have noted that *genuine* PTSD related to military action or war is earmarked by the following characteristics of the patient: (1) attempting to minimize the relationship between his symptoms and the action, (2) blaming himself, (3) having dreams about traumatic events and feelings of helplessness and guilt, (4) denying the emotional impact of combat, (5) being unwilling to recount combat stories, (6) experiencing guilt over having survived, (7) avoiding environments that resemble the combat situation, and (8) feeling angry at the personal inability to overcome PTSD. Phony war heroes often fail to present this picture when creating their symptoms.

Factitious PTSD has also been diagnosed in people who fabricate motor vehicle accidents and say they have flashbacks and excessive startle reactions as a result. One man in Scotland claimed that he was depressed and drinking heavily because he had killed a six-year-old child in an auto accident. He showed symptoms of depression and post-traumatic stress disorder. He said that he had tried to commit suicide by cutting his wrists and that he was contemplating shooting himself. Inconsistent details of the accident weakened his story, and he fled from the hospital under questioning by suspicious doctors, who were later told by police that they had no record of any such accident. Doctors who reported this case in the *Journal of Clinical Psychiatry* (February 1969) candidly noted that "were it not for the inconsistencies in his history and the contrast between the history and objective mental state examination, his presentation closely mimicked that expected of persons presenting after a real accident of this type."

Factitious PTSD or depression has also been reported in that group of patients briefly noted earlier who falsely claim to have been diagnosed with AIDS. In the first reported case of factitious AIDS to include physical and psychological symptoms, Drs. Steven E. Nickoloff, Vernon M. Neppe, and Richard Ries describe in the Summer 1989 issue of the journal *Psychosomatics* a 33-year-old man who was referred to an emergency room because of suicidal ideation. He told doctors that he had already attempted suicide by taking an overdose of antidepressants and that he was becoming increasingly depressed and angry because he had failed to end his life. Complaints ranging from not sleeping for days at a time to rapid weight loss and pronounced mood swings gained him admission to a psychiatric ward. There he fed doctors a dramatic psychiatric history, saying that he had bipolar disorder (a malady that is marked by manic and depressive episodes), had tried to commit suicide four times, and had long abused alcohol and drugs. He said that many different types of therapy had failed to help him and demanded that doctors treat him with electroseizure therapy. He also said that he had experienced the trauma of learning that he had tested positive for HIV and that one of his friends had died of AIDS.

In highly involved cases such as this, where pseudologia fantastica plays an important role in the hoax, patients tend to forget some of the lies they tell or details they provide, and inconsistences lead to discovery. Such discrepancies and other questionable information, such as the patient's claim that he had not slept at all for 18 consecutive days before his admission to the hospital, instilled doubts in his doctors' minds. When they asked for permission to contact his family and past caregivers, he refused. When he developed lesions on his legs, which he claimed were Kaposi's sarcoma (a disease of primitive vascular tissue sometimes found in AIDS patients), biopsies revealed that they had actually been caused by heat or chemicals. He signed a consent form for an HIV (AIDS) test (signed consent is required in many states), but before the results were available he left the hospital. His HIV test was negative, and his doctors never heard from him again.

Drs. Nickoloff, Neppe, and Ries found that the "most important factor in successful management is early recognition. When presented with an atypical history or lack of appropriate physical findings for any disorder, the physician should promptly obtain previous medical records and communicate with other health care providers. It is likely that our patient's true colors would have shown earlier if we had made continued hospitalization dependent on consent for release of information."

CHAPTER 12

THE DEADLIEST GAME OF ALL: WHEN FACTITIOUS DISORDERS BECOME CHILD ABUSE

It is easier to be dishonest for
two than for one.

John Fowles

Т he cruelest and deadliest form of the factitious disorders is Munchausen by proxy (MBP). In this bizarre variant of the mainstream disorder, instead of creating signs of illness in themselves, adults claim or induce illness in children. Tragically, such actions are usually taken by seemingly loving, caring parents or guardians and almost always without the knowledge of their marital partners or other family members.

Clinical awareness and swift action are critical weapons against MBP, a form of child abuse that falls under the criteria contained in the federal Child Abuse Prevention and Treatment Act of 1974. This Act defines child abuse and neglect as "the physical or mental injury, sexual abuse, negligent treatment, or maltreatment of a child under the age of 18 by a person who is responsible for the child's welfare under circumstances which indicate that the child's health or welfare is harmed or threatened thereby." In other words, it is any maltreatment of a child or adolescent by a parent, guardian, or other caretaker. The four main types of child abuse are physical abuse, sexual abuse, physical neglect, and emotional abuse and neglect. Subtypes of child abuse include nutritional neglect, intentional drugging or poisoning (apart from MBP), neglect of medical care, neglect of safety, and Munchausen by proxy.

Though MBP currently accounts for less than 1,000 of the more than 2.9 million cases of child abuse reported each year in the United States, that figure is almost certainly an underestimate of the actual cases of MBP because of underdiagnosis. Indeed, one author, reporting on infants brought to his facility as a result of apparent life-threatening episodes, believes that 1.5 percent of the cases represented possible MBP. *Not every case of child abuse is Munchausen by proxy, but every case of Munchausen by proxy is child abuse.*

A small body of statistics is available for MBP, and the data are staggering: hundreds of cases of MBP have been documented in medical journals; mothers are the perpetrators in an astounding 98 percent of the cases; and, in a study of 117 cases of MBP, 9 percent of the children died.

In 1993, MBP was added to the *Diagnostic and Statistical Manual of Mental Disorders (DSM-IV)* as "factitious disorder by proxy." The original term *Munchausen by proxy* was coined in 1977 by Dr. Roy Meadow, chairman of pediatrics at the University of Leeds in England. Dr. Meadow created the term as a way of distinguishing these cases from other forms of factitious disorder. (It has also been called Meadow's syndrome.) In Munchausen by proxy, a child may undergo an extraordinary number of unpleasant and often painful diagnostic tests and be exposed to numerous pointless medication trials and/or surgeries, with all their attendant risks. Some children have had as many as 300 clinic visits and 14 hospitalizations in their first 18 months of life! One paper reported that the youngest victim of MBP was eight weeks old; in reality, however, the youngest involved an assertion of "fetal illness": a 25-year-old woman continually claimed during her second and third trimesters that her fetus was not moving, but repeated testing showed that the fetus was normal, as was the child at birth.

MBP is perpetrated most commonly against infants and toddlers who are too young to talk. When the child begins to talk and can describe things, the probability is much higher that the parent will be detected. However, MBP doesn't necessarily end with the development of the child's verbal skills. Young children are not always able to see relationships between events and people, so children who are being victimized through illness may not make the connection that a parent or trusted other is making them sick. Besides, parents of legitimately sick children must usually fight to get medicine down a child's throat, so children who are the target of MBP aren't necessarily going to understand when ipecac or a laxative is being forced on them needlessly. It is also well-established that many abused children "internalize" the problem and blame themselves rather than their parents, believing perhaps that they "deserve" the illness because of some wrongdoing on their part.

Older children may not disclose the true sources of their illnesses out of fear of abandonment by their mothers if they stop being "sick." Other elements may creep into the MBP picture as victims and abusers enter into an almost symbiotic relationship, much the same as hostage and hostage taker; children protect their abusers and resist making revelations to the medical and social service personnel who might rescue them. Dr. Meadow has noted that as these children grow older they may in fact come to believe that they are disabled or actually participate in the medical hoaxes, ultimately developing factitious disorders.

Signs and symptoms created in children include fabricated apnea (sometimes children are actually smothered so that signs of breathing difficulty will appear on monitors), seizures, blood and bacteria in the urine, unremitting diarrhea and bloody stools, vomiting, rashes, dehydration, fevers of unknown origin, depression, hypernatremia (abnormally high concentrations of sodium in the blood), heart arrhythmias, bacterial arthritis, skin lesions, vaginal and rectal bleeding, coma, and cardiac arrest. One of the most shocking revelations to emerge from the medical literature on MBP is that a number of Sudden Infant Death Syndrome (SIDS) casualties may actually be due to suffocation as part of MBP that went too far!

The most common among these MBP signs and symptoms are seizures, apnea, vomiting, and diarrhea. In one case of MBP, a two-week-old girl was seen at the University of Mississippi Medical Center after allegedly suffering respiratory arrest (apnea) while breast-feeding. Although all tests were negative and a sleep disorder center found nothing wrong with the child, the mother continued to make claims that her daughter suffered from vomiting, diarrhea, and apnea, and she asked for a home apnea monitor. Doctors thought that the mother was misreading normal changes in the baby's breathing and motor activity, and they refused the monitor, which the mother then wangled from a doctor in her community. When the baby was nine weeks old, that same physician referred her back to the sleep disorder center because of "continued apnea." During this hospitalization, doctors noted that when the baby was with her father, grandmother, or members of the hospital staff, she was well. The baby's maternal grandmother confessed that she thought her daughter was making the baby ill.

The abuse was uncovered when a nurse who was assigned to watch the mother and baby secretly witnessed the woman giving her infant a rectal enema, then removing the enema liquid with a bulb syringe and putting it in and around the baby's mouth to mimic vomiting. The mother, who was found to have symptoms of somatization disorder (a history of multiple physical complaints without demonstrable basis), told psychiatrists that her own haywire existence, which was punctuated by family problems, rape by her brother-in-law, and a personal history of sexual abuse as a child, had put her over the edge and set in motion her own pattern of abusing her child. However, she still contended that her baby was ill. Her child was placed in foster care and remained in a state of good health.

Another mother began making emergency room visits with her daughter when the girl was six months old. By the time she was three years old, the child had had at least nine hospitalizations for alleged apnea. Because the mother's account of her child's illness was so believable, doctors disregarded the normal test results and prescribed a home apnea monitor, also treating the child with an anticonvulsant medication. By the time this child was five years old, some of her caregivers had become suspicious. A visit to the home revealed that the child's room had been organized by her mother, a former nurse, to look like a hospital intensive care unit; it even included an in-home laboratory!

Doctors learned that her mother had reported not only symptoms of near-miss SIDS but also blood in her child's urine and feces, seizures, hypoglycemia, unusual eating habits, and bowel and urination irregularities. They found that the child had been subjected to a host of pulmonary, cardiac, endocrine, gastrointestinal, neurologic, and urologic exploratory operations. Even though the child's test results were consistently normal, the conviction with which the mother continued to report symptoms led physicians to treat this child with a variety of medications. None of the physicians knew that other doctors were involved in the child's care; she even received physical and occupational therapy and special education for the disabled!

A psychiatric examination of the mother, performed under the ruse that she was receiving counseling to help her deal with her child's "illness," revealed that she was alternately concerned with and disengaged from her child's care. Both of the mother's sisters had backgrounds fraught with vague medical complaints, and her husband was typically detached from the child's and his wife's problems. Doctors believed that this woman had been preoccupied with making health care professionals believe that her daughter was ill because she felt so unhappy and abandoned in her marriage.

According to doctors' reports, this mother and child benefited from long-term therapy. The girl was thus able to live at home with her mother. Oddly enough, however, the psychiatrist had difficulty getting doctors to stop prescribing the unnecessary medications.

Manipulations in MBP run the gamut from sad to horrific. Mothers may put their own menstrual blood in their child's urine specimen, or they may inject feces into the child's intravenous line or directly into the child. An extraordinary number of different substances, including prescription and over-the-counter medications, have been utilized to cause diverse clinical presentations. Diuretics have been used to induce dizziness, ipecac or salt to force vomiting, narcotics to create breathing problems, laxatives to produce intractable diarrhea, barbiturates to cause lethargy, antidepressants to trigger coma, and insulin to manufacture hypoglycemia. One mother pricked her own finger and added the blood to her five-year-old child's urine. Another mother produced the illusion of diabetes in one of her children by putting sugar and acetone in the girl's urine, but produced actual illness in another of her children by poisoning him with medication to induce seizures.

In one case, a mother induced seizures through coercive training rather than through the use of drugs. Her four-year-old stated that he was "epileptic," and on numerous occasions was observed lying on the ground at school, trembling as if having a "fit." However, suspicion grew when the child was easily roused by the mention of his favorite food. He later told his teacher that his mother had trained him to simulate epilepsy, and rewarded him with food when he acted in this manner. The child was placed in foster care and his "epilepsy" resolved.

Children often have to endure far more than that four-year-old did before their "illnesses" are resolved. Children have even been subjected to unnecessary operations, such as removal of part of the intestines and removal of the pancreas. One child was unsuccessfully treated for five years for strange ulcerations on his back; it was only discovered much later that his mother had been rubbing oven cleaner on his skin. Another mother altered test results and stole sputum from patients with genuine cystic fibrosis (an hereditary disease affecting the exocrine glands, which include the mucous and sweat glands) to make her child appear to have that disease. And another woman gave her child ipecac to cause the appearance of bulimia.

In a case that is unusual because a father was the culprit, an 11-year-old boy's dad reported that his son had a long history of cystic fibrosis. This claim was easily disproved by testing. When confronted, the father readily backed down from his claim, which contrasts with the tenacity generally seen with mother-perpetrators. Another father added cooked meat to his son's urine samples to create the impression of hematuria (blood in the urine).

Medical investigators warn that sometimes an initial tip-off that a child may be a victim of MBP is a deceased or chronically "sick" sibling, because if there are several children in a family, abuse may not be reserved for just one. In one case, MBP was found to have affected four siblings after one child died at the age of two years and another at the age of 12 months. A third had suffered for six years before MBP was discovered. One mother repeatedly brought her infant twins for medical attention, claiming that they were vomiting blood. While one of the babies was hospitalized, she reported that he had vomited blood and displayed blood-stained clothing as proof. The mother and child had different blood types and analysis showed that the blood on the clothing did not belong to the child, but to the mother. She was later caught pricking the lip of one of the infants with a pin to create bleeding, and the children were removed from her by a protective services agency. Seemingly preoccupied with this medical condition, the mother later complained to doctors that she herself was coughing blood. In another family, illicit insulin administration was found to have occurred to a one-year-old girl. Doctors then looked at the history of her siblings and found that there had been 30 separate episodes of factitious illness in four family members. In a recent study of 56 children who had been victims of MBP, it was discovered that 11 percent of their siblings had died in early childhood of unidentified causes; MBP may have been involved in many of the cases. Furthermore, researchers believe that the high illness and mortality rates for the siblings are almost certainly an underestimate.

Further evidence of multiple MBP victims in the same family can be found in an Australian case in which a woman's son had 18 hospitalizations in his first 18 months of life and her daughter had 15 hospitalizations in her first 9 months of life. Police were able to intervene only when the mother was seen trying to choke her daughter, and the mother was sentenced to six years in jail.

Although their actions are heinous, the typical mother who participates in MBP is described as a "helicopter mother," always hovering around her child, concerned and anxious to work with the nurses to "help" her young one. She's generally the kind of mother whom nurses think is a wonderful parent. Health care professionals may never suspect that a mother would create symptoms in her child. Caregivers need to be more aware of MBP, but they also need to be able to distinguish Munchausen-by-proxy mothers from mothers who are actually loving and attentive but who, out of misguided concern and not an effort to deceive, exaggerate minor problems that their children develop from time to time.

A strange example of this misguided concern is being seen in the Ukraine in the aftermath of the 1986 nuclear power plant accident at Chernobyl. As many as 75 percent of the children of the Kiev area have reportedly been affected by "vegetative dystonia," a condition characterized by such vague symptoms as pallor, inattentiveness, and poor school performance. Researchers, however, say that many of these children are actually healthy, and that rather than representing genuine illness, the diagnosis of vegetative dystonia may reflect parents' fear that their children were physically harmed by the accident. According to Dr. E. Richard Stiehm of the University of California at Los Angeles, children have been diagnosed with vegetative dystonia in the absence of physical signs of illness because anxious parents and doctors are convinced the children are sick. "Thus vegetative dystonia is CFS [chronic fatigue syndrome] by proxy, assigned to the children by their parents and doctors," says Dr. Stiehm. "The medical response to date is not part of the solution, but it *is* a good part of the problem!"

It is often difficult to differentiate between overly concerned mothers, such as the women of Chernobyl, and MBP mothers because most Munchausen-by-proxy mothers seem so normal. Even psychological testing does not typically reveal them to be as disturbed as one might expect. One way to help differentiate between caring mothers and potentially lethal mothers is by being suspicious of a mother (or father, grandparent, foster parent, or other) who shows a peculiar eagerness to consent to having invasive procedures performed on the child. Most parents will ask lots of questions and feel reluctant to allow that.

Also, a pattern often emerges in which the child is sick and the mother stays continuously at the hospital for several days. She then becomes exhausted, goes home to rest at the urging of staff and, during that time, the child suddenly gets well. The mother returns after a couple of days and the child gets sick again. The symptoms closely parallel the mother's presence.

Researchers put the perpetrators of MBP into two subtypes: the "active inducer" (someone who actively produces alarming symptoms in a child and maintains that activity over an extended period of time), and the "doctor addict" (someone who wants to be around physicians and delights in fooling them, reporting symptoms which are often vague to justify frequent visits to the doctor). We know of one mother—a doctor addict—who took her three sons to doctors so frequently that, though her husband was gainfully employed, she had to get a part-time job just to keep up with the portion of the bills that their insurance company didn't pay. The vague symptoms she reported, and which she insisted were signs of chronic illness in the boys, ranged from pallor and headaches to tiredness and sprains. As the boys grew older, the "complaints" issued by the mother worsened to include asthma, chronic allergies, sinusitis, and arthritis. Apart from some valid sports-related injuries and the occasional cold, however, doctors never found anything wrong with the children. Nonetheless, they missed blocks of time from school and their activities were curtailed because their mother insisted that they were ill and that doctors had misdiagnosed them. She also managed to talk doctors into prescribing antibiotics and other medications for her children on the strength of her descriptions of their "symptoms." She kept a medical reference book in her home, and frequently checked it to match symptoms with illnesses.

This woman, who appeared to be the epitome of the concerned parent, admitted that she had always wanted to be a nurse, but said she couldn't go to school to fulfill her dream because her children were "always sick." She had a keen interest in medicine and often accompanied relatives on doctor visits. She seemed to thrive in a hospital or doctor's office, and she readily displayed her knowledge of medications and illnesses, often steering conversations in that direction. She was also infatuated with one of the doctors to whom she brought her sons. Her MBP tapered off when her boys were in their teens and old enough to resist going to doctors for what they described as "nothing," but by that time one of them showed signs of a factitious disorder himself, complaining about vague symptoms without prodding from his mother.

Most cases of MBP involve active inducers whose intense emotional needs motivate the illness portrayals in their children. They may simply love the attention MBP produces for them. Having an ill child brings them a certain kind of misguided status. Their child's illness is their "claim to fame," and they bask in accolades from medical caregivers about their devoted parenting. These parents often have communication barriers with their spouses. For example, the father may be out of touch with both mother and child and unconcerned about or unaware of the child's illness. On the other hand, the child's illness may bring about a closer relationship between the parents, and this closeness may suit the perpetrator. Some MBP mothers openly admit that they hate their children because the child interferes with the mother's having a satisfying life, and repeated hospitalization of the child allows the mothers to escape the responsibilities of parenthood. Others need to feel that the child is totally dependent on them, and they force this dependency through induction of illness.

If medical personnel can obtain a complete, accurate history in these cases, they will likely discover that the MBP offender has always used somatic symptoms as a way of coping and may even currently meet the criteria for a factitious disorder or Munchausen syndrome. MBP in these settings represents a type of extension to the next generation. The abusers tend to have severe personality disorders, and have not learned more appropriate ways to obtain attention and nurturance. They are inclined to be extremely selfish in that they harm their children to benefit themselves.

Several variants of MBP have emerged over the years, causing doctors to urge vigilance among all health care providers, including *veterinarians*! An equivalent of MBP is seen by veterinarians in which a person, usually middle-aged, fabricates medical signs and symptoms in a pet. For many people, a pet is a substitute for a child, and the animal's illness is also a way of maintaining a relationship with the pet's doctor.

Another variant of Munchausen by proxy is being plied by therapists who seem with remarkable consistency to see child abuse histories among their patients, whether the patients remember the abuse or not. One patient's therapist repeatedly told him that he was the victim of childhood sexual abuse by his father, despite the fact that the patient claimed he couldn't remember it. The therapist's answer was, "Of course you can't remember it, but how else could we explain your personality problems?" A tremendous amount of suggestion was involved here, almost certainly without a basis in fact. We also see such behavior among some physicians who overdiagnose and overtreat and seem determined to find certain illnesses or diseases in their patients.

A bizarre variant of MBP surfaced a decade ago in Israel. A symbiotic relationship between a man and two women partners resulted in the first known incident of what doctors termed *Munchausen by adult proxy*. The central figure in this case, a 34-year-old man, began inducing illness in his wife in 1979 by putting sleeping pills in her coffee. While she was sedated, he injected gasoline into sections of her body to create abscesses. The devotion and concern that is often seen in other MBP perpetrators was manifested in this man, who kept an almost around-the-clock vigil at his wife's bedside, under the guise of assisting in her care. She died from the illness he had induced, but his crime was not discovered.

Three years later, the perpetrator hired a nanny to help him care for his daughters, and eventually he proposed marriage to her. When she was unenthusiastic about his offer, he drugged her coffee and injected gasoline into her breasts, neck, and buttocks. Extensive lab tests ultimately led to his being discovered, and he was sentenced to 46 years in prison for the murder of his wife and the assault on his companion. He confessed that he had feared his wife—and later the nanny—would leave him. Through their "sicknesses," he had been able to force each to stay, if only for awhile.

This man became publicly known as the Gasoline Injector. He became a model prisoner and was given a job working in the prison medical clinic, where he was able to obtain syringes, needles, and other medical supplies. In time, the prisoner became attached to his cellmate, who was serving a life sentence for murder, going so far as to write to his cellmate's mother asking her to convince her son to trust him unconditionally and to tell him to "drink whatever I give him." To gain further access to the fellow inmate's emotional life, he even wrote letters to his cellmate impersonating a girl who wanted to marry him. The man ended up repeatedly putting his cellmate to sleep by administering sleeping pills mixed with alcohol and then injecting him with turpentine, which he had stolen from a storage room. He also sexually abused his cellmate. The cellmate became critically ill and was saved through emergency surgical intervention. The Gasoline Injector was convicted of attempted murder.

Prison provided the perfect environment for someone as emotionally dependent as the Gasoline Injector. People with dependent personalities often adapt extremely well to prison. It's not surprising that this man became a model prisoner because he wasn't an overtly violent man. He was really looking for approval from other people, and he wanted to take care of them to get that approval. Sickness is one of the mechanisms by which humans are bonded to one another in perverse ways. The Gasoline Injector demonstrated that he could play this game beautifully in prison, and he was actually helped along by the curious job he was given.

A sad finding in MBP is that most of the offending adults were abused as children and followed the pattern of the abused becoming the abuser. In one case, a seven-year-old girl was victimized by her mother for six years. During five of those years the child was seen 126 times at different clinics and by a private physician and was treated for several disorders, including a condition that required pressure equalization tubes to be placed in her ears. The fever of unknown origin (FUO) that finally led to the discovery that her disorders were factitious began when she was only one year old. The FUO supposedly continued as the child grew, but each time she was admitted to a hospital, her temperature would quickly return to normal and diagnostic tests that included cultures of blood, urine, stool, and spinal fluid were negative.

At the age of four, based on the medical history supplied by her mother, the child was put on medications for asthma and allergic rhinitis (inflammation of the mucous membrane of the nose caused by allergies). By the age of six, she was receiving five asthma medications that had been prescribed by her primary care physician, and her diet was limited to 10 "safe" foods. Despite the way the child was being forced to exist, she had shown no signs of wheezing, and skin tests for inhalant allergens were normal.

This girl lived with her mother, stepfather, stepbrother, and stepsister. Her stepfather was a blue-collar worker and her mother was an emergency medical technician. The child was supposedly so ill that she couldn't attend school and had at-home tutors. When she was seven, she was admitted once again to a hospital for a FUO, but doctors found her afebrile and healthy looking. Every time doctors tried to discharge the child, however, her symptoms recurred, and at one point she developed severe diarrhea and vomiting requiring administration of intravenous fluids. She then developed the symptoms of theophylline poisoning (theophylline is an asthma medication). Her mother, who had refused to relinquish an active role in monitoring the child's vital signs and administering her medication, denied playing a role in this latest medical dilemma. However, the baffling constellation of physical problems, which came and went, and the onset of theophylline poisoning finally alerted doctors to the likelihood of MBP.

They moved the child to a pediatric intensive care unit, and notified her stepfather, a children's protective service agency, legal counsel, and her primary care physician. The child's mother finally received psychiatric evaluation and treatment. It was discovered that she had a chronic history of abuse as a child and also as an adult at the hands of her first husband. By devoting her life to "helping" her "sick" child, she could, in her eyes, be a nurturing, martyr-like mother, unlike her own abusive mother.

A court ordered the child to spend six months in an alternate setting away from her mother. When she returned home, she was thriving without medications and was regularly attending school.

After studying two cases of MBP in his landmark 1977 report, Dr. Meadow observed that while many mothers who stay in a hospital to help care for their children are uneasy, bored, or irritable, the MBP mothers "flourished there as if they belonged, and thrived on the attention that staff gave to them." Both mothers in the Meadow paper had falsified their own medical histories and tended to be overly dramatic. Dr. Meadow noted that in many ways these parents seemed to be using their children to get themselves into the sheltered environment of a hospital, and that one of the mothers appeared to be projecting her worries about her own health onto her child. "We may teach, and I believe should teach, that mothers are always right," Dr. Meadow has written, "but at the same time, we must recognize that when mothers are wrong they can be terribly wrong."

Just as there are degrees of factitious disorder with physical and/or psychological symptoms, Dr. Meadow notes that there is a mild form of MBP of which many parents are guilty. This form is manifested in the way parents may exaggerate symptoms or mildly deceive caregivers about a perceived illness in a child, sometimes simply out of overprotectiveness. Because doctors are accustomed to seeing this type of behavior, and because health professionals are hesitant to admit that they've been tricked, Dr. Meadow warns that the realization that a child is a victim of MBP evolves slowly. The point at which intervention should occur, he says, depends upon the amount of proof a doctor is able to accrue and the level of danger faced by the child.

Proof is what doctors at Yale University School of Medicine in New Haven, Connecticut, were after when they set out to catch a mother who they believed was creating chronic diarrhea in her infant son. The 18-month-old child developed severe diarrhea when he was only 2 days old, and was first admitted to a local hospital when he was 3 months old. He was then transferred to Yale-New Haven Hospital where he underwent costly and comprehensive bacteriologic, radiologic, endocrinologic, and metabolic studies, all of which had normal results. After two months, the diarrhea suddenly stopped and the child was sent home, where he thrived for six months. Then once again he was readmitted for diarrhea after having been treated with several antibiotics for an "unresponsive" inflammation of the middle ear (otitis media).

Unsettled and spare, the child had to be fed through a catheter instead of his mouth, and he was given a multitude of antidiarrheal medications.

Still the diarrhea could not be controlled. As part of their investigation into the cause of the depleting illness, doctors examined every aspect of the child's hospitalization and noticed that his diarrhea subsided when he was sleeping or away from his room for tests. A common denominator during all of his episodes of diarrhea was his mother, a vigilant guardian who stayed by her son day and night to assist in his care. She spent so much time at the hospital that she cultivated friendships with some of the nurses, who offered her food and money because she complained that her husband was stingy and uncaring.

Doctors convinced the mother that she needed a rest from the hospital. She boldly predicted that her son would improve while she was away and he did, but as soon as she returned, so did the diarrhea.

This case presented an unusual set of circumstances to the child's caregivers, who wanted desperately to help him. They took equally desperate measures to root out the cause of his chronic illness, which they feared could lead to his death. They were reluctant to approach the boy's father because they were uncertain about whether he might have a role in the child's illness or might warn his wife. Doctors, nurses, members of the hospital's house staff, and a social worker banded together to gather the proof they needed, which was essential to enable a protective service agency to step in. With guidance from hospital attorneys and administrators, the hospital security team arranged for video camera surveillance of the child; this approach had been effectively used at another hospital in a case of MBP involving twins who repeatedly suffered cardiopulmonary arrest.

A closed-circuit camera was installed above the bed in the private room and staff members were instructed to monitor the child's bed around the clock. If they saw the mother doing anything dangerous, they were to contact a security officer and confront her. Within 24 hours, the video camera showed the boy's mother giving him three doses of a substance which she administered orally with a syringe. She was taken into custody, and a search of the child's room turned up syringes and a number of different substances that would cause diarrhea.

Because doctors had been concerned about what this woman might do to herself or her child when confronted, they had alerted the psychiatric emergency room staff beforehand and asked them to be ready for any eventuality. As predicted, the woman became extremely upset when she was confronted with the evidence and, after being brought by hospital security guards to the psychiatric emergency room, she had to be committed to a psychiatric hospital. The child, whose diarrhea once again stopped in his mother's absence, was released into the custody of his father.

After she was hospitalized, the mother's complicated personal medical history surfaced, which included 15 admissions to psychiatric institutions for such problems as major depression and borderline personality disorder. She also had a number of general hospitalizations, resulting in surgeries which included cholecystectomy (removal of the gallbladder), appendectomy, and hysterectomy (removal of the uterus). The mother, who had worked as a nurse's aide but was terminated for stealing patients' medication, also allegedly had fainting spells and chronic insomnia. During her two pregnancies, she was hospitalized for severe vomiting and diarrhea, the causes of which were never determined. Her records had all the indications of someone who was suffering from a factitious disorder if not Munchausen syndrome. After the discovery of her MBP involvement, she received the kind of intensive therapy that doctors hoped would make a difference in her mental health.

While this mother was detained by hospital security guards and afforded immediate psychiatric care, many others who have subjected their children to MBP have had criminal charges brought against them. As awareness of MBP grows among health care professionals, law enforcement agencies, and the judicial system, more and more offending parents are being prosecuted for doing harm to their children. Many cases like these have cropped up around the country in recent years:

- In 1985, a 20-year-old Texas woman was charged with attempted murder after allegedly trying to smother her baby. In an action that mirrored the one taken by Yale-New Haven, the hospital had installed a television camera in an air-conditioning vent in the child's room and a nurse interrupted the smothering episode. The suspicious death of an infant daughter had occurred two years earlier.
- In Iowa in 1988, a 30-year-old nurse was arrested and charged with repeatedly cutting off air to her two-year-old son. She had supposedly done the same thing to him in Illinois and Texas, causing the boy to be hospitalized an estimated 20 times in two years.

- A two-year-old Minnesota boy named Michael had more than 20 hospitalizations for a variety of severe infections. Doctors noted infected puncture marks on his thigh, but his mother claimed that they were from pins in a quilt. Ultimately, Michael told a family friend, "Mommy gave me shots." Police searched his home and found syringes and sodium chloride solution. Michael was placed in foster care and has been healthy ever since. In 1991, his 24-year-old mother was charged with felony assault.

Although these women are suffering from a mental disorder, it cannot be used as an excuse for abuse. We believe that psychiatric diagnoses should have rather limited use in explaining crime. And that's true for Munchausen by proxy. We say we can explain some of the behavior on the basis of personality disorders, but as long as they know right from wrong, we hold them responsible. Most of these patients are not psychotic; in fact, very few of them are, and they almost always meet the legal definitions of sanity and responsibility. In a similar way, pedophilia is listed by psychiatrists as a mental disorder, but certainly we proceed with the prosecution of adults who feel driven to abuse children sexually.

Some health care professionals have accused the medical, legal, and social service worlds of collusion with MBP perpetrators through their ignorance of the illness and their failure to recognize the disorder and intervene swiftly. In a 1987 paper, Dr. Basil J. Zitelli, social worker Miriam F. Seltman, and nurse Rose Mary Shannon stressed early recognition of the illness to help professionals from becoming "unwitting collaborators" with MBP parents. They emphasized that participation from all involved health care professionals is generally necessary to identify the factors that contribute to this type of abuse.

Detection depends upon an awareness that MBP exists. In a 1988 study of a pediatric nursing staff, 55 percent had never even heard of Munchausen by proxy, and more than 70 percent felt professionally and personally unprepared to deal with such a case if it arose. Education is the key to early detection and treatment, and education is the primary reason for this book.

Initial suggestions that MBP is at work may be viewed angrily by other staff members. Health care professionals don't want to believe that they could be duped so completely, especially by someone who presents a caring and loving appearance, who flatters the staff, and who develops strong and positive relationships with them. Also, in our litigious society, doctors may worry about the consequences if they make an accusation of MBP and are proved wrong. But even when confronted with ironclad evidence, staff *still* may be reluctant to believe that the parent is the cause of the child's illness. Doctors and nurses are basically trusting and see no reason to be suspicious, especially because gross evidence of child abuse, such as burns or bruises, is uncommon in MBP cases. And these cases are further muddied by the mother's falsification of the child's medical history and background. The child's birth date may be the only accurate information the parent provides.

Videotaping, as we have discussed, is the hospital staff's most definitive way of proving MBP. When the mothers are confronted with videotaped evidence, they may claim that "this is the first time" they've ever engaged in this behavior. Videotaping may therefore represent only the beginning of the medical investigation that must follow. Checking on the real histories of the child and his or her siblings (with the help of other family members and caregivers) often leads to the real story.

These are significant warning signs that should raise the question of Munchausen by proxy:

- The apparent disease is extremely rare.
- Mother is less anxious than the medical staff regarding the inability to diagnose the cause of the child's illness.
- Mother has medical or nursing training herself.
- Mother has a history of feigning or inducing illness in herself (and may even have Munchausen syndrome) or she has somatization disorder.
- Mother refuses to leave the child.
- Another child in the family has also had unexplained illnesses.
- Mother gets into conflicts with other parents over whose child is "most ill."
- Child has been to numerous caregivers without a cure or clear diagnosis.
- Experienced physicians state they have never seen a case like this before.

- Signs and symptoms occur only when the mother is present.
- Medical problems do not respond to appropriate treatment.
- Mother is extremely willing to have the child undergo diagnostic procedures and treatments.

Several strategies can be used to help detect MBP:

- Separate the child from the mother and see if illness persists (the child, however, may resist separation or develop apathy and passivity until reunited with the abusive parent).
- Analyze the medical course for a temporal relationship between illness and the presence of a parent or guardian, usually the mother.
- Retain specimens for detailed investigation.
- Obtain psychiatric consultation if the question of MBP arises.
- Station a nurse near the child's hospital room to observe the mother's interactions with the child.
- Ask the child directly about abusive behavior whenever possible.
- Request specialized testing. Examples include testing for laxatives in the child's stools; seeing if blood in urine samples matches the mother's (but not the child's) blood type; and performing an EEG (electroencephalogram), which may reveal brain effects from surreptitiously administered drugs.
- Spend time with the child's mother during regular visits. Ask gentle questions about the mother and about the child's homelife; the answers may be enlightening and give the pediatrician insight into the mother's personality.

Once MBP has been detected, the child's safety must be the first priority in the treatment process, and removal from the home is almost always indicated. Legally, suspicions need to be reported promptly to law enforcement or child protection agencies. Caregivers must also recognize the need to protect other children in the family, including those not yet born. The abused child's health status must be monitored on an ongoing basis to ensure that any subsequent medical treatment is appropriate, and care should be consolidated at a single medical center where physicians are familiar with the history. The doctors who diagnosed the MBP should be involved to counter the skepticism that seems inevitably to creep into these cases as time goes on.

Victims of MBP may be permanently damaged physiologically and/or psychologically, either directly by the mother's manipulations or by the treatments and tests administered. For example, children may develop brain damage or cerebral palsy from induced anoxia (inadequate oxygen to the tissues in the body), or severe damage to internal organs from recurrent infections. Children may miss a lot of school and suffer educationally and socially. They may go on to display intense anxiety or hyperactivity, fearfulness, or passivity and helplessness. Some of these children may develop Munchausen syndrome themselves or become convinced of their own "invalid" status. One healthy 26-year-old was confined to a wheelchair because his mother had persuaded him he had spina bifida (a defect in the spinal column through which spinal membranes may protrude).

Although it is often an essential course of action, separating children from their parents becomes a major issue in MBP cases. When children are taken away from their parents, the major issue becomes the separation, not the disease. Children who are taken out of their parents' custody often don't do well, especially when they've had a very traumatic first few years. Because abused children may assume they're to blame, they often have difficulty separating from their parents.

Many of these children are returned to their parents, sometimes with disastrous results. To achieve a situation in which children can be reunited with their parents and live stabilized lives, we usually recommend continuous surveillance of the situation for an indefinite period of time. There should be family therapy, and the goal of that therapy should be to acknowledge, understand, and communicate about the behavior of all family members. Once dysfunctional behavior is no longer dealt with as a secret, it is less likely to occur again, especially if the child is checking in regularly with an authority.

Although preserving the family unit whenever possible is important, protection of the abused child must be the primary concern. While it can be important to be optimistic, the therapist still has to keep in mind that the bottom line is the safety of the child. There are setbacks in any therapy. The exploration of some issues goes well, but pursuit of other topics goes poorly. In Munchausen by proxy, the consequences are high if the work of therapy is going poorly. The therapist has to be realistic about what can be accomplished. If the child's been reintroduced into the family, he or she may have to be pulled out of the family again, and the therapist has to be fully prepared to make that recommendation. There is no doubt that these children also require intensive individual therapeutic work. These are heavily conflicted, compromised children.

The individualized approach to making therapeutic recommendations must take into account the seriousness of the threat to life which the parent's behavior generated. Someone who is highly dangerous to life must be handled differently than someone who is manipulating a thermometer to create the appearance of fever.

Being able to follow through on treatment recommendations made to MBP perpetrators is just as difficult as getting cooperation from any other factitial patient, primarily because of their denial. These parents are usually emotionally fragile and vehemently deny the allegations of abuse. There are several cases of mothers or fathers attempting or committing suicide after detection and confrontation. Regardless of the dangers, this is one disorder where the offending parent should be approached when alone; otherwise one parent tends to defend the other, sometimes very angrily. The suspected parent should also be approached first, so that his or her spouse does not have the opportunity to signal doctors' suspicions. Unsuspecting fathers in these cases tend to be distant and often seem determined to avoid recognizing what their wives have been doing. They often have jobs that require prolonged separation from the family and therefore add to their spouses' denial out of their own ignorance about the abuse.

The denials from these child abusers may be so convincing that the doctors involved start to doubt the evidence themselves. Mothers may turn to others, such as the family pediatrician, to marshal support. They are usually intelligent, articulate, and absolutely believable: one perpetrator got five physicians to testify to her integrity as a parent. After discovery, mothers tend to refuse treatment and seek medical assistance for their children elsewhere.

Doctors need to point out to an MBP parent that his or her actions are harming the child but that help is available for the entire family. It is best not simply to accuse but to redefine the problem as one for which ongoing treatment will be provided, even though the abuse *will* be reported. The consulting psychiatrist should strive to maintain an alliance with all of the individuals involved: the child and family, pediatricians, attorneys and protective service workers, and other mental health professionals.

The impact that MBP has on hospital staffs is intense and lasting. Twenty nurses at a midwestern children's hospital who were questioned after dealing with an MBP patient were typically reluctant to admit that they had been duped and equally unwilling to accept that the seemingly doting mother was the perpetrator. The case with which they had been involved concerned a 17-month-old girl who was hospitalized for recurrent urinary tract infections with hematuria, fevers, weight loss, vomiting, hypoglycemia, and developmental delays. Her three-year-old sister, who had recurrent hematuria, had had approximately 13 hospitalizations. The mother had some training as a licensed practical nurse, and she enjoyed strong camaraderie with some of the nurses. Once the MBP was confirmed, the child was released into the custody of the paternal grandparents and the father. The mother, who was charged with attempted murder and neglect of a dependent, pleaded guilty to battery causing serious bodily injury and received a five-year suspended sentence and probation. Long-term psychotherapy was ordered by the court.

Cases such as this may lead nursing and other staff members to be less trusting of other parents. They may also feel shame and sadness when they realize that they helped administer extensive and painful procedures that were unnecessary. We need to do a better job alerting physicians, nurses, and other professionals as part of their training. We also need to alert attorneys and court officials proactively to facilitate appropriate prosecution of these cases when they come up. One judge dismissed a Munchausen by proxy case, stating the charges were defamatory; he didn't believe such a phenomenon could occur. In another case, the lawyer representing the state on behalf of the child responded that no mother would ever behave in this manner. Defense lawyers and their expert witnesses may attempt to dismiss the whole phenomenon of MBP as "overblown" or "exotic and fashionable."

The allegations are often seen in the legal community as bizarre, and so legal arrangements may be made that do not adequately protect the child. For example, one judge ordered a psychiatric evaluation of the parents, but it was performed by one of their friends; the child was returned to the parents and later died of unknown causes. Doing something as simple as sending reprints of published case reports to court officials and others, such as protective service workers, may be very helpful.

Most of the nurses who were involved in the midwestern study had never heard of MBP during training and were unaware that such a syndrome even existed. Mary Sheridan, Ph.D., of Pali Momi Medical Center in Hawaii is co-founder of the National Association of Apnea Professionals and the Munchausen by Proxy Network, and she knows the devastating effects MBP can have on children and caregivers alike. She finds it hard to accept that there are still health care professionals, including pediatricians, who don't believe this behavior occurs.

Mary Sheridan:

Members of the National Association of Apnea Professionals have been so troubled by mothers with MBP that we formed the Munchausen by Proxy Network as a means of exchanging information and promoting education. Apnea professionals see MBP because so many of these mothers use smothering to create the appearance of apnea.

I think that health care professionals actually have to be exposed to MBP before they understand that it's a reality and want to know more about it. Full-blown MBP is not something that we see a lot of, so many caregivers don't have much of a sense of its symptoms. The experience of dealing with a full-blown MBP situation is extremely painful and difficult, especially if you don't know anything about it when you're starting. Most people don't, even within the mental health and medical professions. They don't know that this disorder exists. It's not been well-publicized or well-identified.

My first case was a very difficult situation of a mom who, we believed, was creating the appearance of apnea in her child through smothering, although we never proved it. A typical baby with apnea usually doesn't have severe episodes. If he or she does, there should be one or two at the most. With proper treatment, the child should get better over the course of time. This child, according to her mother, was constantly having very severe episodes and we couldn't keep her out of the hospital. Every time she went home, her mother reported, she would have another severe episode.

When apnea episodes recur with great frequency, caregivers have a little checklist in their minds that they run through to determine what's causing them. We work our way down from the most likely to the least likely, and children whose symptoms are being induced don't fit the pattern. The tests come back normal. They don't respond to medication the way they should. So, it becomes a very difficult intellectual challenge because we're working our way farther and farther down the list into more and more esoteric diagnoses. We consult colleagues who come up with more and more exotic possibilities. It's very easy to get emotionally sucked into one of these cases if you don't know what's going on. Later you stand back and look at the process that you've been through, and you look at the number of hospitalizations, and the number of ambulance calls, the diagnoses that you were considering and the timing sequences. After the dust has settled, you say to yourself, I should have recognized this a lot sooner.

I didn't know about MBP before I first encountered it several years ago. I came to believe it was occurring because nothing else made sense anymore. When I started to wonder if it was possible, I kept telling myself, while I didn't believe that it was happening, it was possible that *I* was wrong. I was grappling with these feelings when one of the residents at the hospital saw an article in a medical journal about MBP and gave it to me, saying, "This sounds just like the family you're dealing with. Do you think it's remotely possible?" A mother had been caught smothering one of her children at a hospital in Texas and they recorded it on video. The similarities to our patient were striking. The case history was the same and the profile of the mom was the same.

Then I discovered that there's a body of literature on MBP, and I read as much as I could and I found that so many of the cases had the same pattern. That's when my faith in the mother started cracking. Our apnea director was also heavily involved in this process. He suspected the mother before I did. Ultimately, we reported the case to child protective services. They confronted the mother, the child was placed in foster care, and the apnea episodes ended. I found out that the mother was known to have actually created illness in herself as a teenager. A look at the mother's medical record showed that there were plenty of indications of current problems—problems we hadn't been told about.

Painful is the word that comes to my mind when describing the whole process of being involved in such a case. It was very, very difficult for me to believe that a mother had done this. Just before the child was placed in foster care, I believe the mother unconsciously told me what was going on. She did it in a very subtle way. She knew at that point that anything that she said to us would be checked. She happened to mention that a relative of hers had just had a child die of SIDS. It was a fabrication. I believe that at some level she knew that I'd go straight to the SIDS coordinator and ask if that was true. One of the things that one does after one begins to suspect a parent is to take any piece of information that's checkable and use it to establish a pattern of truth-telling or falsification. When the child was placed in foster care, the problems resolved immediately. Eventually the apnea monitor was taken back and so my involvement with the patient was over. Later the child was returned to her mother. A couple of years after that, there was a segment on the television news one morning in which this same mother was claiming that some chemical which was being used near her home was making her child sick! That was the last I heard of them.

We had another case in which the physician confronted the mother and was met with complete denial. However, the child got steadily better after the confrontation, and then all of a sudden the family disappeared with the child. We had two or three cases around the same time and all of them were pretty typical of factitious apnea.

A survey conducted by Dr. Sheridan and Dr. Michael Light (published in *Clinical Pediatrics*, March 1990) found 54 cases of suspected MBP. Sheridan and Light followed up on 32 of the 54 cases and found that they were replete with reported life-threatening episodes. Three of those 32 infants and 5 of their siblings are known to be dead.

CHAPTER 13

VICTIMS OF
THE GREAT
PRETENDERS

There's one way to find out if a man is
honest—ask him. If he says, "Yes," you
know he's a crook.

Groucho Marx

rançois duc de La Rochefoucauld wrote: "It is more ignominious
to mistrust our friends than to be deceived by them," (*Moral
Maxims*, 1678). So we give them the benefit of the doubt rather
than risk ruining the relationship over our own shameful suspicions
about their illnesses. As a result, we—literally meaning everyone who
feels sympathy for others—can all become unwitting players in the
sickness game, victims of the great pretenders.

Because they are directly victimized, the children who are preyed
upon through Munchausen by proxy are the most obvious casualties in
factitious disorder cases. But there are also many indirect victims; for
example, the emotionally drained, guilt-ridden health professionals who
unknowingly put children through the torture of unnecessary tests and
procedures, and the horrified family members and friends who had
unintentionally lent their support to an abusive situation. As in MBP
cases, every form of factitious disorder leaves casualties in its wake.
Virtually everyone who comes in contact with a factitial patient becomes

a victim of emotional rape to some degree, and the longer and more intense the relationship, the more profound and devastating the experience can be.

Previously published accounts (by M.D.F.) drew letters from people across the nation who had been victimized by men and women suffering from factitious disorders. All of the letters were fraught with emotion and most were explicitly confidential; but several writers, including a woman whom we shall call Laurel Martin, agreed to share their stories here, for the benefit of others. Laurel's poignant initial letter reflected the confusion, disbelief, and self-recrimination that is experienced by most victims, whether they are health care professionals or laypersons. She wrote:

> A friend of mine recently gave me an article from the *Los
> Angeles Times* about a patient of yours with factitious disorder. I
> read this story with horror and fascination. More than a year has
> passed since my close involvement with a young woman who did
> the same thing. I find myself still vastly impacted. How could I
> have been rooked so completely? Why did I allow her to swear
> me to secrecy? Why did I give myself so willingly to her service?
> And most difficult of all, how do I take responsibility for having
> enabled her in her sick game?
>
> Her ruse of cancer caused her to adopt some extreme measures.
> She did not lose weight, which was always mystifying to me, nor
> did she shave her head. But I cared for her each Friday evening
> following her alleged chemo treatments when she would vomit
> for hours. . . .
>
> As I write this to you I ask myself once again how I could have
> been so stupid. It is the most implausible series of events one
> might imagine. And yet, there was immense suffering in her
> eyes. That, I am convinced, was *not* contrived.
>
> Dr. Feldman, please help me understand more about this strange
> disorder. I have not yet fully recovered from the loss of
> confidence, self-esteem, and integrity resulting from this
> "friendship."

Laurel is a well-educated, articulate woman whose experience does more than shed light on another extreme case of factitious disorder. It illustrates the strange, dangerous dependent/codependent relationship that develops between the "teller of make-believe" and the "believer," to use Laurel's words. The longer the relationship lasts, the more difficult it becomes for a victim to end it. These relationships often become so complex that it is impossible to differentiate between the dependent and the codependent.

Laurel's first letter led the way to an ongoing dialogue (between her and M.D.F.) and, ultimately, to the complete revelation of what she had endured at the hands of a woman whose fantastic ruse made her at once pitiable and despicable. Here, in her own words, is Laurel's account of life with "Marie." Her story has been edited to preserve confidentiality. Our comments appear parenthetically in italics.

Marie: A Case History

The story of Marie cannot be told apart from my own story, for every teller of make-believe needs a believer, and I was a believer through and through.

(People in our society generally respond to someone who is afflicted with a chronic or terminal illness with unconditional compassion. This is what creates the "believers" who are so crucial to a successful disease portrayal.)

My job was to recruit and retain disadvantaged students in vocational programs, and it was my first paying job in two decades. For years I had given my time away in various social service capacities, reared children, and attended school, but now I was to receive a salary for my work. I was fired with enthusiasm and eager to serve, with lots of heart and little formal experience. Still, heart was the most important component of this job and I knew it.

(Laurel felt important again, and receiving compensation for her work increased her confidence and self-esteem. The nature of her job allowed her to have a positive effect on peoples' lives and primed her for Marie, who made her feel needed and successful.)

Even now, even after being thrown from the lofty pedestal of my idealism, I believe that my primary effectiveness with students came from my genuine high regard for them, my compassion for their plight, and my desire to help.

Marie was my first student, so in some ways I became her student, too. She was to guide me in my practice with other students. From me, she learned math and study skills. She was bright, sensitive, motivated—in many ways the perfect first student to build my confidence. She was quick with math, praising me in my ability to explain and simplify concepts. Even in that first meeting I now see how she began working me by appealing to my vanity, my desire to help, and my need to matter. In that lengthy first meeting, Marie also shared something of her personal circumstance, revealing just enough to arouse my curiosity, withholding enough to maintain my intrigue, and responding warmly and appreciatively enough to elicit from me a feeling of self-empowerment.

(By building up Laurel's confidence, Marie began turning her into a codependent and laying the foundation for the time when that role would be reversed. New at her job and anxious to succeed, Laurel needed the reassurance which Marie so willingly gave. Marie was supportive of Laurel, and this was her way of making Laurel subconsciously indebted to her. Marie proved to be a master at emotional manipulation.)

My initial attraction to Marie, a 30-year-old medical technician in training, was based on her unique qualities. She was a black woman with Hispanic ancestry. Although overweight, she had an exotic beauty. She suffered from a slight paralysis of her right arm but carried herself regally.

Marie was very perceptive. As we became closer in our relationship, I found she could read my inner disposition through touching my hand. At first I saw this as a remarkable gift which could become an asset in her work with hospital patients; but as the touching became more of an essential feature of the relationship, I grew increasingly uncomfortable with it. Comments which she made at the most intense moments between us now seem to indicate that she may have been seeking a sexual intimacy, but I did not read them as such at the time. In the beginning, her touch was an attractive quality. Her hand in mine was a validation of my trustworthiness and a sign of her willingness to let down barriers, at least with me. She told me many times that I was the only person in her life who was permitted to touch her. I admit to having felt an egotistical satisfaction in this.

(Marie further endeared herself to Laurel by appealing to her ego and bolstering her sense of self-worth and importance. She used physical contact as a way of strengthening the bonds between them.)

There was an attractive artistry in Marie's style. Gestures, facial expressions, and a poetic ability with words all combined to create a powerful magnetism. She intrigued me with stories of her bizarre childhood, her unusual family, and horrifying epic tales related to the cause of her disability, as well as the recent death of her mother from breast cancer, and the lonely role she played as her mother's caretaker.

(These tales could have been evidence of pseudologia fantastica. It's hard to tell whether they were factual or fictitious, and they could not have been easily checked because there was such a flood of incomplete personal information. If her mother had indeed been afflicted with cancer, and Marie had indeed been her caretaker, she would have learned about the disease through close observation. However, through her schoolwork Marie had excellent access to information about cancer as well.)

The stories, intriguing in themselves, were enhanced by her extraordinary gift with words and told with dramatic flair.

With Marie's daily drop-in visits, our relationship quickly strengthened, but as my student caseload grew, drop-in visits were no longer possible. Marie stated her resentment over having to schedule appointments "like everyone else," and although this was expressed in a playful way, it was clear to me that she felt threatened. My own feelings were conflicted. I had come to care deeply about Marie. Her emotional needs were obvious, but I did not believe she needed my academic support and I had many students who did.

In late October, approximately two months after our first meeting, Marie came to my office seemingly distraught, visibly tense, and unable to speak her awful fear. She seemed to greatly desire the intimacy that resulted from sharing herself, but the act of unveiling was an immense struggle for her. Long, painful silences were prerequisites for each new revelation, and patience became my hallmark. After numerous aborted attempts to share her secret, she finally told me that she had discovered a lump in her breast. She was frightened and asked if I would feel it and tell her what I thought. I did, in fact, feel a disc-shaped lump. I told her I thought she should have it evaluated without delay. I tried to reassure her. Even if cancerous tissue were found, treatments can be highly successful. Why didn't she make an appointment right away to ease her mind?

A week passed. She had done nothing toward seeking medical attention. I argued with her, appealing to her sense of reason. She was, after all, a student in the medical field.

(This proved to be part of Marie's game because her failure to seek immediate medical attention caused Laurel to be more concerned about her and focus more energy and time on her.)

Two weeks passed. Still no doctor's appointment. I was becoming genuinely distressed by her lack of action. My arguments made no headway with her. She was too terrified to see a doctor. She cried. She wanted her mother.

About the third or fourth week after revealing her fear of cancer (although she never used the word *cancer*), she appeared at my office door. She looked pained and depleted. Something else had happened, so awful that she couldn't tell me. What would I think of her if I knew?

This was a consistent pattern with Marie. Shame, silence, secrecy all combined, emitting the same tantalizing message: "Come and get me. Come pull me out, if you are able, and I will reward you with a magnificent secret." I waited. She put her head in my lap. I held her and whispered words of reassurance. And I knew at this moment, even before she told me her new secret, that this woman was not well in ways that went beyond her physical condition. I stroked her hair and wondered what to do now.

Her story emerged slowly and painfully. Just as she had never spoken the word *cancer*, she could not say the word *rape*, but her meaning was clear. Her assailant was white, drugged up, armed. He used racial slurs against her while committing his vile act. She cried audibly and convincingly, but I remember registering that I saw no tears. In a brief flash of doubt, I remember thinking at that moment, Would she possibly go to such lengths to gain my attention? I was immediately repelled by my own question. That, I thought, is exactly why women don't tell.

She presented me with several poems expressing the depth of her pain and, as I read them, I felt a fear rising in me like an advancing tidal wave. These were powerful expressions—beautiful, poetic expressions of suicide.

I talked with her at length until I felt reasonably secure regarding her intentions. She was adamant against my suggestion to report the rape. I didn't push this idea. In light of her fragile psychic state, I worried about the risk of police involvement.

I did, at this point, tell her that she needed much more than I could give her, that a crisis counselor was imperative, that the situation was entirely too big to handle alone. She was passionately insistent that no one must know and she swore me to silence. In her agitated state, her breath became short and labored. She began searching wildly in her purse for something. I remember my amazement at seeing her stockpile of pill bottles—six or eight medications she routinely carried with her. She needed an atomizer, she said, and it was at home.

I was determined to see her safely home. Before we reached her apartment, she was in a full-blown asthma attack. I had never witnessed an asthma attack before and it was a frightening scene. As I frantically searched her apartment for the atomizer, I remember thinking, My God! She is going to die and I am doing nothing to help her. Later on, as we became more enmeshed and her circumstances more difficult, I found myself perverting this statement to, My God! She is going to die and it is my fault.

(Marie had gradually made Laurel feel responsible for her well-being. Laurel had unwittingly accepted this role, falling victim to a 'God complex' which made her believe that she had control over Marie's ills and could somehow fashion a cure.)

In the days that followed, I felt a rising desperation to get Marie the help she needed. She was not dealing with the breast lump. She was not dealing with the rape. But her body was registering what her mind refused to recognize. Her speech had acquired a child's tone. She appeared as a hunted animal, continually looking over her shoulder, vigilantly guarding, it seemed, against potential attack. Everything startled her. Even the softest voice or the gentlest touch evoked a frightened response. She flinched at my slightest movement.

With her stress circuits so overloaded, I was amazed at her ability to successfully continue her schoolwork. How was she functioning in the clinical setting? How was she managing to maintain her academic standards? As depleted as she appeared, she nevertheless attended all classes, keeping pace with the rigors of her educational program, and continuing to perform adequately if not excellently. I couldn't understand it. I kept waiting for her teachers to notice.

Perhaps she was diverting all her anger and energy toward her medical goal. But I had another goal. And while she struggled so hard to keep up appearances, I began a thorough phone search for the perfect counselor. I felt an utter and absolute responsibility in this regard. I was still gathering information when she came to me with a new crisis. She was experiencing uterine pain, she said. She was not feeling well and had missed her period.

I insisted that she seek immediate medical attention. She was visibly frightened, but I promised to see her through. I stood beside her while she placed a call to her doctor and then scheduled her appointment on my calendar. This was the first of many times I was to accompany her on such a trip, although I would never speak with a doctor or hear firsthand the nature of her many illnesses.

On the scheduled day, I left work early to take her to the doctor. Following the examination, she remained silent. On the ride home I finally asked her what the doctor had said. "The doctor said I have an infection and that my uterus is enlarged," she said. "What do you think that means?"

This, I thought, is a mature woman with a medical background. How can she not know what that means? I attributed this apparent naivete to stress. "What do *you* think it means?" I asked.

She hesitated. Her voice was barely audible. She covered her face with her hands and moaned.

I put my hand on her shoulder. "When will you know for sure?" I asked. She told me that the doctor would call. It did not occur to me at the time that pregnancy test results are rarely delayed. With dread and anxiety I waited for the anticipated call. Two days passed before Marie received word. She came to my office to deliver the message in person. "The doctor called," she told me. "The test result is negative." Emotionally spent, I wept with relief and gratitude.

In this theater of the absurd I was the perfect foil to Marie's protagonist. She was the experienced star, I the supporting player. Her performance was flawlessly executed, mine poorly improvised. In little bits she spun out her lines, watching me squirm in the sticky substance of her script. It was a game, I think, that never wearied her, but I did not see it as such at the time.

Each new dramatic conflict was introduced in just this way, and the conflicts were now arising in rapid succession. The next one followed soon upon our small victory regarding the test results. One morning she appeared in my doorway looking sad and defeated. Her head was bowed and her shoulders sagged. How could she ever tell me what an awful person she truly was? I would never forgive her for what she had done.

What could she possibly have done this time? I thought. Suddenly I felt a rush of excitement, an anticipation of something—some reversal of fortune. I knew then that she was about to tell me that she had lied. That it had all been a lie from the very beginning. My hands were shaking with anticipation. I struggled to maintain a calm voice.

"It's okay," I promised. "Anything you say here is okay."

"You will hate me," she countered.

By now this was an old familiar pattern.

(Actually, it is a classic case, complete with the expert use of suspense to build up to the lies which are used as bait to keep the victim hooked.)

I knew I must be patient and that I must follow the script exactly.

(And that is what Marie counted on.)

"Nothing you can say will make me hate you," I promised.

She threw her arms around me and cried. "I lied! I lied!" she sobbed. My heart dropped from my throat to its normal position. All the tension in my chest and shoulders released itself to this moment. I held her gently and stroked her face. "It's okay," I said. "I understand. You were so scared. You didn't want me to go away." Suddenly, aggressively, she pushed me away and looked me fiercely in the eyes.

"What do you mean?" she asked. I felt my heart racing.

"What do *you* mean?" I countered.

"I mean that I lied!" she shouted. "I mean that I *am* pregnant." I stared at her in horror.

I was no match for Marie. With my supervisor's approval, I called a rape crisis counselor and set up a secret meeting in my office at one of Marie's scheduled visits. This was entrapment, pure and simple. It was a measure of my desperation, and I struggled with my conscience over resorting to such tactics.

The meeting was a troubling affair. Marie was predictably enraged and humiliated. She refused to speak with the counselor. She hung her head and remained silent throughout most of the session. The counselor tried every avenue to reach her. It was the topic of pregnancy that finally elicited a response. As pregnancy options were gently broached, Marie appeared confused. She seemed to have no understanding of abortion, seeking clarification from me. This is unbelievable, I thought. Could she really not know?

The counseling resulted in no decision regarding the pregnancy, and Marie had still received no diagnosis regarding the lump on her breast. Neither reasoning nor pleading moved her to action. I watched her slip day by day into steady decline, her jerky, startled responses becoming worse, and weakness and physical instability becoming apparent. It was during this period that she entered my office one afternoon appearing disoriented and unable to express herself. Before I could respond, she collapsed to the floor.

I immediately secured approval to take her to an emergency public mental health clinic. Weakened by her physical condition, her protests were easily overruled. I considered it a stroke of good fortune that the on-staff psychologist was a black woman. A gender and culture tie might help Marie feel more at ease. At Marie's request, I was permitted to remain with her throughout the session. Little by little, with my encouragement, Marie revealed her story to Diana, the psychologist. I noted my vast relief. I no longer had to be the sole repository of these terrible secrets, and finally we were receiving the professional help we so urgently needed.

I am not sure at what point I shifted my thinking from "she" to "we," but I see now how I had clearly come to regard this as "our" problem.

(This was the result of Marie's having made Laurel responsible for her well-being, and Laurel's believing that Marie was her charge. It was also part of the codependency web that Marie had woven and the emotional reliance that they had come to have on each other.)

My dreams were indicators of this odd interlacing. I was experiencing insufferable insomnia at this time, often awakening with nightmares. In my dreams, I was the one with cancer. I was the victim of rape.

Diana believed that Marie's condition warranted hospitalization, but succumbed to her adamant protests. She settled instead on having Marie sign a contract that she would not harm herself and would seek further help through the clinic. Much to my relief, another appointment was scheduled.

At the same time, Marie was given a doctor's referral and instructed to have the lump on her breast evaluated. She was told that if she abided by the terms of the contract, she could spare herself enforced hospitalization. Marie promised to live up to her agreement.

The doctor's appointment was immediately scheduled, and I was given permission to accompany her on work time. As always, I had no personal contact with the doctor but learned from Marie that she had seen in the doctor's eyes "how bad things are." She told me that further tests were required by an oncologist. Marie followed up on this referral independently and within a short time reported back. The oncologist, she told me, had confirmed the presence of cancer and chemotherapy treatments were needed. I expressed amazement that no surgery was required. She explained that due to her blood condition, resulting from sickle-cell trait, she was a poor surgical risk and that the doctor believed that chemotherapy was her best option.

The first of 10 chemotherapy treatments was started. She, the medical technician, became my patient and I, her long-suffering servant. The great leaden load of her misery settled over me and I gave myself up to her illness, suffering with her and for her. The practical demands in themselves were exhausting, but suffering is another matter. It extracts its price at a deeper level. For the first time in my life I began relying on sleeping pills to see me through the night.

My Friday nights with Marie following her chemo treatments gave me a glimpse of hell's torments. The vomiting was wretched and relentless. It started within the hour and continued solidly throughout the night. But the headaches were even worse. Like shards of hot steel, she told me, they pierced her skull. She writhed in agony, her face contorted in pain and her cries begging for release. Once during such an episode, I massaged her scalp while presenting visual imagery in opposition to the pain. Suddenly in an unexpected flash, the thrashing and contortions abruptly ceased, her features softened, and she stared at me as if I were a beatific vision. I felt an eeriness creep over me. "It's gone," she whispered, her voice full of awe. "How did you do it?"

Oh, how I wanted to believe her. I took hold of her words until the words took hold of me. I believed that she had opened in me some magical, healing touch. That I could remove her suffering and give her a new, clean life. I went home that night and without medication slept soundly and peaceably. I believed somehow that I could save her and whatever it took from me, that was my intention.

It is difficult to believe, even now, that Marie's condition was not the result of cancer. Not only were there the obvious signs of vomiting, pain, and weakness, but she took care to provide me with reinforcing evidence of her illness. No detail was overlooked. For example, once upon my arrival Marie led me to the bathroom sink where she displayed large clumps of hair. She exhibited great distress, but I attempted to comfort her by demanding that she look into the mirror. No thinning was remotely apparent. "No one will ever notice," I assured her. And that was the truth.

Another time, I went to the store to buy ice chips and returned to find her incontinent. Her humiliation was utterly convincing. I now believe that both these incidents were part of her elaborate ruse.

Some weeks later, after the onset of radiation treatments, I noticed black ink markings on the affected breast. When I questioned her about this, she quickly covered the markings. Lowering her eyes in apparent embarrassment, she told me that the markings were used to correctly position the radiation scope.

Similar ruses were adopted to fit the circumstances of her "pregnancy." With the stresses incurred from radiation and chemotherapy, Marie's pregnancy soon aborted, but only after she had begun to plan and dream about the prospects of becoming a mother. Idyllic and dreamy, her fantasies of impending motherhood appeared to have boosted her morale and given her something to live for. Any attempt to help prepare her for the inevitable loss incited her anger and denial. This child, she told me, was her only hope. The spontaneous abortion was therefore received as another devastating loss.

To satisfy Marie's penchant for drama, she introduced an additional conflict. It was not enough to present her abortion story as a mere psychological loss; it must also garner sympathy for her physical plight. The abortion, she told me, had resulted in unbearable pain and severe blood loss. I was incensed at what she said was her doctor's simple instruction to stay off her feet. She appeared in need of serious medical attention, and I took this home remedy approach as a sign of the poor quality of care rendered to Medicaid patients. Throughout this ordeal, Marie continued to attend school, dragging herself through classes and clinicals, and appearing steadily weaker with each passing day.

I puzzled over the fact that Marie remained so plump, but her condition showed a decline in other ways. Her lack of balance worried me, and her general state of health appeared exceedingly poor. I began to wonder if she were clinically safe. I shared my concerns with my supervisor. We had a responsibility, I knew, not only to our clients but also to the institution we served. We weighed the problem carefully before determining that it was time to break the silence. The justification was not only the safety of Marie's patients, but also her own personal safety. A lowered white blood count, due to chemotherapy, could increase her susceptibility to infection. What if she died because I didn't tell? On the other hand, I worried excessively over what she would do if I did tell. I believed she would see this as the ultimate act of betrayal. I believed suicide to be a real possibility. The only relief I found in those torment-ridden days was the sweet sleep that came with Halcion.

When the secret was finally revealed, Marie's supervisor required her to obtain a note from her doctor acknowledging her fitness for clinical practice. She continued her studies, so I had assumed she had obtained the note. (Months later, when our relationship ended, I requested an instructor who had become familiar with Marie's case to search her file for the doctor's note. I was plagued by a desire to verify once and for all the reality of her disease. The instructor returned to inform me that no such note was in Marie's file. Impossible, I told her. She needed a doctor's note to return to clinicals. The instructor checked the file again. No note was found.)

By that time, I was beginning to encounter other troubling doubts that had previously been censored by my compassion and guilt. For example, early in Marie's diagnosis, I sought financial assistance for her through a special cancer scholarship fund. She had refused to fill out the application, indicating that she did not wish to be stigmatized by her illness. As she appeared to be having serious financial difficulties, I was insistent. Her chosen field, her minority status, and her academic record made her an excellent candidate. Still she refused. Some time later, upon the insistence of Diana, her psychologist, Marie reluctantly filed the application. When weeks had passed with no word from the awarding agency, I placed a call. The woman with whom I spoke remembered Marie's application. She said she remembered it because it had been missing pertinent information, therefore the application had never been processed. The woman could not recall exactly what information had been missing, but I had some grave suspicions.

My "betrayal" of Marie in breaking the bond of secrecy placed a great strain on our relationship. She punished me in numerous ways but did not reject me altogether. She still permitted me to continue my caretaking role, but I was now sharing the responsibility with Diana, who was also becoming equally involved with Marie. The personal assistance which Diana provided gave me some much needed relief as well as a confidante with whom to share my burden. Diana and I spoke frequently to each other by phone. This contact allowed me to see through another, more experienced set of eyes the manipulative tactics that Marie employed. She became despondent, for example, at the mere mention of home health care. I knew that, with a doctor's referral, Marie would qualify for hospice home care, but she refused to hear of it. She wanted only Diana and me to care for her. No one else, she insisted, could do it as well.

In the midst of her worst illness, her elderly grandfather died. I began receiving phone calls at 2 A.M. to talk her through her enormous grief. I was exhausted by my lack of sleep and her seemingly relentless suffering, and I was growing increasingly resentful of her stubborn resistance to outside help.

(Resentment was a natural outgrowth of Laurel's increasing suspicions and the toll that Marie's difficulties were taking on her devoted friend's health. The more Marie was questioned, the harder she pushed Laurel. It was her desperate pushing, however, through the use of a seemingly endless supply of problems, that weakened her hold on Laurel. Marie's efforts to perpetuate the ruse only created more uncertainty about her truthfulness and made Laurel more determined to find others who were willing to share the burden.)

Through the efforts of one of her instructors, Marie was eventually encouraged to join a hospice support group to help her deal with the family loss. She did not, as I had hoped, reveal to the group her personal fight with cancer. But this contact did provide another support person in the form of a hospice counselor, Patrice, who began calling Marie on a regular basis.

Meanwhile, our relationship became more and more unstable. Prior to Christmas, Marie told me that her doctor said she could not get better. She told me that cheek scrapings had revealed cancerous tissue inside the mouth. She wanted to do one thing before she "got too sick." She asked me to take her to the seaside for a vacation. This was a dying woman's simple wish, I thought, but it seemed too big for me. She was already experiencing difficulty making it to the bathroom. How were we to manage on a beach?

After giving the matter some serious thought, I told her I would take her on the trip but only upon the advice of her doctor. Some weeks before, this subject had surfaced in regard to her general care. Following a chemo treatment she became very ill and was hospitalized, she told me, because of a toxic buildup in her system. She had not drunk enough water the previous night while in my care. An overnight hospitalization did, in fact, occur at this time. According to Marie's neighbor, Marie had fainted in the hallway of her apartment building, and the paramedics were called to the scene. I told Marie that I was concerned that I was not caring for her properly and wanted to speak with her doctor. "What would you ask?" she wanted to know. "I am a med tech," she said. "I can tell you everything you need to know."

I gave in to her then, but was determined to hold my ground on the vacation issue. When she could see that I was implacable, she made a patronizing reversal. "If you are too unsure of yourself to take me to the ocean," she said, "then let's do something that will be more comfortable for you." I was too weary to confront her unfairness.

I took her to see a performance of *The Nutcracker*. It was our last evening together for nearly three weeks, as I was planning to spend Christmas in the mountains. Though I knew that the separation would be healing for me, I wrestled with my conscience over leaving her. I was uncertain as to whether she would survive that long.

In early January, I returned to work and to Marie, but my sojourn in the mountains had given me the time and space I needed to make some decisions in support of my own health. I had worried about Marie, but I had also given more thought to myself, noting the obvious effects of stress on my body, my uncomfortable reliance on sleeping pills, and the knowledge that all the energy normally given to my family—my husband and children—was used up with Marie. I returned to work determined to establish an appropriate boundary.

Marie's physical status remained unchanged, but she was now the victim of a new crisis: the death of her younger brother. When she began, once again, actively threatening suicide, I called for help. Diana was unavailable, but the hospice counselor, Patrice, responded readily. I was called in as a secondary support.

The events that followed allowed me to see Marie with different eyes. She sought affirmation from me by questioning my loyalty and by accusing me of caring little for her. I had lost my heart for this game. Each verbal attack became a wedge which increased the distance between us. I marshaled my inner forces and fixed my line. She did not cross over this time.

That evening Marie called me at home. Sensing, perhaps, my inner shift, she appealed to my sympathy by grossly misrepresenting the intentions of a friend. I was incensed and told her that I was left to wonder if she distorted *my* words in the same way. She hung up on me.

Shortly afterward, Patrice called. She revealed to me her strong belief that Marie's cancer was a hoax. Marie displayed none of the classic symptoms, said Patrice, and by all norms could not have survived so long. "Marie has probably convinced herself that she is afflicted," said Patrice, "but cancer? Not a chance."

Her words bypassed the brain and stuck a blow directly to my body. I reached for the wall to keep from falling.

Upon returning to work, my relationship with Marie was formally broken. My supervisor remained with me as a support and a witness. I did not confront Marie with Patrice's charge, but I did confront her on other matters that concerned me. I told her I had been wrong to allow her to depend on me so completely as this had prevented her from seeking the psychiatric care she clearly needed. Her sick, sagging frame shot up straight and strong. Her weak voice became loud and commanding. She jabbed her finger at me and flung accusations, but my boundaries held well. I had no need to return her fire. Enough had been said.

Although she remained in school, I took great care to avoid her so that we did not see each other again. Four months later, Marie graduated and took a position with a large hospital. Several weeks following her graduation, Marie made a sudden, unannounced visit. She had come, ironically, to forgive me. She missed me, she said, and asked if she could hug me one more time. It was a familiar hug. It felt warm and genuine, and for all that had happened, for all that I now knew to be true, I felt an abiding grief in that parting hug.

For me, many unanswered questions still remain. But the answered questions have validated this unhappy experience. With the help of my therapist, I have come to understand that my attachment to Marie is linked to my feelings for my emotionally disturbed brother. Because of Marie, I am learning to establish boundaries and set limits. And I am discovering that it is possible to love without losing myself in the process. Marie has been a good teacher after all.

Diana, who was deeply affected by the extent of Marie's suffering, became personally involved in much the same way I did. The first signs of this were evident when Diana decided to leave her employment with the public mental health clinic where Marie had received counseling to take a job at another facility farther away. My first concern was for Marie's continuing treatment, but Diana assured me that she had no intention of abandoning Marie. She continued to assist her through telephone contact and by seeing Marie privately on her own time and at no charge.

Diana and I remained in close phone contact throughout Marie's ordeal. In some sense, we drew our strength from each other. After Marie's "chemotherapy" treatments were underway, Diana decided that she could provide some relief for me by sharing the caretaking role. She also served as Marie's advisor on practical issues related to her finances and her schooling. She even tutored her in certain subjects and assisted her financially.

As my relationship with Marie became more intense and more unstable, Diana urged me to break free of Marie. As an experienced professional, she recognized Marie's powerful tactics and yet was apparently unable to free herself from Marie's hold.

I do not believe that Diana ever saw herself as truly "sucked in." I think she saw herself as having the professional insights that I, perhaps, lacked, and believed herself more capable of handling Marie's manipulations.

(If only this psychologist had had insights into factitious disorders. . . .)

She was certainly aware that Marie's secrecy was hiding something significant, and when the cancer story was revealed as questionable, she hardly seemed surprised. Nevertheless, she continued her involvement with Marie long after mine ended.

Several months after I had released myself from Marie's hold,

Diana called me at home. I had not heard from her in a long time. She told me that she was getting married. "Who is the lucky man?" I asked her. She told me that she had fallen head over heels for Marie's brother."

(That gives new meaning to the expression "family ties.")

Although Laurel's association with Marie may sound extreme, it is entirely characteristic of the traumatic and lasting effects factitial patients have on their victims, from clergymen to nurses to spouses and coworkers. A common thread running through accounts from victims is that they believed their experiences were unique until they read about Jenny's case. One man wrote of a woman who also feigned cancer:

> I was involved with a woman for almost 12 years who convinced not only me, but an entire group of friends and associates, that she was diagnosed with terminal bone cancer. The woman in our situation has never been confronted. Rather, she has built a new life entirely, without past associations: new friends, a new job, and so on.
>
> Until I read about your study I thought that I and my friends were entirely alone in our experience.

Victims have, for the most part, silently endured the indignity, anger, pain, and embarrassment imposed upon them by factitious disorders without knowing such diagnoses even existed. The victims of Jenny's deception were far more fortunate than most because Jenny agreed to treatment, and thus they were alerted to the exact nature of her illness. This knowledge did little to assuage their feelings, but at least they knew that they were the victims of someone's illness rather than willful malice.

No one is immune to such victimization. As we saw in the case of Abby (described in the first chapter), clergymen are likely candidates for the codependent role because of the supportive nature of their work. One minister told us about a parishioner who he believed had faked accidents and injuries. She had staged an auto accident and even faked reports of brain cancer. Whenever the minister tried to get her to be specific about one incident or illness, she'd evasively move on to the next. He said that he couldn't help but feel that he had been used.

Another victim reported to us that he had developed an intimate relationship with a woman whom he had met while vacationing in Canada. She turned up on his doorstep in the United States soon after he had returned home to Virginia, and moved in with him. She pretended to seek employment while accepting money and gifts of clothing and jewelry from him. After several weeks, when he began questioning her stories about jobs promised or lost, she started spending more time at home with the excuse that she wasn't feeling well. Gradually, her minor complaints escalated into major displays of pain and exhaustion, and she began drinking heavily, which worried her partner and distracted him from work. She assured him that she was under a doctor's care. When he pressed for details, she told him that she had a bladder infection which was being treated with antibiotics. She said that she was drinking to numb the pain, and that she would have to postpone her efforts to find a job because of her illness.

After several weeks, when her condition remained seemingly unchanged, he expressed doubts about her story. "I have a right to know if something is really wrong with you and, if you *are* sick, why you're not getting better," he insisted one night during a heated argument. "I can't function properly because I worry about you day and night."

His lover, who acted her part with great flair, took him in her arms and confessed: "I didn't want to worry you over something we can't change, but I suppose you need to know. I have ovarian cancer."

He was overwhelmed with a sense of guilt at having doubted her. He begged for more information, talked about seeing specialists, and offered to accompany her on visits to doctors and to pay for her treatments. She told him to be brave and have faith, and to carry on as he had all along. She assured him that she was in good hands.

Months slipped by without any physical changes, and with her providing only sketchy details about her "treatments." When he was at last financially and emotionally depleted and on the brink of losing his job because of his deteriorating performance, he once again began questioning her condition. "If I get fired, who's going to pay for your treatments?" he demanded to know. "My savings are almost gone. I've given you everything I have!" She told him that her doctor, who had also immigrated to this country, had taken pity on her because she had no roots and no means of income here, and the doctor was going to be treating her gratis. She stonewalled him when he tried to check details of her story, and eventually he told her that he didn't believe her. She accused him of callous indifference, and said that she couldn't live with a man who treated her so harshly. She promptly returned home.

In a desperate attempt to get at the truth, he contacted her uncle and learned that his lover was alcoholic and frequently feigned symptoms to elicit pity and emotional and monetary support. His lover knew that he enjoyed traveling and, after learning that he had discovered the truth about her, she waged a campaign of terror by telephone, threatening to kill him if he returned to Canada.

We believe that this woman posed a serious threat to her victim. Her actions reflect an antisocial personality disorder, and her web of lies goes beyond a reckless disregard for the truth. There's a willful focus on being dishonest at every possible opportunity. We have to contrast this with Jenny, who acknowledged that there were victims to her deception, was remorseful, and wanted to know how she could move on and make her life different. This woman showed no remorse.

Such threatening behavior is not typical of even the hard-core Munchausen patient. Most of them have sociopathic traits, but they aren't particularly violent or physically threatening. This is an extreme case in which the woman appears to have strong criminal tendencies, and her sociopathy emerged in full force when her deception was uncovered. Whatever the cause of her ills, she had quite an impact on this man's life.

The scope of the negative influence factitial patients have on the lives of their victims varies with the magnitude of their deceptions. Most families suffer in silence, unaware of what they are dealing with, and knowing only that it is destroying their lives. One family was constantly under siege because of a daughter who faked illness. Her mother wrote: "We just don't know what to do. We are so frustrated. She's made a real mess out of our lives. We have no idea about how to proceed with psychiatric treatment because nothing seems to work for her. We have a dresser full of medical bills that arrive regularly. We don't even open them anymore. We just put them in the drawer."

Their adult daughter was running up medical bills because of her disease portrayals and telling the hospitals and doctors who took care of her to send her parents the bills, even though they weren't legally responsible for them. In some way her parents had to learn to cut themselves loose rather than continue to allow her to wreak such havoc within their lives.

Sometimes anger is the tool that performs the cutting. A resident physician called the father of a woman who was putting blood up her urinary catheter. He wanted to tell him that she was in the hospital and to talk with him about her case. The father got very angry, saying, "I'm sick and tired of dealing with this. I get hassled all the time. I've decided I don't want anything to do with it anymore."

With guidance from counselors, families may contribute to the treatment of factitial patients but, for various reasons, most of them never seem to get the chance. There is a surprising lack of information concerning the origins and families of these patients. They hit the hospital ward, cause tremendous uproar, arouse a lot of interest; when caregivers discover that they've been had, the patients disappear. Many of those who have allowed doctors to put them on psychiatric units won't allow contact with their families. Only a small percentage of them get their families involved in their treatment.

Still, it makes good sense to try to contact families whenever possible, even if just to build an accurate medical history. Once the boiling rage many of them feel has been reduced to simmering, they may provide help by fleshing out the possible motivations behind the faker's ruse.

Long after the anger and frustration of victims have subsided, a sense of aloneness arises, along with the feeling that one must be foolish to have been duped this way. Victims of factitial patients need counseling and adjustment time. They must first acknowledge the problem and not be reluctant to turn to health care professionals for advice and support.

If you suspect that you are a victim of a factitial patient, first talk to someone who can objectively listen and has enough medical knowledge to know whether or not a factitious disorder is a possibility. You may want to confront the person you suspect of the factitious illness by saying, "This is what I believe is going on and we must seek help if you want to continue a relationship with me." And the next step, depending on the seriousness of any financial consequences endured by the victim as a result of the portrayal, might be to contact an attorney. (More on the legal issues in the following chapter.)

As a victim, your own therapy might focus on fully letting go of the other person. Although it may sound harsh, especially when you've been so close to a person, you have to cut your losses and worry about how you can protect yourself. You may not be able to change the other person, so you will have to focus on how to distance yourself from the problem and carry on a healthier life.

Victims must remember that these patients are very glib and tend to say what people want to hear, just as we saw in Laurel Martin's experience. Fakers have been known to talk family members out of believing that any ruse occurred. Victims, or people who regard themselves as potential victims, have to steel themselves against further manipulation by focusing on objective evidence.

Some victims, however, are as immovable as the perpetrators when it comes to making attitudinal and/or behavioral changes. They feel a need to take care of sick people as much as factitial patients need to be taken care of. For such budding martyrs, acknowledging that the illness is a hoax is extremely difficult. The duty to take care of the sick is drummed into all of our heads throughout our lives. Traditional wedding vows obligate spouses to care for each other "in sickness and in health." But if your spouse *makes* himself or herself sick, should the obligation be called into question? We assert that it must be redefined to take into account the fact that, faker or not, a factitial patient is indeed sick—albeit mentally—and still deserves care. That care, however, must be taken over by mental health professionals so that the victim can focus on his or her own much-deserved recovery.

Recovery for the victims begins with information about the disorder. Information is liberating. So say all the victims with whom we have talked. The single most curative event for most was simply finding out that there is a name for this disorder. In sharing experiences they have had with this bizarre psychological malady, people have felt as if a burden has been lifted off their shoulders. They no longer have to feel foolish or ashamed about falling for a false illness once they realize that they certainly are not the only ones who have been misled in this way, and that they have been dealing with a true, recognized mental disorder.

CHAPTER 14

THE LEGAL
AND ETHICAL
BOILING POT

Honesty
isn't so simple:

a simple honesty is
nothing but a lie.

Don't the trees
hide the wind between

their leaves and
speak in whispers?
  Denise Levertov
  The Third Dimension
  (1957)

A host of legal and ethical questions swirls around these great pretenders, further muddying the already darkened waters through which health care professionals must peer when dealing with them. As cases in this book have illustrated, bold moves, which in some instances were ethically and legally questionable, have been taken by medical professionals who had no other alternatives if they were going to diagnose and/or treat factitial patients. But such actions are dicey at best, because they simultaneously expose doctors, other caregivers, and hospitals to the risk of character assassination, accusations of misconduct, and legal actions.

One of the foremost legal considerations for doctors who encounter factitial patients is the danger of being sued for malpractice. Doctors may feel less vulnerable in a case that turns out to involve a factitious disorder than in other cases. They assume that whatever happens regarding a factitious illness is entirely the patient's fault and that any jury would agree. Quite a few physicians might view it as inconceivable that they could be sued in a factitious disorder case. But they're wrong. Factitial patients can and sometimes do bring malpractice suits against doctors. Only very infrequently are judgments rendered against the physicians. But whether or not damages are awarded in the end is the least of the concerns involved in a malpractice action. Of greater importance is the toll on the doctor and his or her family as the suit drags on for months or even years, as such cases often do. As we saw in the situation of the woman who was enamored of her surgeon and infected her surgical wound with feces, even though her legal efforts ultimately proved unsuccessful, the case had to be appealed and the surgeon went through a lengthy, very frightening experience.

We know of one case in which a young woman who feigned cancer later sued 35 physicians collectively for $14 million because they had failed to recognize and treat her for a factitious disorder, treating her instead for a disease she never had. Rather than face a battle, the insurance company settled out of court for more than a quarter of a million dollars. This case underscores the message that health care professionals must recognize factitious disorders as early as possible.

Another critical legal dilemma involves satisfaction of debts incurred by these patients. This conundrum has hospitals and professionals grappling with the question of whether or not factitial patients are guilty of criminal fraud. Many factitial patients rely on insurance carriers, the Veterans' Administration, or public assistance programs to absorb their medical costs. Others, who have no funds and no medical insurance, simply don't pay their bills. Some doctors believe that all factitial patients should pay for their medical care with their own resources; otherwise, they say, they are guilty of fraud. In some states this thinking is supported by the law. In North Carolina, for example, it's a crime to seek medical care under fraudulent circumstances.

An additional important legal issue is whether or not factitial patients are committable for involuntary psychiatric hospitalization. The only time doctors can force people to make themselves available for treatment is through commitment, which is a serious matter involving adjudication by the courts.

Commitment does not mean that treatment itself can be forced, only that the patient will be made *available* for it. An individual can be committed and refuse medications and, except in exceptional circumstances, that refusal must be honored. If doctors believe that a person can't appropriately decide about treatment, then this becomes a question of competency to make medical decisions, and this question must also be decided by a court. Just as the lab technician who was bleeding herself was permitted to run away, we have to allow any factitial patient, including those we are sure we could help, to leave the hospital if they do not meet commitment criteria.

These restrictions are essentially the same in all states, although the specific laws and thresholds for commitment vary. Physicians have to recognize the limits of their authority. People have the right in our society to make unfortunate decisions about their lives. There are few cases in the United States in which a patient has indeed been committed solely on the basis of a factitious disorder. In one instance, a patient had presented to a hospital with factitious hematuria after she catheterized herself and injected the catheter with her own blood. Although her behavior wasn't suicidal, a judge found that she was nevertheless placing herself in serious medical danger, which might well result in her death, and he committed her for psychiatric treatment. Unfortunately, she was released one week later by a misinformed psychiatrist who said that by definition of her factitious disorder she was untreatable and therefore did not meet the state's criteria for involuntary hospitalization. It is true that, in some states, treatability is a criterion for commitment; like this psychiatrist, many doctors may believe that factitious disorders are inherently untreatable. In all cases, it requires a leap for judges and lawyers to view a factitious disorder as a mental illness; when it comes to commitment, they're usually looking at disorders such as schizophrenia and suicidal depression with the risk of imminent overt harm to self or others.

In most states, the only criteria for commitment are the presence of a mental disorder with overt and acute suicidal risk, overt danger to others, or the incapacity to care for one's basic needs, such as those for food, shelter, and clothing. Factitious disorders do not generally fulfill these criteria. Perhaps recognizing this fact, in a case in Oregon a judge set up a medical conservatorship as an alternative to commitment. In the conservatorship, one person was appointed to make all medical decisions on behalf of the patient. This approach, designed to eliminate unnecessary care, is eminently reasonable, and other states might consider amending their laws slightly to permit such actions in cases involving factitial patients.

Other legal questions involving individual rights have arisen from secret surveillance and surreptitious searches of patients' property and hospital rooms, which have sometimes yielded evidence used to confirm factitious illnesses. Such actions were seldom questioned in the not-too-distant past, but today they are considered likely invasions of privacy. In the last three decades, the medical community's concept of patients has changed. Thirty years ago, when people were hospitalized, the staff took away all their clothes, including their shoes. Patients had no rights and were treated like two-year-olds; frequently the staff and many doctors even spoke to patients in a kind of baby talk. They told patients what to do, how to do it, when to do it, and where, and patients were allowed to keep few, if any, of their personal possessions.

The issue of privacy arose in a case in which a woman was suspected of inducing vomiting to cause an electrolyte imbalance. Doctors secretly performed tests (not explaining what they were really for) to monitor serum and urinary electrolytes. They were able to determine that the electrolyte loss was through vomiting. Was it ethical for doctors to perform that kind of diagnostic study without telling the patient what they were doing and why?

Another questionable practice is the use of "truth serum" on patients to induce them to admit their ruses. It is unlawful to administer a chemical without informed consent solely for the purpose of trying to extract the truth. Regardless, the method is very often ineffective; a patient who is highly motivated to maintain a deception can resist the effects of such a drug, so it doesn't really "force" truthfulness.

Some doctors have argued that there is a therapeutic privilege that allows them to forgo the conventional process of getting informed consent before administering such substances, but we don't agree with that. Even such procedures of very low risk are not entirely *without* risk.

Imagine the scenario of a doctor's administering a drug without informed consent and the patient's having a life-threatening reaction. It would be considered a criminal offense. Doctors cannot afford to practice with disregard either for potential liability or for individual rights.

Some doctors believe that room searches may be legally and ethically justifiable to help confirm a factitious illness. But unless the patient has accepted the possibility of room searches as a precondition to admission, the days of such actions are long gone. When a person enters a hospital today, that person does not give up any civil rights. Hospitals are even required to post a bill of rights for patients. Technically, informed consent should be obtained for every procedure and medication. There is no blanket form that allows doctors to do to a patient whatever they deem necessary, without regard for the patient's wishes.

Doctors still do have some options for catching disease forgers, and one is to incorporate the informed consent process into testing. For instance, a doctor who suspects someone of feigning an illness can sit with that patient and explain, "I don't know what's going on with you yet, but one of the possibilities is that you are producing this disease yourself. Because I'm considering this among the diagnoses, I need to do a series of tests that will rule out that option as well as other possible diagnoses. I'm telling you beforehand to ask your permission to go ahead with the diagnostic workup." This statement is very hard for doctors to make because it immediately strains the doctor-patient relationship. If the patient does have a factitious disorder, he or she may find an excuse to check out of the hospital and slip off to another hospital to perpetuate the same behavior. But the direct approach could make a big difference in helping to identify selected cases of factitious disorders and perhaps result in proper treatment for those patients. Through this approach, doctors could also avoid participation in the pattern of unnecessary medical and surgical intervention.

As we pointed out earlier, using video cameras as watchful eyes can be very helpful in diagnosing Munchausen by proxy. Videotaped documentation of abuse may be made part of the child's permanent medical record for review by protective services personnel. However, video surveillance in MBP cases might be seen as an invasion of privacy and could be challenged as illegally obtained evidence which should not be admissible in court. As soon as doctors become suspicious of MBP, they should contact the hospital's attorney and administrator, and possibly consult with an ethics committee. They should also consult the hospital's risk management office and local authorities on any proposed detective work. If the worrisome behavior is occurring outside a hospital, a doctor should contact his or her attorney or a legal advisor with the American Psychiatric Association or American Medical Association.

In cases of possible MBP, doctors in the United States *must*, by law, share their suspicions with the proper authorities. (This differs from other countries in the world, such as England, where there is no mandatory duty for doctors to report child abuse.) With reporting comes immunity from any type of prosecution or lawsuits for defamation, as long as the report was not filed with conscious malicious intent to injure a person.

Against this complex legal backdrop, doctors who recognize a factitious disorder in a patient find themselves in a quandary. The actions physicians must take are largely determined by the laws and professional practices of the community. For example, a physician cannot unilaterally terminate active care, suddenly saying, "I think you're faking and I'm not going to see you or treat you from this moment on." A physician must in some way provide warning to a patient that, on a certain date, he or she will no longer care for that patient. There also has to be some reasonable hope that the patient can obtain other medical care to the extent that it is needed, and the physician may be required to assist in getting the patient that care.

Typically, when dealing with a factitial patient, it is recommended that the primary care physician, in the company of a psychiatrist, conduct a therapeutic confrontation with the patient by saying: "We have discovered that you don't really have the disease that you wanted us to believe you had. It is clear that you were simulating it or inducing it yourself. You must be very distressed if you feel you have to do this to get help. For the type of problem you are experiencing, we recommend that you get help from the psychiatrist who is here and who has the skills to help you deal with emotional matters." In this way, doctors attempt to renegotiate the therapeutic contract and redefine the problem rather than simply get rid of the patient. The patient will typically say, "Doctors, you're crazy. I don't know what you're talking about, and if you continue to talk this way I'm going to sue you." If the impasse can't be broken, the primary care physician must be prepared to say, "I cannot be forced to commit malpractice by pursuing tests and treatment which are not medically sound; therefore, I am letting you know that, effective in 10 days, I can no longer be your doctor." The physician should send the patient a certified letter restating this information and offering recommendations for follow-up treatment and potential providers of that care.

The ethical dilemmas presented by factitial patients are as complex as the sampling of legal questions raised here. For instance, the American Medical Association's "Principles of Medical Ethics" holds that physicians must respect the confidentiality of patients and deal honestly with them. But if a patient is not playing by the rules of the doctor-patient relationship, does the physician have to play by them? Except under certain conditions, the physician clearly does.

According to the *Clinical Handbook of Psychiatry and the Law* by Drs. Paul Appelbaum and Thomas Gutheil, disclosing information without a patient's consent may be legally justified, or even necessary, but only in a limited number of circumstances. These include:

1. *When an emergency is present.* When a patient's physical well-being is at stake, a doctor or therapist, acting in the person's best interests, may deem it necessary to disclose appropriate information about a patient. For example, if a patient is in a hospital emergency room and refuses to volunteer information, a clinician contacted by hospital personnel may feel obliged to reveal information pertaining to the diagnosis, medications prescribed, or any illicit drug use to insure proper evaluation and treatment.

2. *When a patient is incompetent.* If a clinician believes that a patient is not legally competent to give or withhold consent, he or she should seek consent from an appropriate guardian or relative. In the absence of such a person, the clinician can release information that will serve the patient's best interests.

3. *When a patient must be hospitalized or committed.* When information is needed to voluntarily or involuntarily hospitalize a patient, such disclosure is permitted in most states. There are restrictions, however, in some parts of the country, which should be clarified with local authorities.

4. *When third parties must be protected.* In the past, psychiatrists' obligations to protect others from patients' violent acts were limited

and did not require breaching confidentiality. A 1976 decision by the California Supreme Court, however, stated that all mental health professionals have a duty to "take whatever steps are reasonably necessary" to protect their patients' potential victims. In this decision, the court recognized that warnings might have to be issued to the potential victim and/or the police. Courts in a number of other states have rendered similar decisions. The *Handbook* suggests "ordinarily first considering other measures which can be taken without breaching confidentiality, such as changing therapy to focus on feared violence, adding or changing medications, expanding therapy to include a threatened intimate of the patient, and hospitalizing the patient. The duty to protect has been extended by some courts to include property damage and harm caused by dangerous driving." The duty to protect may also apply to protection of sexual partners of persons infected with HIV. Some states forbid such disclosure while others allow it. The *Handbook* notes that it is "generally agreed that efforts should first be made to get the HIV-infected patient to make the disclosure, and to bring his or her partner for counseling. The American Medical Association and American Psychiatric Association have issued statements indicating their support for disclosure when necessary to protect a sexual partner."

5. *When there are requirements for disclosure.* The obligations of health care professionals to report specified conditions and behavior vary from state to state. Clinicians who fail to meet mandatory reporting obligations in their areas may be subject to civil and criminal penalties. It is crucial for health care professionals to be aware of local statutes and laws pertaining to these issues.

6. *When supervisors or collaborators are assisting.* It is not generally considered a breach of confidentiality to disclose information to professionals who are assisting a primary caregiver in a patient's care, including supervisors, members of a hospital's milieu staff, and colleagues who are directly involved in a patient's treatment. Once taken into a primary physician's confidence, however, they are obliged to maintain the same respect for confidentiality as the primary caregiver.

Despite the legal priority for confidentiality, what about matters of conscience and collegiality in cases of factitious disorders? Aren't doctors obligated to warn each other, hospitals, and insurance carriers about factitial patients to forestall the misuse of medical resources? The case of Joan Nelson in England is a frightening example of what can happen to someone who is misdiagnosed as having Munchausen syndrome; she was subsequently treated inappropriately by a physician who was "warned" about her. But what about a person who really *is* feigning illness and unnecessarily using up vital health care resources?

One doctor tried informally to alert his colleagues to a woman whom he had seen as a patient and believed was suffering from a factitious disorder. Feeling concerned about her well-being and obligated to warn his fellow physicians, he contacted a number of doctors who he had learned were currently seeing this patient. He was offhandedly dismissed by every one of them. He was shocked by how willing his colleagues were to accept the compelling tales of his former patient.

Other health care professionals have taken concrete steps to warn people inside and outside the medical community about specific factitial patients. Writing in *Nursing Times* (August 1990), nurse Philip Kinsella recounted a case in which a 24-year-old man named Richard was admitted to a hospital for what appeared to be post-traumatic stress disorder. Richard told a harrowing tale of a fire on the Norwegian ship of which he was the captain. The fire left six crew members dead, including his girlfriend's father. Talk of depression and suicide peppered his narration, and he complained of terrifying "flashbacks" and sleeplessness. He openly craved human touch after his frequent and lengthy "flashback" episodes. When a hospital discharge paper accidentally fell out of his pocket, doctors learned that the patient had recently been discharged from another psychiatric institution. This fact contradicted the personal and medical history that Richard had given his new caregivers. Doctors contacted the other hospital and then, in direct defiance of the patient's instructions, contacted his parents. They learned that the patient had never been in a fire the likes of which he had described, but had simply read about one; in addition, he had never been a ship's captain, although members of his family had been seafarers.

Richard had a long history of psychiatric admissions. In view of the disclosures, he was discharged, leaving his caregivers to deal with other patients who had been supportive of him and who were now angry and hurt. Because this man had had such an adverse effect on his fellow patients, nurses contacted other hospitals to warn them that he might try out his hoax at their doors. Nurse Kinsella even suggested a computerized registry of factitial patients "to manage them more successfully."

Other health care professionals have also argued in favor of instituting a national registry of factitial patients to help monitor and curb their activities, an idea that we believe is ill conceived. Disease portrayals can end at any time. In many cases, once a person's emotional needs are met, the portrayals seem to end and the individual moves ahead with his or her life. Generating a list of these patients and sending it to every hospital in the country could create a myriad of problems. A primary concern is that if a person on the list became authentically ill he or she probably wouldn't receive treatment.

Other measures have been suggested to try to identify and track factitial patients, including posting their pictures on hospital bulletin boards and circulating flyers about them to emergency rooms. However, access to bulletin boards and flyers is uncontrolled and so these measures would involve breaching confidentiality. In *General Hospital Psychiatry* (1985), Dr. Frederic C. Kass postulated that to strike a happy medium, physicians should consider each individual case when deciding whether or not to identify a factitial patient. He recommended taking into consideration such factors as the frequency of the disease portrayals, the jeopardy in which a patient places himself or herself because of the factitious illnesses, and the nature of the disease or diseases being feigned. "Disclosure is more justifiable with patients who present as candidates for emergency surgery," he noted. "Less virulent forms of the syndrome probably warrant less vigorous identification efforts."

A number of papers have been written for professional journals with the explicit intention of disclosing the identity of a particular patient. In this way, other professionals would become aware of the patient's existence. For example, a dental journal carried an account of a patient with Munchausen syndrome who received treatment from at least 25 dentists in the New York metropolitan area. The characteristics of the patient and the syndrome were described to alert the dental community to this patient, who was believed still to be living in the area. Some older papers written by doctors, especially in Europe, have contained actual patient names, or accurate initials and so many specific details that it would be easy to identify the patient. Physicians have had to become more and more careful over time about engaging in this sort of disclosure.

Some physicians believe there are ways of circumventing confidentiality and suggest that it is not breached if, for example, doctors simply drop blatant hints that there is a story behind a patient that can't be told. Some suggest writing a letter to a referring physician about the patient in question, noting, "I have been forbidden to comment on whether or not this patient has a factitious disorder." However, such techniques merely finesse the issue and do not directly confront it. We believe that such actions are no different from other breaches of confidentiality.

Physicians must be extremely sure of themselves if they are going to violate the fundamental rules about patient-doctor relationships. At present, there must be clear evidence that such a violation is in the interest of the patient. However, there are no explicit guidelines about what constitutes the interests of other parties. One way to clarify the appropriate behavior for physicians would be for the American Medical Association and/or other professional organizations to take positions on factitious disorders and say publicly, "In terms of our code of ethics, there are certain circumstances in which confidentiality no longer holds and these include situations in which patients have been fraudulent in producing information and/or have surreptitiously produced their own diseases. As a result, it may not be necessary for the physician to maintain the standard level of confidentiality with these patients." At the present time, these patients actually have an unfair advantage over doctors. Through their portrayals, they are saying, "I don't have to play by the rules of being a patient, but you still have to play by the rules of being a doctor. You can't tell my family or other doctors the truth about me."

There is another argument to support limits on doctor-patient confidentiality when factitious disorders are involved. These patients use physicians' time and services often without paying, and they are therefore stealing. However, because they are identified as patients, stringent ethical and legal constraints block communication of this information. If someone walks into a store, however, and takes merchandise without paying for it, there's no expectation that "confidentiality" will be preserved. Yet both situations are thefts.

Another factor that keeps the ethical and legal pot boiling is that the only way a physician can distinguish between a factitious disorder and malingering is by apparent motive. But how can a doctor read the mind of a patient to determine whether the patient's primary motive is the sick role itself or some external gain?

Munchausen by proxy, unlike most types of medical deception, is acknowledged to be a serious crime. Legal intervention, with the central aid of health care professionals, has resulted in the arrest and sometimes the conviction of the perpetrators. The number of MBP cases reaching the courts is growing steadily, and we believe it will continue to burgeon as knowledge of factitious disorders spreads in legal circles. An ethical responsibility for health professionals is to educate judges and attorneys. If court officials can be made aware of the unique characteristics of Munchausen by proxy, they may be better prepared to attend to the objective evidence when the perpetrator comes into court with protests and denials.

In a 1991 article for *Juvenile & Family Court Journal*, Beatrice Crofts Yorker (a nurse and attorney) and Bernard B. Kahan examined a sampling of MBP cases that made it into the courts to highlight the different actions taken against accused parents. One of these cases, *People* v. *Phillips* (1981), has been credited with helping the legal community to recognize MBP as a form of child abuse. In this case, the California Court of Appeals upheld the use of psychiatric expert testimony to describe MBP and to render an opinion on whether or not the mother in question fit the profile of such an offender. The mother, a child abuse agency volunteer who claimed she had never harmed her children, was accused of adding sodium to the formula of her adopted infants. She was found guilty of having murdered one of the children in 1977 and of having willfully endangered the life of the other.

Yorker and Kahan contrasted that outcome with one in which a mother was accused of giving her son diuretics. Syringes and vials of a diuretic were uncovered in a search of her home. The judge in that case found that the child needed assistance, but on appeal the boy was returned to his parents under supervised custody. In a third case, one involving laxative administration to an infant by her mother, the court found evidence of a number of warning signs of MBP, including the mother's inordinate attentiveness during her child's hospitalization and the child's marked improvement in her absence. This case is significant for the court's acknowledgement of the reluctance of legal authorities to believe that a parent who seemed caring could actually cause her child's illness. Two nurses provided evidence in this case linking the mother to laxatives in the bottled formula. The court found the mother guilty of child abuse, placed the little girl with her father under the supervision of the Department of Social Services, and ordered monthly visits to a pediatrician and a psychiatrist. A six-month court review was also required.

Going beyond the Yorker and Kahan paper, a 1992 judgment in Ohio is worth noting as well. In this case, the Court of Appeals expressed concern about the evidence attributing MBP to the mother. Indeed, while the psychiatric expert had pointed out that the parent's infant daughter had been repeatedly hospitalized for minor medical problems, there was no evidence that the mother had ever induced any medical problems. Instead, the court viewed her as unreasonably worried about medical issues but not overtly hurtful. This court also acknowledged that the legal community has at times been an obstacle to the prosecution of MBP cases because of its skepticism about the entire phenomenon. The court reported two trends in its review of earlier cases: on the one hand, the judicial system has been likely to find that a child was abused whenever a parent has introduced a foreign substance into the child's body to induce symptoms; on the other hand, even in the absence of indications of such overt abuse, courts have frequently terminated parental rights based upon a finding of MBP *combined with* other factors (such as general parental instability or lack of employment).

Yorker and Kahan stress that "comprehensive coordination of services is critical to all interventions with children," and point out that hospitals should provide their own guidelines for handling MBP cases. "Legal guidelines for searches and seizures, covert video-surveillance, and appropriate risk management should be instituted in health care settings," they say. "Hospital ethics committees should be involved when competing interests of patient and family privacy are weighed against child protection."

A new dilemma may emerge with the inclusion of factitious disorder by proxy in the new edition of the *Diagnostic and Statistical Manual of Mental Disorders (DSM-IV)*: the potential exists for misuse of the diagnosis as a psychiatric defense in cases of premeditated murder! Someone could mimic the case of the Gasoline Injector, for example, to commit murder and then use the diagnosis of factitious disorder by proxy as a defense. This could lead creative criminals to commit more medicalized types of murder. Such offenders could then claim that as victims of this mental disorder, they "only" intended to make a person sick, and that the eventual death was accidental.

A well-coordinated, multidisciplinary approach is crucial for health care professionals who are trying to address any case of factitious disorder. It becomes even more essential when trying to build a legal case in these situations. Whether the case involves a parent harming her child or an adult poisoning himself, once suspicions are voiced, the burden of proof rests with the accusers.

To date, we know of no civil cases instigated against factitial patients by their victims, although such cases are certainly conceivable. Lawsuits would be one way to turn the tables on factitial patients for the damage they've done; however, as in the example above, such patients might attempt to argue that they were the "helpless victims" of mental illness. One woman who defrauded several doctors through false claims of illness and who repeatedly impersonated an insurance company official pleaded guilty in a recent criminal case. Given this, the odds are good that someday a precedent-setting civil case against a factitial patient will be waged and won by a victim.

CHAPTER 15

DISCOVERY, CONFRONTATION, TREATMENT

The ability to discriminate between that which
is true and that which is false is one of the last
attainments of the human mind.
James Fenimore Cooper (1789–1851)

Being able to prove that someone has a factitious disorder, whether in a hospital or a court of law, is unquestionably one of the most challenging tasks any physician could face. Most doctors will never find themselves in that position, however, because the majority of factitial patients are falling through cracks in the health care industry, cracks which have been created by lack of knowledge and, in some cases, indifference. A number of physicians have wagged fingers at their colleagues, scolding them for letting factitial patients slip by them without detection. A central reason is that scores of cases have involved repeated exploratory operations and invasive procedures, including the removal of healthy organs, in attempts to isolate the causes of what ultimately proved to be feigned illnesses. Time after time, doctors have prescribed medications and other treatments for factitial patients, even when costly tests proved inconclusive or negative.

Weeding out factitial patients begins with one supremely basic yet critical factor: awareness of the phenomenon. Obviously, the burden of proper diagnosis rests with physicians who, we would hope, are acting in tandem with the other health care providers attending to these patients (to the extent they are aware of these other providers). The goal of the medical team must be to confirm or disprove suspicions and then take proper action. As simplistic as this sounds, this path is not being followed on a large scale. There's an old saying in medicine that the first step in diagnosis is a high index of suspicion. If you're not aware of a particular disorder or don't know about its characteristics, you're not likely to consider it, and the diagnosis is not likely to be made.

Education about factitious disorders is important for all people involved in medical care, not just doctors. Because nurses and ancillary workers, such as nurses' aides, generally have lengthier individual contacts with patients than doctors, they, too, must be knowledgeable about this particular diagnostic group. If they're not educated about it, they won't have the information to communicate to doctors. Good medical care, regardless of whether an illness is factitious or not, involves good communication within the entire multidisciplinary team.

A number of researchers have worked to educate the medical community through professional journals, urging them to be on the alert for these great pretenders and pointing to areas of special concern. The knowledge, for example, that AIDS is being feigned with increasing frequency is critical if doctors and others are going to avoid misdirecting precious resources needed by real AIDS patients. Writing in the journal *Clinical Infectious Diseases*, Drs. Abigail Zuger and Mary Alice O'Dowd warned that 15 cases of factitious AIDS had already been reported in the United States, Canada, and Europe as of 1992, each replete with elaborate personal and medical histories and classic AIDS symptoms; each also bore characteristic signs of factitious disorders, such as pseudologia fantastica and additional feigned illnesses. Contributing to the convincing nature of these presentations was the fact that most of these patients, who were typically young adults, were members of groups at high risk of developing the HIV infection, such as people with drug dependencies.

Drs. Zuger and O'Dowd cite one case in which a 31-year-old woman turned up at a hospital in April 1989 with facial trauma (the disturbing evidence of an assault by a sex partner) and abdominal pain. She told doctors that she abused drugs and had been diagnosed with AIDS. She also claimed to have already had two bouts of *Pneumocystis carinii* pneumonia (a type of pneumonia that occurs in persons with depressed immune systems). She was admitted with the diagnoses of AIDS and pelvic inflammatory disease. During emotional interviews with infectious disease and psychiatric consultants, she explained that she had been denied certain types of AIDS therapy because she had just one kidney (the other kidney had been removed in 1979 because of an infection) and, consequently, certain drugs were contraindicated. She added dramatically, however, that even if she could have these drugs she no longer wanted treatments that would extend her life. After being discharged, however, she followed up at an infectious disease clinic. She was also referred to a psychiatric outpatient clinic for AIDS patients, but she did not return there for therapy.

In July 1989, she was readmitted to the hospital at which she'd been treated in April, this time with severe headaches and recurrent right-sided weakness. During this hospitalization, a permanent central catheter was placed in one of her veins so that she could receive nutrition intravenously when necessary. Only one week after being discharged, she returned to the emergency room with an infection in the skin surrounding the catheter. Readmitted to a ward for AIDS patients, she was placed on a regimen of antibiotics. The patient displayed such high spirits and cooperation that she earned the respect of the nursing staff, who marveled at her incredible courage. She began showing signs of improvement; however, days before she was to be discharged, the patient developed a fever and additional signs of infection. The catheter was removed and she was treated with more antibiotics. Infection recurred again, and she was finally discharged after 65 days!

This patient periodically visited the infectious disease clinic, voicing her complaints of headaches and weakness. She accepted home nursing assistance, counseling on death and dying, and other social service support, and she executed a living will. In the interim, she told doctors that she had become addicted to a prescription pain killer (hydromorphone), and she was placed on methadone maintenance therapy. In January 1990, after this young woman had received 10 months of treatment and observation, doctors reviewed her chart before ordering additional tests and x-rays. They were stunned to realize that none of her caregivers had ever actually documented HIV infection. When she was told this, the patient cleverly feigned relief that she was "doing so well." Two subsequent HIV tests were negative. Informed of those results through her social worker, the patient reversed herself entirely, now reacting angrily because the medical staff had treated her as if she had had AIDS.

After the negative HIV tests, doctors requested this patient's records from the hospital at which she had supposedly been treated for AIDS-related pneumonia. While it was true that she had been seen at that hospital five times between 1985 and 1988, the visits were only for complaints of bloody urine and pain, not AIDS complications. During one emergency room visit, her complaints of bloody urine *were in fact diagnosed as factitious disorder with physical symptoms*! Her history was also marked by five psychiatric hospitalizations for depression and thoughts of suicide. During one of these admissions, she was treated for AIDS after claiming that it had been diagnosed at another hospital. She had also gained hospitalization for allegedly taking an overdose of a drug used to treat AIDS. In retrospect, doctors believed that following the insertion of the central catheter this woman had induced her own infection, probably with feces.

Like many factitial patients, this woman's past was overshadowed by an abusive alcoholic parent. Doctors suspected that she was introduced to the supportive hospital environment as a child when she was treated for a broken leg. In later life, when she felt abandoned and alone, she turned to the AIDS-therapy network for comfort and support, just as Jenny had turned to a cancer support group. This patient also tried to control her physically abusive boyfriend, albeit unsuccessfully, with her "diagnosis" and "symptoms."

Drs. Zuger and O'Dowd warn that "high-technology, high-cost treatments for HIV infection may be distributed haphazardly while the basics of health care, such as careful chart reviews, are overlooked. Our patient's physical appearance, remarkably similar to that of a patient in the late stages of HIV infection, allowed her to receive medical care, disability income, and social support services for a year."

There is no doubt that careful reviews of medical charts and personal histories can help alert doctors to factitial patients. However, unless doctors know the warning signs of factitious disorders, examination of these records will be of little value. When a history is unusual, or when no positive findings support a patient's claims, doctors should make every effort to track down records and speak with other health care providers who have, or supposedly have, treated the patient. Some physicians have even suggested that continued hospitalization should be contingent upon the patient's providing accurate information and signing releases which can lead to the compilation of a complete history. Medical records are enormously useful in detecting factitious disorders. High use of medical care, for example, which is highly associated with concurrent psychiatric diagnoses, would be revealed through a person's records. Evidence of high utilization does not prove whether a person has a real or a phony disease. It does, however, provide a big clue that something more than a physical ailment may be wrong with the patient. For example, people who are depressed as well as physically diseased use two to three times the medical care of people with the same disease who aren't depressed. Concurrent anxiety jacks up medical use as well. Somatization disorder increases use of health care up to six or eight times the norm. High medical utilization means that the physicians, nurses, and other caregivers should be highly suspicious that the patient has a psychiatric diagnosis. These considerations should include factitious disorders.

Age and profession rank with high medical utilization as potential clues to factitious disorders. At greatest risk for a "simple" factitious disorder are unmarried women in their thirties who are working or have worked in a medical profession. Nurses are at increased risk for a factitious disorder because of their unique position as caregivers. They give and give, filling dependency needs of sick people, and thus their own emotional supplies are drained all day long. Yes, that's their job, but if they're not getting very much nurturance themselves, they frequently flip their roles and become the recipients of care. Nurses have a lot of somatization problems in addition to factitious disorders.

In contrast, patients with true Munchausen syndrome tend to be men in their forties and fifties who have had multiple hospitalizations and are socially unconnected. They have no family involvement, and that issue becomes important in itself for these patients. The greater prevalence of Munchausen syndrome among men has less to do with gender per se than with confounding variables. For example, antisocial personality disorder, which is often seen in men with Munchausen syndrome, is more common in men in general. The greater frequency of Munchausen syndrome among men may also have to do with the different ways in which men and women are socialized. Aggression is more tolerable in our society when it is expressed by a male. The lack of roots, willful disregard for others, and edge of criminality that are seen in Munchausen patients occur more in men because society allows and tolerates more of these characteristics in them.

Although not all signs of factitious disorders are seen in every patient, any combination of them can be telling. Some clues are obvious once health caregivers know what to look for. For example, a startling number of scars on a patient's body can indicate that he or she has undergone multiple exploratory surgeries because of vague symptoms. Old scars in unusual patterns often betray factitial wounds and have been described as an important clue to the existence of this problem. (Factitious lesions are produced on the body within easy reach of the dominant hand. These lesions usually have bizarre shapes and linear or geometric outlines.) When suspicions about wounds arise, Dr. Jack C. Fisher, writing in the journal *Resident & Staff Physician* (September 1985), recommends getting a second opinion without the patient's awareness, or hospitalizing the patient so that he or she can be observed continuously by the nursing staff. Another important clue to self-inflicted wounds, says Dr. Fisher, is that they heal quickly in hospital settings when a patient is being watched. This factor often leads patients with factitial wounds to resist admission. They may also be kept out of the hospital by their insurance carriers. "If I think I can learn something by having a patient suspected of factitial [skin] ulcer admitted, I will overstate my case on paper in order to achieve that goal," says Dr. Fisher. "For example, I will state that the wound is infected, which is usually true. I justify my action based on the belief that accurate diagnosis will, in the long run, save money."

Other overt signs, which we've discussed elsewhere in this book, are evident in factitial patients, especially those with Munchausen syndrome. Remember that these people are very disruptive and demanding in the hospital and that they become angry and offer new physical complaints when told that their tests are negative. They also have a fascinating knack for being able to divide the staff and create tension and hostility among caregivers. Other frequently seen indicators are the use of pseudologia fantastica; an inclination toward social isolation with few or no hospital visitors; a history of drug or alcohol abuse; a history of considerable travel; medical savvy; willingness to undergo diagnostic procedures and exploratory surgeries despite the inherent pain and risk; evasiveness about personal and medical histories; the ability to manipulate others, especially doctors and hospital staffs; the ability to control their own symptoms; the vociferous demand for treatment and hospitalization; and a history of signing out of hospitals against medical advice. They often show up at emergency rooms late at night or on weekends, when less experienced staff members, including young house officers, may be working and when insurance and medical information is more difficult to verify. Health care professionals should also remember that, while exaggerating or creating symptoms, these patients usually go to extremes to ensure that they will receive treatment and/ or hospitalization; thus, any exotic case should be carefully reviewed. Hospital employees may discover carelessly discarded syringes or concealed drugs in a patient's room. The medical staff may find evidence on drug screens of surreptitious use. When checking outside records, doctors may learn that factitious illnesses have occurred before, and that the information these patients provide is inconsistent. Talking with family members may also reveal a history of such deceptions.

Other clues to factitious disorders can be far more subtle. It is here that intuition stemming from knowledge and experience can be extremely helpful. Doctors note, for example, that the most critical factor in assessing post-traumatic stress disorder is the clinical interview with the patient. This precious time with the patient can provide insights into the true malady and help clarify the patient's motivations in order to ascertain whether deception is present. "Exaggeration of symptoms for personal gain is not synonymous with malingering," Dr. John A. Fairbank pointed out in the *American Journal of Psychiatry* (February 1986). "Certainly the clinician may be confronted with the task of evaluating a treatment-seeking or compensation-seeking veteran who actually has symptoms of posttraumatic stress disorder, yet exaggerates these for fear of not receiving a diagnosis. Thus, the evaluation of posttraumatic stress disorder is often extremely difficult and the clinician needs assessment procedures [such as standard psychological tests, which can help betray feigned psychological illness in general] that help to increase the accuracy of clinical judgment."

Neurologic ailments such as epilepsy (a group of brain function disorders which are characterized by seizures) and multiple sclerosis have found their way onto the list of diseases of choice for factitial patients because they draw such a swift response from doctors and because signs can sometimes be difficult to prove as fraudulent. False seizures (or pseudoseizures), for example, are often seen in factitial patients, but not all false seizures are factitious. Some patients with genuine epilepsy, for instance, are chronically concerned about having a sudden epileptic seizure and develop pseudoseizures as a result of their anxiety. Others with genuine epilepsy have learned that seizures are a powerful means of eliciting responses from others and may have "seizures" when they are needed. It takes a keen observer to distinguish which seizures are real. One means is to obtain continuous and simultaneous videotape and electroencephalographic (brain wave) recordings.

One of us (M.D.F.) encountered a man whose grand mal seizures occurred at seemingly selected times. In addition, his body movements weren't rhythmic, nor were his limbs coordinated, which made his seizures less than convincing.

Dr. Feldman:

During one of his alleged seizures, I told him that if he opened his mouth the seizure would stop. The patient opened his mouth and the seizure did indeed suddenly end. Had the patient been in the throes of a real seizure, he would not have had such excellent control over his body.

I participated in another ruse to unmask a patient with a psychologic overlay to her neurologic illness. A woman was hospitalized for what appeared to be epilepsy, but the history was questionable. Her neurologist believed she was either having factitious seizures or pseudoseizures but wanted to be certain before accusing her. We came up with a little plan, which also assessed her suggestibility. We told her that in order to test the intensity of her seizures we needed to administer a liquid that would precipitate a seizure in a controlled environment. We also assured her that we had another medication available, an antidote. In reality all we had was saline (salt water) solution, which would have no ill effect on her whatsoever and certainly wouldn't induce a seizure. She readily agreed to let us give her the liquid, and as the saline started flowing into her arm, the neurologist said, "In about five seconds you're probably going to have a seizure." Moments later, her head tipped back and her eyelids started fluttering, and she enacted a full-blown seizure. She instantly "came out" of it when we gave her the so-called antidote, which was more saline.

Other doctors have employed tests to ensnare patients who they believed were creating their own illnesses. In one instance, a 23-year-old woman was admitted to a hospital for chronic diarrhea and weight loss, but a house doctor suspected that she was guilty of a hoax when no cause for her illness could be found. Though she denied using laxatives, the doctor performed a test: he placed sodium hydroxide on a sample of her stool, and the color turned pink. This indicated that she had indeed used a specific type of laxative.

One of the studies ophthalmologists routinely perform when patients say they can't see is to test the visual fields. A patient is shown a chart and asked to draw what he or she can see. The patient is then told to step back and draw the visual field again. Factitial patients mistakenly believe that if they move back, they will be able to see less; therefore, they reproduce less of the chart. In reality, however, if you move back, your vision becomes broader. Doctors also sometimes test people who claim to be blind by throwing a soft ball at their faces without warning. Blinking and protective movements give away sighted people. Another trick designed to uncover factitial blindness is far more coarse but equally effective. A person purporting to be blind is asked to read a series of eye charts, one of which says, "I know you're faking, you (expletive)." If the person can't see anything, he or she has no reaction to this message. But if the individual can see, the immediate response is shock, which reveals the hoax. Such "tests" may demonstrate that a symptom is psychogenic but they do not indicate whether the initiation of the symptom is deliberate (as in malingering or factitious disorders) or unconscious (as in conversion disorder).

Subtle calls may be required when diagnosing factitious disorder with psychological symptoms. A tip-off occurs, however, when the patient's overall clinical appearance is uncharacteristic of any recognized mental disorder, and psychological tests (which are often refused) reflect a layman's concept of a mental illness instead of providing consistent evidence for a specific disorder. Doctors must also watch for approximate, vague, overemphatic, or random answers. When attempting to assess the legitimacy of a given case of multiple personality disorder, doctors should be mindful that fakers have difficulty maintaining different personalities over time, often confusing or forgetting details and characteristics. People with factitious disorder with psychological symptoms may also fail to respond to medications that would have been expected to help in genuine illness, or they may demonstrate a positive response to medications not expected to be beneficial.

As we've described, a host of challenges is associated with diagnosing factitious disorders, not the least of which is the cleverness these patients display in creating and mimicking symptoms. However, we believe that medical knowledge, when properly applied, can prevail most of the time.

As stated, recognition is the first step in treating any illness. The second step is bringing news of the diagnosis to the patient. Revealing one's suspicions and the diagnosis of a factitious disorder is unlike any other revelation that can occur between physician and patient. How this information is presented is crucial. It is the pivotal point in each case, the time when a patient either denies the statement and signs out of the hospital or concedes and accepts treatment. Some doctors advocate a strong confrontational approach with such patients. This approach essentially entails telling patients that the curtain has come crashing down on their acts, and everybody now sees through the disguise. In a review of 12 patients with self-induced infections who had been directly confronted in this way by their physicians, 1 patient admitted to the factitious disorder; 5 of the other 11 patients stopped producing their symptoms even while denying their involvement in them; and 2 of these had not repeated their factitial behavior after two years (researchers could not keep track of the others). None of the 12 threatened suicide or experienced psychotic reactions after they were confronted.

Other researchers, who consider factitious disorders to be protective defense mechanisms, fear that confrontation might lead patients to escalate self-injury or precipitate psychosis. They recommend a nonconfrontational therapeutic style in which the primary physician and a consulting psychiatrist approach the patient in a noncondemning but firm manner. At the same time, they convey a wish to help and extend an offer of psychiatric treatment and ongoing medical evaluation which, as in Jenny's case, might include hospitalization. The psychiatrist can also assist the medical and nursing staffs, who may be very angry, by explaining the nature of the disorder and the psychopathology involved. Writing in the *Journal of Clinical Psychiatry* (March 1978), Dr. Vincent J. D'Andrea pointed to the anger and indifference experienced by physicians who have treated patients whose illnesses proved to be factitious. "No one enjoys being duped or used. The common denouement in the more dramatic cases is for the patient to arrange for the hoax to be uncovered, followed by angry condemnation by the staff and rapid discharge," said Dr. D'Andrea. "This exactly fits the dynamics of the patient who wants nothing more than to prove that in their system of belief, in the end, caretakers are unreliable and don't really care. They then repeat the cycle. Moral judgements and labeling have no place in the care of such patients. It is for this reason, along with concern about underlying dynamics, that non-confronting or minimally confronting techniques be used, and the patient referred to psychiatric consultation in an attempt to cut short the cycle of hospitalization-discharge, etc., etc."

Despite the review alluded to previously, there seems to be a growing consensus that heavy-hitting confrontation too often causes these patients to flee. They may flee regardless of how they are approached, but we agree with others who say that this technique usually drives patients to another physician or hospital. There are ways to confront a patient without being hostile. For instance, doctors spoke with a patient who had been secretly taking medication to lower the level of sugar in her blood, and she offered an emphatic denial. To avoid a direct confrontation, one of the doctors said, "You must have been taking it in your sleep." She replied, "I guess that was the explanation for it," and afterwards her behavior changed and she no longer took the medication. Research has found that after such indirect confrontations roughly one-third of the patients ended their hoaxes. They vigorously denied what they were doing, but if the doctors somehow allowed them to save face the behavior stopped, at least for a time. The embarrassment of discovery was lessened.

The psychiatric examination following confrontation should be non-accusatory and impartial; the physician should remember that discovery has already weakened the patient's defenses and he or she may act rashly to preserve what little is left of the facade. Approaching the patient in a supportive fashion will to some degree obviate the need for the symptoms to recur. These are such fragile people that they will accept support from wherever it comes. In a therapy situation, those emotional supplies are provided by the physician. For example, one Munchausen patient told stories so wild that they were clearly unbelievable. She once said that she had been pregnant with twins and gave birth to one in Texas and the other in Tennessee! A woman medical resident took an interest in her. The resident saw the patient once a week for 30 minutes in a follow-up clinic and the patient stayed out of the hospital for six months. When the resident was transferred from the clinic and couldn't see her anymore, the patient ended up back in the hospital. With all of these patients, one needs to be consistent, fairly nonconfrontive, and supportive, while gratifying their underlying needs.

Once a patient has been diagnosed as having a factitious disorder, if he or she agrees to treatment, psychological testing can be helpful in pinpointing the underlying personality dynamics. Here, again, doctors must be mindful of the factors that generally characterize these patients: a poor sense of self; poor sexual identity and adjustment; low tolerance for frustration; strong dependency needs; absence of psychotic thinking; narcissism; and intelligence quotients that range from average to above-average.

There are no comprehensive studies on treatment, nor is there a definitive treatment. When considering the course of action to take with one of these patients, physicians must consider how long the patient has been feigning illness, whether or not there were early disturbances in personality development, and the nature of the stressors that sparked the factitious symptoms; all weigh heavily in choosing the type of treatment and determining the patient's prognosis. We believe that if a patient does agree to treatment, it must begin with the gradual development of a therapist-patient alliance. Through this consistent relationship, patients ideally learn that they don't need to use ostensive illness to elicit interest from others. In general, however, the prognosis for true Munchausen patients will remain guarded. Their inability to tolerate frustration and almost compulsive tendency to lie contrast sharply with individuals such as Jenny, who remained open to psychotherapeutic and behavioral treatments and was thus able to turn her life around. Some reports suggest that very lengthy psychotherapy makes a difference for certain patients, but the psychodynamic issues vary in each case and so the treatment must vary as well.

Usually the goal of treatment is not to "cure" these individuals but to help them act out their "illnesses" to a lesser extent. If a patient has an emotional disorder for which we have a specific treatment and the factitious disorder is only secondary, we can treat the primary disorder while simultaneously dealing with the issue of feigned illness. In this regard, we believe that patients whose factitious disorders stem from major depression have the best prognosis of all factitial patients. On the other hand, if a person has a severe personality disorder and little ego strength, the prognosis isn't going to be very good because it is difficult to alter character. Munchausen patients are the most refractory to treatment, so with them the focus is on early recognition for damage control—trying to prevent the patient from the bodily damage that comes with repetitive, unnecessary operations and invasive diagnostic procedures, and trying to save hospitals the costs of unreimbursed medical expenses.

Caregivers must tolerate lapses during which factitial patients in treatment "fall off the wagon." These lapses don't mean that the doctor is a failure or that treatment should be abandoned. These disorders demand perseverance. Caregivers must also anticipate that when they prescribe psychotropic medications for specific associated psychiatric diagnoses, the patient may not take the medication or may even end up misusing or abusing it. Physicians must continue to pursue whatever treatment appears to be effective and hope that the periods of health become longer and longer. If a physician can reduce hospitalizations in a single patient by 50 percent, psychotherapy has been effective. To increase the chances of a positive outcome, physicians must also look at the potential for alternative social support for factitial patients. Can they be hooked into a more nurturing social support system that will reduce the need for symptoms? A support network, even the small but powerful one that was waiting for Jenny, is crucial for a continued positive outcome.

Writing in the *American Journal of Psychotherapy* (October 1984), Drs. James P. Mayo, Jr., and John J. Haggerty, Jr., noted that up to the time of their report 37 factitial patients were known to have agreed to extensive evaluation or treatment. Twenty-two of these patients received outpatient psychotherapy for months to a year or more, and 10 reportedly improved. In contrast, only one case of Munchausen syndrome has been reported to be successfully treated, but to achieve that outcome the patient had to remain in a hospital for three years. Compared with the countless factitial patients who enter hospitals every year, these statistics are slim, but they hold promise. And although some of these patients do not remain in therapy for long, they may benefit in limited ways. Drs. Mayo and Haggerty recount the story of one of these patients, a 22-year-old woman who called a hospital pretending to be a psychiatrist referring herself for inpatient treatment for "psychiatric Munchausen syndrome." While her admission was being arranged, she conned her way into the medical unit of the hospital by saying she had a peptic ulcer. She ultimately confessed to having Munchausen syndrome, but when offered psychiatric hospitalization she declined, accepting outpatient therapy instead. Surprisingly, this patient stayed in treatment for 70 sessions over 16 months. During that time, she had lapses during which she cancelled sessions and she was also hospitalized several times for feigned illness. These hospitalizations neatly coincided with absences by her therapist, which she perceived as intolerable abandonment. Although she ultimately left treatment and moved on, she had shown definite signs of improvement in symptoms and behavior during the middle 8 months of therapy.

Multimodal treatment which centrally incorporates behavior therapy principles may be valuable in some cases. Elizabeth A. Klonoff, Stuart J. Younger, Douglas J. Moore, and Linda A. Hershey reported a case in the *International Journal of Psychiatry in Medicine* (1983–84) in which a 29-year-old woman was admitted to a medical intensive care unit for weakness in her left arm and legs. She had been diagnosed three years earlier as having multiple sclerosis and epilepsy. Watchful nurses noticed that her seizures increased in frequency when she was angry with hospital workers or with her parents. They also detected movements in her "paralyzed" arm. A psychiatric consultation, interviews with her parents, and a review of her records disclosed that from the time she was a little girl, she dreamed of becoming a doctor. During her high school years, she began visiting doctors with vague complaints and when, as a college senior, she was rejected by several medical schools, she began complaining of neurologic symptoms. Frequent hospitalizations characterized her life, and she once spent eight months in a rehabilitation hospital where she was suspected of feigning illness. Factitious disorder was confirmed when she had a "convulsion" during an electroencephalogram but the recording of brain waves didn't change as it would have during a genuine seizure.

Once this woman agreed to treatment, her therapeutic team devised a treatment plan and set goals that included increasing her sense of control and self-esteem; helping her to build better relationships; promoting interests that were appropriate for her age; and curbing her self-destructive behavior. Treatment included co-therapy by two psychologists; biofeedback, which was used to monitor minute changes in muscle tension in her "paralyzed" arm and legs; and operant conditioning procedures, such as telling her family to flatly ignore her "seizures." The woman was seen weekly for nine months and monthly for the following six. During that time, her most serious symptoms—such as paralysis, seizures, apnea, and urinary incontinence—almost disappeared; the number of days she spent hospitalized decreased; she entered a college that offered degrees in health professions; and she began to function socially in ways that suited her age.

A creative approach was taken in the treatment of a patient whose fraudulent illness involved paraplegia. Treatment included a physiotherapy machine which utilized electrical current to deliver a painful massage. The discomfort was intended to convince the patient that she was receiving powerful treatments for her useless legs, ones that would "increase circulation and stimulate nerve endings." The machine turned the skin a rosy hue, which was pointed out to the patient as a sign that it was working and that recovery was possible. The patient was told, however, that if goals weren't reached, the massage would be extended by one minute. Conversely, the treatments would end as soon as she recovered function of her limbs. Reporting on this case in the *Journal of Behavioral Therapy and Experimental Psychiatry* (1990), Carol Solyom and Leslie Solyom noted that their strategy was simple: they told the patient that they had accepted her illness and were going to treat her for it. After the first painful "treatment session," the patient was informed that the second session would occur the next day. Three hours later, she was walking! This patient remained in follow-up for 1½ years and, although she tried to be rehospitalized, her efforts were unsuccessful. The Solyoms wrote: "There are people whose vitality thrives on untruthfulness both towards themselves and the world at large. We must, therefore, consider all the more carefully what cure means and what are the limits of psychotherapeutic effort."

Therapy should not be reserved for factitial patients. It must extend beyond them to their victims, many of whom are caregivers. To this end, the psychiatric consultant can offer assistance to the hospital staff while the patient is still on the ward, and long after he or she has left the hospital. Even if a patient entirely refuses therapy, a psychiatric consultant still has a role to play with the staff. Caregivers can't help but feel some anger, betrayal, and even contempt toward these patients. The staff has to be shown how to manage those feelings so emotions don't get in the way of patient care. Offering staff education and understanding is critical both during and after an encounter with a factitial patient. The staff feels outrage, and everyone must be given an opportunity to discuss the emotions that are evoked. Because the nursing staff spends so much time with the patients, nurses are especially vulnerable to these pretenders. Some hospitals offer group therapy and support sessions for anyone who has been involved with such challenging patients.

The Journal of Psychosocial Nursing (March 1986) recognized the special role that nurses play and offered guidelines to help them manage factitial patients. They advised: avoid displaying hostility; demonstrate that you can be aware of the deception without rejecting the patient; ensure that your expectations are realistic; provide an interdisciplinary approach to care; guard against being overly fascinated by the patient or the syndrome; and be sure to support suspicions with facts. Nurses should be taught about factitious disorders from school days on. This education will not only help them when dealing with such patients but also may help them avoid becoming one of them. Nursing programs have come to realize this and to understand that nurses need social support and programs that quietly fulfill their emotional needs.

Immediate gratification, control over life, an abundance of warmth and nurturance from loving, caring people—these are the goals of men and women who are plagued by factitious disorders. Simply put, factitial patients want nothing more than what the rest of us want. The problem for them is that they don't know how to achieve these ends in healthy, socially acceptable ways. Thus, they find themselves on urgent quests which become bizarre and convoluted and usually end up causing physical harm to themselves and emotional abuse to their caregivers and loved ones.

Factitial patients lose sight of what they are doing to their bodies and to those who care about them. They are fully aware of their actions, but they feel they must continue on this path. Their needs become the driving forces in their lives, overshadowing all they do; everything and everyone else becomes secondary.

Factitious disorders become a lopsided game of chess in which the factitial patient dictates the moves of the other player. But despite their illusion of mastery and control, these great pretenders must be viewed as real, not false, patients. Despite the waste and repulsion by the medical community, humanity must prevail. As socially and medically unacceptable as their actions often are, factitial patients deserve an opportunity to receive psychiatric treatment, even if it is ultimately rejected.

In all disorders, the best form of treatment is prevention. Proper education of all health care professionals and the public is crucial. If we can find ways to reduce the neediness and desperation so many people feel, if their needs for nurturance can be better met, it may also reduce the incidence of factitious disorders.

There are few Cinderella stories among the scores of cases we've presented here (as well as the multitude of cases that didn't find their way onto these pages). For 99 percent of factitial patients, it is always midnight, the pumpkin is just a pumpkin, and no shining heroic figure ever arrives to snatch them from the twisted fantasy world they have created. But there is promise that more and more of these patients can be identified, and the number of patients and their victims whom we'll be able to help will swell commensurately.

INDEX